ROMANCES
of the REPUBLIC

ROMANCES · · · · · ·
of the REPUBLIC

Women, the Family, and Violence
in the Literature of the Early
American Nation

SHIRLEY SAMUELS

New York   Oxford
Oxford University Press
1996

Oxford University Press

Oxford   New York
Athens   Auckland   Bangkok   Bogota   Bombay
Buenos Aires   Calcutta   Cape Town   Dar es Salaam
Delhi   Florence   Hong Kong   Istanbul   Karachi
Kuala Lumpur   Madras   Madrid   Melbourne
Mexico City   Nairobi   Paris   Singapore
Taipei   Tokyo   Toronto

and associated companies in
Berlin   Ibadan

Copyright © 1996 by Oxford University Press, Inc.

Published by Oxford University Press, Inc.
198 Madison Avenue, New York, New York 10016

Oxford is a registered trademark of Oxford University Press

Library of Congress Cataloging-in-Publication Data
Samuels, Shirley.
Romances of the republic : women, the family, and violence in the literature
of the early American nation / Shirley Samuels.
   p.   cm.
Includes index.
ISBN 0–19–507988–4 (cloth)
1. Historical fiction, American—Men authors—History and criticism.   2. United States—
History—Revolution, 1775–1783—Literature and the revolution.   3. American fiction—
19th century—History and criticism.   4. American fiction—18th century—History and criticism.
5. National characteristics, American, in literature.   6. Literature and society—United
States   7. Man—woman relationships in literature.   8. Violence in literature.   9. Family in
literature.   10. Women in literature.   I. Title.
PS374.H5S26   1996
813′.0810902—dc20   95–13816

9 8 7 6 5 4 3 2 1

Printed in the United States of America
on acid-free paper

For my family

Acknowledgments

Many people have encouraged or challenged me as I worked out the terms and readings of this study and I am very grateful for their generosity. This work shows the traces of early discussions with Walter Michaels and Michael Rogin; it was especially influenced, through example and conversation, by Mark Seltzer and Eric Sundquist. Cathy Davidson, Emory Elliott, and Jane Tompkins were encouraging at valuable points. The friendships and collegial exchanges offered by a number of women have given personal and professional salvation: I am especially grateful to Lauren Berlant, Laura Brown, Susan Gilman, Mandy Merck, Harryette Mullen, and Lynn Wardley. I would also like to thank warmly Cynthia Chase, Jonathan Culler, Carol Flynn, Lora Romero, Neil Saccamano, Karen Sanchez Eppler, Annette Schwartz, and Sally Shuttleworth.

I have a large family and there's a long history of support and love to draw on. For the record: Larry, Nils, Rolf, Lisa, Joel, and Maya are great siblings; each has at some point given me what I needed and I hope I have sometimes reciprocated. My grandmother, Helen Briggs, has been a wonderful example for me, and my parents, Margaret Ann, and Larry, and Lucia, have shown me endurance and faith. I also thank Mark Seltzer for many years of thoughtful affection, and his family, Sara Seltzer, Tasha Vigoda, and Ann Pangborn. My son, John Briggs Seltzer, distracted me in the best sense.

Work on this project was supported by a fellowship at the Society for the Humanities at Cornell and by grants from the American Council of Learned Societies and the Northeast Modern Language Association (for work at the American Antiquarian Society). Versions of several chapters have been published previously. The short essay that eventually became part of the introduction appeared in *American Quarterly* (Fall 1986); a somewhat different version of the chapter on *Arthur Mervyn* was in *Criticism* (Summer 1985), two incarnations of the chapter on *Wieland* first emerged in *Early American Literature* (Fall 1987 and Fall 1990), the chapter on Cooper's *Last of the Mohicans* was in Daniel Peck, ed., *New Essays on "Last of the Mohicans"* (Cambridge University Press, 1992), and a slightly different version of the last chapter appeared in Shirley Samuels, ed., *The Culture of Sentiment: Race, Gender, and Sentimentality in Nineteenth-Century America* (Oxford, 1992).

Ithaca, New York   S. S.
November 1995

Contents

ROMANCES
of the REPUBLIC

The Family, the State, and the Novel in the Early Republic

One of the first pictorial representations of America, the Philipp Galle portrait of America as a muscular Indian woman (1592), suggests both the threat of the Medusa and the story of Judith and Holofernes, two related allegories of politicized violence conjoined with sexual desire (Fig. 1). Her body appears seductive and yet indifferent to its seductive force—the eyes gaze up and out of the picture's frame, eluding our look. Incongruously graceful long hair covers her genitals; the spear clutched in her left hand is not quite balanced by the severed head dangling from her right. This woman's powerful body evokes the recurrent origin story of national victories secured through the ability of a woman to behead her enemy; and it makes visible the castration panic marking such stories.[1] The peculiar fetishism of this new world order involves the symbolic substitution of a woman's body for the male enterprise.

The image also reverses the historical scenario—that is, it seems necessary to imagine this threatening Indian woman's body in order to justify slaughtering the bodies of those she represents. In this complicated mingling of seduction and threat, she resembles the Brazilian cannibal princess in the 1580 illustration of Vespucci greeting America, with its concomitant question of how a sexual threat is mirrored by and engaged in the cannibal threat (Fig. 2). To figure woman as threat seems to allow for slaughter. And since, in these representations, woman figures national origins, it is as if the violence to be *enacted* is simply *projected*—the threat *of* the male nation-making enterprise is presented as the threat *to* it. In these reversals of gender positions, the female *agent* of nation formation is thus portrayed as the natural enemy of that enterprise. The female body operates as a shifter term in this merging of colonizer and colonized, victor and victims. Yet if the male enterprise is figured in the fetishistic and symbolic substitution of the female body for the male project of nation making, then a lingering anxiety persists that

3

Figure 1. "America" (ca. 1581–1600). Engraving by Philipp Galle. *Source: Bibliothèque Nationale.*

nation making might be refigured in the violent taking apart of the male body.

"Americus rediscovers America: . . . and thenceforth she was always awake."[2] The ambiguity of such wakefulness is that America at once invites and heralds with her right arm and points to the scene of human consumption

Figure 2. "Vespucci 'Discovering' America" (ca. 1580). Engraving by Theodor Galle. *Courtesy of the Burndy Library, Dibner Institute, Cambridge, Massachusetts.*

beyond. The allure of her fleshy body competes with the implication that it is, as the scenes of cannibalism in the background suggest, nourished by the bodies of white men. While fears about this threatening woman seem to have been invoked in order to justify attacking her, there is a residual appeal in her languorous body.[3] Perhaps what makes these images interesting is not so much their transparency as indices of colonization as the ambiguity they reveal about the relation of national enterprises to representations of gender and race.

Sixteenth-century Europeans pictured the attraction and horror of the "new land" by personifying the Americas as an Indian princess, seductively naked before the white male European, but threatening to devour him.[4] In order to question how such embodiments operate in the construction of American national identity, this introduction traces a short series of such images, figures that in effect conflate national identities with women's bodies. I want first to consider the relation between sixteenth-century pictures of discovery and conquest and late eighteenth-century representations of national struggle. Such figures can embody menacing power (cannibalistic women) and its antithesis (debased and mutilated victims). Between seduction and violence, or incorporating violence as seduction, the image of the simultaneously alluring and devouring female centers cultural figurations of national conflict.

The paradoxical logic of this pictorial lesson, and the intimacy of its identification of national values, continues to structure accounts of American national identity produced in Europe as well as the Americas. Almost two hundred years pass between the appearance of these images and one of the best-known Revolutionary cartoons, "The Able Doctor, or America Swallowing the Bitter Draught" (British, 1774 [Fig. 3]). And yet there are iconographic as well as ideological connections. The message of impending political violence is clearly conveyed through threatened sexual violence: between the image of Boston—proleptically shown cannonaded in the background—and the written political protest—the Boston petition (against closing the port) torn in half in the foreground—America lies helpless. Represented as a prostrate Native American woman, she appears to have been both symbolically and euphemistically forced to swallow tea. The scene resembles a gang rape: America lies on the ground, her arms held and her legs restrained. While he holds America's legs, a man has lifted up the sheet that covers her torso and appears to be peeking at her genitals. On the right side of the cartoon, a soldier with a drawn sword labeled "Military Law" wields a phallic object that suggests a further joining of violence and sexual violence. Elsewhere represented as justly punished for having been seduced away from her duties, America is here literally a fallen woman.[5]

Again, a complicated set of reversals and inversions operate in the form of a masquerade. This masquerade alludes to but reverses the actions of the male American citizens who dressed up as Indians and dumped tea—here the tea is forced into the body of the native American woman by the British male ruling order. The fetishistic substitution of the woman's body for the male masquerade occludes the racial identifications. Showing little of the musculature or sexuality of the earlier images, America appears more vividly as the prostrate object of the voyeurism of onlookers than as the symbolic register of national conflict.

The violence of political cartoons may be traced to their obvious need to mobilize as well as explain political scenarios. On one level such cartoons are themselves presented as a form of military or state violence. The eighteenth-century British satirist Gillray, for example, was famous for fighting Napoleon; and Abraham Lincoln claimed that the Civil War cartoonist Thomas Nast was his "best recruiting sergeant."[6] Further, if "violence is the most important means available to a political group to inscribe meaning upon the world," as the political theorist Anne Norton has argued, "the source of those passions, appetites, and institutions that bind the individual to politics" is "sexuality."[7] These images of revolution thus conjoin a libidinal attachment to a political position with the violent inscribing of that political position on sexualized bodies. Although such cartoons may be understood to contain founding gestures of a sort of national eroticism—and the novels I will examine produce national identifications from romance plots—I am more interested here in

Figure 3. "The Able Doctor" (1774). Engraving by Paul Revere. *Courtesy of the American Antiquarian Society.*

demonstrating how their libidinal attachments operate to correlate political questions and threatened bodies.[8] This introduction defers a later concentration on violent familial strategies in order to look at mothers and daughters in the iconography of eighteenth-century political cartoons. These illustrations of the early American nation not only displace political violence onto sexual violence; they also code sexual violence in a way that both covers for the political/sexual threat and emphasizes its terrors.

A later Tory cartoon, "Britania and Her Daughter" (1780), finds America on her feet again, confronting her "mother" in a charged crossing of anxieties about parenting and nationhood (Fig. 4).[9] The stanzas that caption "Britania and Her Daughter" combine metaphorical justifications for the revolt against England—that England is a "bad mother" and that America has "grown" and should now be independent—with the scurrilous accusations leveled by Federalists about the licentious association with France:

> *Miss America North, so News-paper records;*
> *With her Mother Britania one day had some words,*
> *When behold Monsieur Louis advanc'd a new whim,*
> *That she should leave her Mother for to live with him.*
>
> *Britania beheld her with tears in her eyes,*
> *O! Daughter return to your duty she cries,*
> *But she replies no I'm a Woman full grown,*
> *And long for to keep a good house of my own.*

Figure 4. "Britania and Her Daughter. A Song" (1780). *Courtesy of the Library of Congress.*

Up to this point the language is the familiar conjunction of domestic and national housekeeping. The seduction of a daughter from her duty to her mother—duty, or national allegiance, figured as familialism—is introduced as a "whim" and then justified by her having grown so that she needs to keep her own house. But her mother's tears are answered by a more sinister threat, translating the family romance into a fantasy of violence:

> If you'd used me kind when I was in your power,
> I then had lived with you at this very hour,
> But now on my Lovers so much do I doat,
> That we'r Arm'd and I'll help 'em to cut your old throat.

A series of familial and political scenarios are thus linked, and the tensions among them are as prominent as their mutual reinforcement and support. The poem equates emergent female sexuality with "dangerous" political or revolutionary license; it contains the rebel justification that England's abdication of parental responsibility could explain or excuse such revolt; and it introduces the anxious preoccupation of the early republic: how does the figure of the woman who dotes on lovers and wants to cut her mother's throat become the one who will "keep a good house," or, more generally, how turn this figure of licentious sexuality, the woman involved in revolution, into an emblem of national morality—the woman who will hold the republic to-gether?[10] Finally, how can the republic convert a scene of familial violence into what Andrew Jackson was later to call "one political family"?

The story of the American Revolution told by novels as well as political cartoons repeatedly invokes the seduced bodies of women for its emotional and rhetorical force. Finding in eighteenth-century English novels a source for revolutionary sensibilities, Jay Fliegelman cites, for instance, John Adams's complaint about national vulnerability, "Democracy is Lovelace and the people are Clarissa. The artful villain will pursue the innocent lovely girl to her ruin and her death."[11] The seduction of women in popular eighteenth-century American novels like Susannah Rowson's *Charlotte Temple* (1791) and Hannah Foster's *The Coquette* (1797) clearly conflates national and bodily symbolics. Both Charlotte Temple and Eliza Wharton are seduced from affectionate mothers by rakes whose designs are compared to that of Lovelace. Their stories of ruined virtue, as Cathy Davidson reports, were received as national tragedies inspiring memorial visits to their putative tombstones.[12] While contemporary cartoons similarly portray America as seduced from her mother Britain by the designing French, such iconographic seductions associate violence with not only the sexual but also the racial attributes of women who appear as metaphors for national identity.

When America as an Indian woman is opposed to her Caucasian mother Britain in late eighteenth-century America, as a woman threatening *or* threatened with violence, a form of national miscegenation is intimated. By figuring a national conflict through the bodies of these women, a double substitution is enacted where not only a woman's body, but the body of a native American, twice disenfranchised and paradoxically seen as doubly powerful, manages the stressful business of national violence. In this cartoon, America advances toward her mother wielding a hatchet, flanked by her armed lovers. The ominous sharp implements carried by France and Spain seem on the verge of reaching Britain's body. Presented as a serene warrior, Britain requests: "Daughter return to your duty and let me punish these empty Boasters these base Villains who keep you from your Alegiance and disturb our quiet." America asserts the presence of a new sense of duty and a relocation of a foreign invasion to domestic and internal insurgency, conflating the war front and the home front: "Mother if you would punish these Villains who forced me from my Alegiance and disturb our quiet you must find them at home: These Gentlemen are my Allies, we are now Arm'd and seek your life." Her flanking companions seem to have other forms of alliance on their minds, however. Undercutting America's allusion to "gentlemen," they reply with punning sexual innuendo. Spain sneers, "Signiora Britania, I'll take care your Daughter shall be true to me. I'll make her wear a Spanish Padlock." Allegiance and duty are not political but sexual for Spain, while for France an aggressive courtship emerges: "Sacra Dieu! I vill have your Daughter vether you vill let me or no; and vat you tink besides . . . you shall roast your own Bull for our Wedding Dinner." Turning the symbolic token of British sovereignty into food for a wedding feast, he both makes a pun on John Bull and advertises a form of national cannibalism.[13]

This mixture of familial correction and sexual sadism emerges most vividly in an earlier political image, "The Colonies Reduced" (1768 [Fig. 5]). The severed arms and legs that lie about on the ground in this cartoon echo the cannibalism, figured by a detached leg, in the background of Vespucci's greeting of America as well as the detached arm in the foreground of the Philipp Galle portrait.[14] Where once America appeared as a cannibal Indian princess, now the body of her "mother" England has been presented as if for consumption. At the edge of terra incognita on seventeenth-century maps was a land of women, part of the identification of newfound lands and the female body; now the focus has shifted from a land of women to the land *as* woman. Fallen off the globe and forced to beg, the mutilated Britania finds her spear and shield useless. Yet an ambiguity of conflated bodies appears here: England's body is also the new world's body. Her amputated limbs have been labeled and include Virginia, the hand of Pennsylvania that has dropped the olive branch, New York, and the leg of New England, with a dropped spear pointing ominously toward the torso. This simultaneous revenge and loss of the new world reminds us of the scattered limbs of the earlier cannibal portraits—but who is there to devour these pieces of a national body?[15]

The iconography of the illustrations and political cartoons that accompany or comment on the historical trauma and thrill of moments of discovery depends heavily on allegorical codes. Yet the use of allegory in these pictures at once embodies national conflicts and insists that we read past or through bodies; the violence they exhibit can paradoxically appear so blatant that it can

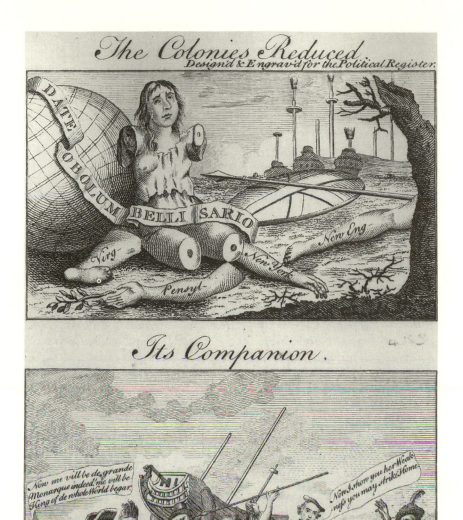

Figure 5. "The Colonies Reduced. Its Companion" (1768). *Courtesy of the John Carter Brown Library at Brown University.*

barely be seen. As one recent commentator on the cultural fascination with the bodies of dead women puts it, "As we focus on the hidden, the figurative meaning, what is plainly seen may not be seen at all. . . . the gesture of an aesthetic substitution is such that what is literally represented—femininity and death—often entirely escapes observation."[16] The substitutions these images enact occlude racial and sexual violence in the name of political allegory. Hence as these allegories advertise a racially coded sexual violence, they both cover for a political threat and emphasize its terrors. Even as fraught attempts to figure the American Revolution by embodying nations as women, for example, almost inevitably require threats in the form of rape, mutilation, and dismemberment to the bodies of combatants, that violence is immediately rendered symbolic. In reading these visual images for *how* they represent a national story, what is literally shown here—femininity and death as a national allegory—can hide the problematic circularity of a national allegory figured by dead or threatened women who stand for the state.

Keeping company with a dismembered body, for example, "The Colonies Reduced" was shown with "Its Companion" (British, 1768), in which a somewhat dizzying cluster of aggressive acts surrounds the representation of England's body (Fig. 5). Three men form a closed triangle on the right side of the cartoon: the British minister Lord Bute holds up Britain's petticoat and stabs her, Spain sodomizes her with his long sword, and a man with a Maltese cross on his back prepares to beat her naked buttocks with a long paddle. As he raises her skirts, Bute exults to the other two: "Now I show you her Weakness you may strike Home."[17] Seeming unaware of what is occurring, Britain raises her spear against America. America rushes into the arms of France who says, stabbing Britain in the eye, "Now me will be de grande Monarque indeed!" A smirking Dutchman carries off one of her ships in the background. And in the foreground a snake (symbolic of America after Benjamin Franklin's famous "Join or Die" cartoon) tries to bite her.[18] The sadism of such overkill—injuring a body with rape, robbery, eyestabbing, snakebite, beating—may appear irrelevant to rather than constitutive of the account of national violence it is intended to illustrate.

To repeat, the political use of allegory at once embodies national conflicts and insists that we read *past* or *through* bodies. Allegorical violence appears so blatant that it often cannot be seen as violence. The almost unimaginable aggression de Sade displays in works like *Philosophy in the Bedroom*, where the daughter directs her mother's penetration, poisoning, and mutilation, is suggested by (perhaps even driven by) the extravagant proliferation of penetrations directed against the mother's body in this political cartoon: if all these threatened actions are carried out, she's anally speared, whipped, shot, bitten by a snake, and blinded by a dagger.[19] It may seem irrelevant that her Indian daughter America runs into the arms of her French lover.

Recent historical work has on many fronts established that "gender is a primary way of signifying relationships of power."[20] What I have tried to trace here is how gender implicates race and nation in signifying relations of power.

The primacy of any of these categories can seem subsumed by the violence of iconographic dismemberments and beheadings. Opening with an account of symbolic violence and sexuality in national embodiments, this book will attempt to establish further premises for and scenarios of such violent actions. Tracing sexual, political, and familial accounts of national identity, I want to consider how an identity bound up with racial, ethnic, or gendered embodiments is harnessed to the national project. At the same time, race, gender, and nation are emphatically not casual or isomorphic substitutions for one another: to understand them that way is to overlook the problematic competition of such categories at precisely the points where their identities are most at stake.

The acting out of murderous families in a haunted house preoccupies the cultural scenarios of the early republic.[21] As Carol Clover has noted of a later version of American gothic, "What makes these houses terrible is not just their Victorian decrepitude, but the terrible families—murderous, incestuous, cannibalistic—that occupy them."[22] For example, in *Common Sense*, his famous call to arms for the American national enterprise, Thomas Paine complains, typically, "But Britain is the parent country say some. Then the more shame upon her conduct. Even brutes do not devour their young, nor savages make war upon their families."[23] Although displaced onto the British here, images of people devouring each other and making war on families locate this savage violence as a peculiarly American activity.

The historical events these cartoons illustrate could be understood to invoke such violence as part of negotiating the move from patriarchy to fraternalism. During an age of revolutions, the problem of fraternal violence can appear as at once a symbolic and an actual problem of democracy.[24] Once patriarchy has been succeeded by fraternity, hierarchical stasis supplanted by egalitarian challenge, anxieties about equality produce a struggle for power often figured as a competition over a woman.[25] Such a struggle between brothers, as it is represented for many of these conflicts, requires a deposed mother and a weak or absent father. If revolution as an upheaval in the social order seems most visible in terms of a family analogy, at least in the eighteenth century, it is also *experienced* as a family analogy—succession and competition make it seem necessary to kill members of the family.[26]

The political viability of women was often expressed as an image of republican virtue or power. The backlash against such female imagery might be seen in the formation of a separate domestic sphere. But the move to put women in a separate sphere also meant the politicizing of that sphere. Developing a theory of the relation between the state's reliance on family imagery and the transformations caused in both state and family by the French Revolution, Lynn Hunt asks: "What kind of family romance would replace the one dominated by the patriarchal father?"[27] Crucially, if the new fraternal order lays claim to a nonhierarchical organization of power, the position of women becomes all the more problematic: "Women who acted in the public sphere of politics would be described as transgressing sexual boundaries" and yet "most representations of the republic were feminine."[28] In the years following the

French Revolution, "Male hostility toward women's political participation began to crystallize into a fully elaborated domestic ideology." This domestic ideology, as in the United States, meant that attention focused on the "education of a new generation of republican children" and contemporary pamphleteers moved away from the previous anxiety about women as revolutionary icons to propose that "Marriage prepares the government of the family and brings social order."[29] In France as in the United States, the problem of erring transgressing women was to be "solved" through domesticity. Following this historical and political gendering of the nation, *Romances of the Republic* traces how women and the family stand or stand in for national identity between the American Revolution and the Civil War.[30] In the early national period, romances of the republic present women and the family paradoxically as at once embodiments and abstractions of national values.

II.

"It has indeed often been observed by foreigners, with some surprise," wrote the American novelist Susan Ridley Sedgwick in 1834, "that females here are remarkably absent from the care of the public weal." While "foreigners" may express surprise about finding women "absent from the care of the public weal," what today's readers may find more surprising is that such an absence, in the nineteenth-century domestic novel that presumably encouraged it, should excite comment. Sedgwick's explanation looks at first like that of the early nineteenth-century "woman's novel," which purportedly knows nothing beyond its "separate sphere." She claims, however, that the absence of women from public care is not caused by the constraints of domesticity: "There is a better reason."

Sedgwick finds that American women do not need to concern themselves with affairs of state because "government here, though extending over all its protection and vigilance, is a guardian, not a spy." This "guardian" government protects and watches, but does not invade: "It does not rudely enter our houses, hearts, and consciences; women are not made to feel its existence by an invasion of their tenderest affections, in codes of conscription, dis-abilities, and test-acts." The equivalent status granted here to "houses, hearts, and consciences" collapses the position of women and the world of the home—the interior space of the home is where the hearts and the women are—while at the same time the home seems as thoroughly fixed within women as hearts and consciences. As a guardian, overseeing the operations of the home, American government further appears—"to use a female figure of speech—like a well made garment: it fits perfectly and presses nowhere." To claim that government guards or watches over women rather than spies on them first maintains the separation of home and world that looks like the familiar separation called for in the "cult of domesticity," which held that each had a separate sphere. Somewhat ominous alternatives are posited here in the "codes of conscription," however.[31]

While American government does not "rudely enter" the hearts or consciences—that is, in Sedgwick's equation, the homes—of American women, it "covers" them in such a way that the ostensible difference between the state's position outside the home and its ministrations within the home becomes increasingly difficult to trace. And while Sedgwick claims to be noting a separation of home and world here, she paradoxically calls attention to the ways it is not, or not only, a separation. If government does not "rudely enter" the home, this is in large part because it does not need to: outside the home, as a guardian, it becomes paradoxically all the more effective inside the home, in the comforting form of a garment that "fits perfectly and presses nowhere." How do these oppositions define one another—as the body and the garment, home and government, women and politics, or the female and the civil (that is, not simply male, but opposed to female)?

Relating the place of women in the home and the place of government—or the place of women in the discourses of the family and politics—raises the question of whether they are indeed separate spheres or arranged in a distinct though problematized "fit."[32] As the threat of what might be called female "political sexuality" was alleviated through the concept of the "Republican Mother," "those who opposed women in politics had to meet the proposal that women could—and should—play a political role through the raising of a patriotic child." The displacement of the danger of the politically (and sexually) active woman onto the figure of the mother who will raise political children meant that women were at once implicitly granted political effectiveness and explicitly denied it. Such an "ambivalent relationship between motherhood and citizenship," according to Linda Kerber, "would be one of the most lasting, and most paradoxical, legacies of the Revolutionary generation."[33]

Proclaiming that women act politically through their position in the family, John Adams asserted in 1778 that the "foundation of national morality must be laid in private families."[34] After the American Revolution, with the rise of the "republican family," the family came increasingly to be considered a private space separate from the public sphere of state and government.[35] With such a separation—that is, with a change in the conception of the family from public to private—came a change in the relation of family and state and in the rhetorical strategies for explaining and implementing this change.[36] Familial language was still used to explain state policy with the difference that the family was no longer described as a miniaturized version of the state and indeed might be thought to disrupt the state. The concept of a republican family implied neither absolute separation nor absolute joining of state and family, but unstable relations with permeable and unfixed boundaries.

The permeability of these boundaries was emphasized to the extent that, by 1837, a legal commentator could speak of a "reciprocal action and reaction constantly, though almost invisibly, existent between government and our firesides; and, if insubordination reigns in either, it is very certain, in a short time, to obtain in both."[37] Such reciprocal actions and reactions, balancing the state of the state and the state of the family, meant a strict attention to the operation of the family as well as the operation of the state. It further produced a "conspicuous and persistent public obsession with the well-being of the American household" in the period. This obsession meant the family was both made public and publicized; the image of the family was thus reinscribed in public institutions that maintained its private status while ensuring its public function.[38]

After the Revolution, the announced project of nationalist "young America" was to mold children and instill in them "an inviolable attachment to their country," beginning, as the orator Rufus Choate exhorted, with "the infant in his cradle." This origin of national and political loyalties in the cradle points yet again to the peculiar configuration of national and familial bonds. It has been noted that it "was a convention of American public language between the 1790s and the Civil War to speak of the Union . . . in familial and domestic terms. Political language borrowed readily from 'sweet household talk, and phrases of the hearth.'" Such benevolent familial rhetoric accompanied a more comprehensive strategy: "As society preempted functions that once were monopolized by the family, it looked for ways to model its performance on that of an idealized family."[39]

John Quincy Adams, for example, accompanied the traditional Fourth of July reading of the Declaration of Independence in 1821 with this oration on the family: "The sympathies of men begin with the affections of domestic life. They are rooted in the natural relations of husband and wife, of parent and child" and "spread" to "countryman and fellow-citizen; terminating only with the circumference of the globe." Although this affection spreads from family to country, Adams asserts that "the tie which binds us to our country," while derived from the "sympathies of domestic life," becomes "more deeply seated in our nature." Finally, in the "common Government that constitutes our *Country* . . . all the sympathies of domestic life and kindred blood . . . are combined."[40] Such a description of "common Government" shows both a "natural" continuity between the family and the state and the tension produced by the desire for such continuity. The family is at once a model for government and the socializing unit that will make that government tenable. The country is "constituted" by a common government made of sympathies. But to learn the link to government and country, "all the sympathies of domestic life and kindred blood" are called on.

As Andrew Jackson explained, in his Farewell Address of 1837, "the Constitution cannot be maintained, nor the Union preserved . . . by the mere exertion of the coercive powers confided to the General Government. The foundations must be laid in the affections of the people . . . in the fraternal attachments which citizens . . . bear to one another as members of one political family." Here "affection" establishes, as with Adams, an identification between government and the local government of the family and thus allows for the condensed locution "one political family," joining family and state under one roof.[41] The move from coercion to affection that Jackson relies on became linked with the desire to institutionalize the processes of the family in the early nineteenth century. Institutions, especially the schools, but also asylums, penitentiaries, and factories, were called on to replicate and supplement the order and the processes of the family. Therefore, politics may be viewed as a domestic issue both because the family functions as an allegory for the state and because the state is absorbed through the family, through the way the family is organized, and through the repetition of family organization in other political structures.

An anxiety about disorder within the family is often exhibited in the early sentimental or domestic novel. These novels, which frequently show the family as a model for the nation, also demonstrate the ways it has become an instrument of social control. If politics is not opposed to but reciprocally related to the personal or familial, then the novel's concern with personal and family relations gives it political significance and purpose.[42] The historical novelists of this earlier period frequently turn from historical accounts to concentrate on the "domestic"; the historical realm appears at first to be subordinate to, or merely illustrative of, conflicts in the home. Yet the authors of these novels claim simultaneously that historical details are valuable insofar as they support domestic ideologies (such as free choice in marriage), and that domestic details matter as an exposition of historical change.

The reciprocity and even tautological relation of "separate spheres" might be illustrated by Catherine Sedgwick's closing conviction in her historical novel, *The Linwoods* (1835), that "the cause of humanity and the advance of civilization depend mainly on the purity of the institution of marriage."[43] This attempt to equate humanity, civilization, and marriage, to establish a reciprocity between the contracting of marriages and the advance of civilization, involves establishing a congruence, that is, an identification, among them. Such a congruence brings into mutual interdependence the domestic place of the family—a place marked in the early historical novel by gestures of courtship and the forming of marriages—and the political place of the state—a place determined not only by battles, but also and especially by the endorsements of these marriages. Although typically the action of these novels takes in specific battles, real prisons, and real historical figures such as Washington, the excitement or suspense is often provided by obstacles to the marriages of their central characters. This romantic suspense is not just the formal requirement of the novel plot: the achievement of these marriages represents the very success of the revolutionary contest. Put simply, the marriages of the characters in these novels typically depend on their political commitments and produce a founding of the family that founds the state. Indeed, the reciprocal work of the family posited here seems to be to create selves who create families who create states in the image of the family.

The displacement of the historical onto the domestic is made possible by and depends on their identity, and the achievement of that identity is the story Sedgwick's novel, like others of the period, tells. Such a displacement, however, will eventually lead to the reverse strategy of separate spheres—that is, to a separation of history and domesticity, world and home, politics and the family—a separation that may coincide with the separation, on the one hand, of the popular political-family novels of Sedgwick or James Fenimore Cooper, and the succeeding domestic novels of, by, and for women, from, on the other, nonpopular, "significant" literature by men. The novel itself, limited to domesticity, would ratify this separation. If marriage and politics are identical or isomorphic, then to compare them is to invoke a tautology: marriage equals politics. But much of this fiction hesitates about the equation, so marriage and politics devolve into separate spheres. Such spheres may be mutually suppor-tive, but are nonetheless emphatically distinct. The American marriage may be the "foundation of intellect and virtue"[44] for the new republic, but the insistent rhetoric by which marriage and state are conflated suggests a faltering of a sense of congruence between the government within self and family and that of the larger state. The insistence of the focus on the family thus becomes a way of separating the family from the world; to focus on the family in the name of an alignment of the family with the state may paradoxically lead to the separation of the family from the state.

While the family continued to serve as an exemplary private domain—a private model for public structures—throughout the nineteenth century, this difference between public and private appears as a functional one. In a brief essay on the history of government and the family, Michel Foucault argues that the eighteenth century witnessed a major shift from a notion of family as a "model" or analogue of government to a notion of the family as an "instru-ment" of government.[45] The shift from model to instrument, or rather the shift to model *as* instrument, means that the family as separate and private becomes an instrument of governmental measures of social control even as the separateness of the family from these measures is insisted on. In other words, the very difference between public and private, the separation maintained between the institution and the family, enables us to consider the family's role in the institution.[46] Such a conception of the family in the early republic may paradoxically incorporate the still influential nineteenth-century picture of the family as a "haven in a heartless world." Indeed, if the description of family as a "haven" becomes central to the nineteenth-century concept of the family as a separate sphere, it becomes possible to see how this concept perversely assists the family to relay the very social and economic values it is defined "against."

Exploring the novel in the early republic is central to understanding con-ceptions of women and the family in the period.[47] In particular, the opposi-tion maintained between the "home" and the "world" in nineteenth-century domestic fiction might make the home a part of that sphere to which it has been opposed. If, as writers of the period suggest, the home already incorpo-rates the role of government, the notion of separate spheres may keep such a difference functional. As a *Knickerbocker* reviewer put it, in December 1858, "The novel at present, more than any other variety of literature, becomes a household book, and in some sort a member of the family." Brought into the home, indeed, into the "home's heart," the novel, as I have been suggesting, centrally introduces the relations among home and world, the family and politics.[48] At the same time, both contemporary and current writings about this period exhibit a certain tension arising from the uneasy placement of home and world, of "inside" and "outside."

In specifying the relays between political ideology and family configurations, I seek to bring into play both a truism and a flexible and often powerful tool for reconfiguring governments. What matters about the specificity of this argument almost goes without saying—that a powerful nation constitutes much of its political identity through the language of heterosexual and patriarchal family relations. Its durability and power are certainly bound up with its status as "truism," that is, as a historical construct that tends to be represented as the natural ground of history. Less obviously, it matters that fiction carries this message—that it operates in the dissemination of national presence into families.[49] The machinery of the family works as a conduit for expressing at once violent actions and controlling reactions. Postulating the happy family operates to keep citizens in line with the state as well as to buffer the sensation of state control, and fiction provides the clearest expression of that family.

III.

This book looks at the translation of revolutionary discourse through a number of documents, primarily novels, but also poems, pamphlets, and sermons. In the historical romance, for example, questions of political and national identity become attached to female bodies, and a national subject is formed through the coordination of citizenship and family ideology. The historical romance presents sexual and familial accounts of national identity that perform a political function; the pressure in these discourses is to locate forms of the national body, or rather to produce, historically and politically, a national body and a national family that could reproduce that body. Such a concentration on reproduction opens the intimately related questions concerning the links between the reproduction of bodily states and the reproduction of nation states. Hence, in the chapters on the gothic and on narratives about slavery and the frontier, the study moves from the political structuring of the family to question the ambiguity and instability of bodily identity—the bodily identity of what might be described as the republic in person.

Political and literary discourses both respond to and enact a relationship between the family and the state in America from 1790 to the 1850s. Politicians at the time of the American Revolution frequently linked women and the state—Great Britain as a bad mother, for example—and the historical novels of the early republic subsequently use such family imagery to indicate an idealized concept of how the nation should function, but also the failure of that posited model—the breakdown of heterosexual normativity under the stresses of national violence. The threats of violence at the frontier and in slavery are rehearsed in the specter of a newly transgressive family romance: a romance that uncertainly secures the boundaries of the family, in part through claustrophobic melodramas centering on miscegenation and incest. These accounts appear as rhetorical strategies in novels as well as political oratory, in pamphlets and sermons as well as poems. The idiom of the debates between Federalists and Republicans in the 1790s (focusing on the constitution and the Alien and Sedition Acts) was reinvented, with a difference, by the language of debates between pro- and anti-slavery forces in the 1830s through 1850s. Both debates addressed the ideologies of family and marriage, and, crucially, woman's defined or defining role within them, and they asserted the relationship of the family to two connected larger enterprises: the operations of the state and the threats posed to state or family by some alien force or contagion.

The project involves what might be called a prehistory of the separate spheres concept: the separation of male and female, world and home, that has tended to dominate conceptions of American culture. That concept, however, presupposes precisely the gender and political divisions this book will reexamine. That is, questions of American identity have frequently been taken up, particularly in literary study, apart from national politics and have instead focused on, in effect separated out, gender divisions; this book will relocate gender divisions (which presuppose, I will be arguing, the antinomies of liberal market culture) in relation to models of American citizenship and conditions of national identity.[50]

The first part of this book traces a series of connected changes in the depictions of the American Revolution, the use of the family as a model and instrument of political forces, the relations between sexual, political, and familial rhetoric, and the changes in the formal features of the novel that accompany these political and familial changes. In brief, the early historical novel formalizes some of the more extravagant features of the gothic novel—incest, murder, a vision of the family as a place of horror—while incorporating a sentimental picture of the family produced in the domestic novel. In the first half of the book, I work with early national writers like Charles Brockden Brown, Catherine Sedgwick, James Fenimore Cooper, and Mason Weems, and I argue that the significance of the early American novel lies not merely in its inculcation of national values and its consumption within the home (which aided the promulgation of those values); it also formulated a family structure that, unlike earlier models, was neither patriarchal nor a revolt against patriarchy. Instead, in emphasizing sibling struggles and intergenerational quarrels about marriage, the novel of this period attempted to unite disparate political, national, class, and even racial positions.

The first two chapters place the novels of Charles Brockden Brown in the context of the political and religious controversies of the 1790s. I begin by discussing *Arthur Mervyn* as the register of several related anxieties produced by the French Revolution. The coincidence of a virulent yellow fever epidemic in Philadelphia the same year the Terror ruled in France provided Americans with an implicit analogy between Democracy run amuck and a fatally contagious disease. The association of French democracy and deism was seen as a further danger. While *Arthur Mervyn* implicitly sought to solve his problems by creating a safe family unit, *Wieland* displays the terrors that can be played out within the family. *Wieland* locates danger at once in religious extremism and in the intrusion of an "alien" force into the family. I show how that alien, Carwin, is invoked both because of the concurrent American nervousness about the intrusion of French immigrants (a nervousness that led to the Alien and Sedition Acts of 1797, the year of *Wieland*'s publication) and because of the need to see political and religious dangers as imposed from without, rather than as coming from within the family.

The notion that the family was an appropriate model for institutional as well as political discourse and organization became increasingly powerful in the early republic as schools, prison, asylums, became at once increasingly "benevolent" and increasingly well "managed." In the third chapter, on Catherine Sedgwick's *The Linwoods* (1835) and James Fenimore Cooper's *The Spy* (1827), I discuss the use of the family as a model for the nation and question why women, particularly mothers, are necessarily pictured as threats to the family in novels that treat the American Revolution. *The Spy* shows the American Revolution as a conflict within the family to be resolved by political marriages. In striking contrast to *The Spy*, which ends on a note of family reunion, Cooper's *Lionel Lincoln* presents the failure of the family to contain the violence of revolution. The suspected infidelity of the wife and mother is blamed, and only with the return to England can the family be considered saved. America becomes, in the closing words of the novel, "a remote province of the British empire" (545). As part of a projected series of novels on American colonies during the American Revolution, the book reveals Cooper's misgivings about the American "victory" over England.

An uneasiness about this victory is also prominently displayed in the work of Nathaniel Hawthorne. A central figure of Hawthorne's stories and unfinished romances of the Revolution, for instance, is a huge rambling house, once splendid, now decayed, and displaced by newer and more democratic styles of architecture. In the fourth chapter, I discuss Hawthorne's "Legends of the Province House." These short stories first appeared in the *United States Magazine and Democratic Review*, a nationalist, Locofoco journal founded under the auspices of Martin van Buren and claiming Andrew Jackson as its first subscriber. Taking over the metaphors of the American Revolution and presenting himself as a "second Washington," a second father to his country, Jackson made use of a set of powerful associations already entrenched in American political dogma. In line with this network of literary and political discourses, the novels and other literature of the period share a concentration on the family, a concentration that may be seen to culminate in the rise of novels of domesticity at mid-century. This chapter treats the politics of the family through a consideration of Hawthorne, of Cooper's *Lionel Lincoln*, and of other contemporary historical novels, such as George Lippard's *Blanche of Brandywine* (1846).

The politics of identity in the period of the early American republic involved the cultural production of a national self. The last part of the book moves from the intersection of national values and family conflicts in the early American novel's presentation of that self through dramas about the Revolutionary war to treat dramas about violence on the frontier and in slavery. Debates about slavery and national identity also insisted on the involvement of domesticity and political concerns. Building on the work of historians like Linda Kerber and Mary Ryan, who trace the training of the "Republican mother" in this period, and the work of literary historians like Jane Tompkins, Nina Baym, and Mary Kelley who have sought to bring women writers into the canon, I concentrate on how both slavery apologists and abolitionists use language, paying attention, for example, to the simultaneity of domestic concerns and miscegenation in the writings of Lydia Maria Child. Where domesticity has been treated as a "given" of nineteenth-century American literature, I trace its invention as part of a larger social and literary politics.

In my fifth chapter, I examine how James Fenimore Cooper's *The Last of the Mohicans* (1827) not only stages frontier violence within the family, but also questions the relations of humans and animals, whites and Indians, men and women. In effect presenting violence as a means of reproduction, the novel wards off miscegenation in its attempt to produce a national story. The last chapter considers how nineteenth-century American pro- and anti-slavery debates used the matter of embodied racial identity as their characteristic point of departure for the justification or repudiation of slavery. The difficulty that such claims for or against racial embodiment produce shows up particularly in accounts of incest and miscegenation. Through an analysis of such texts as the pro-slavery epic *The Devil in America* (1856) and Lydia Maria Child's *A Romance of the Republic* (1867), I show the charged political and racial identity of the national family.

In approaching the early republic using feminist social history and the "new historicism" of literary critics, different questions can be asked of nineteenth-century American culture—how it articulates the position of women and the function of the family in political terms; how it describes political structures in family terms; and how these structures and relationships appear in literature that both shapes and reflects the ideological concerns of its production.[51]

The vexed relation between "interior" and "outside" worlds, the uncertain agency of culture, symbolic forms, and bodily dispositions in the making of national identity, the question of the origin of persons and identities: such issues represent the very terrain of these romances of the republic, even as they point to the supposed impasses of new historicism. In exploring this terrain, my project necessarily engages with those impasses. At the same time, the components of these cases are not necessarily "explanations" of them. If it has become customary to locate contradictions and impasses as breakdown points—points at which ideologies demystify themselves—it may be the case that these operate by way of, and not in spite of, such impasses and contradictions. Inasmuch as impasses may be seen as symptoms of such fraught enterprises rather than as explanations of them, the explanation can scarcely abandon such symptoms. What my project seeks to do finally is to draw into relation and test out the difficulties that become visible in the subject of the romance of the republic itself.

Plague and Politics in 1793:
Arthur Mervyn

Infidelity and Contagion: The Rhetoric of Revolution

An eighteenth-century New England minister who wrote a history of the American Revolution once described the need to "dress" his history modestly: "laboured elegance and extravagant colouring only brings her into suspicion, hides her beauty, and makes the cautious reader afraid lest he is in company with a painted harlot."[1] While it seems understandable that a minister would not want his reader to keep "company with a painted harlot," the conjunction of history and harlotry here appears striking. Such nervousness about licentious sexuality in language—particularly language that depicted the still volatile topic of the American Revolution—extended to other writers, ministers, orators, and politicians in the young republic. They protected themselves by claiming to use a conservative rhetoric in their efforts to extradite the "alien" dangers of both deism and radical democracy. They proceeded, however, by emphasizing the dangers of the loose woman and, in attempting to educate the American people about the contagion of her infidelity, paradoxically enhancing the sexual associations they claimed to be protecting themselves against.

The writer "Parson" Weems, known today for his aggrandizing *Life of Washington*, spent thirty years peddling books and tracts with titles like *The Bad Wife's Looking Glass* and *God's Revenge Against Adultery*. Presented as moral lessons, rooted in an idealized concept of sexuality and the family, these tracts also discussed political issues, a mixture so common in eighteenth- and early nineteenth-century writings that the rhetoric of sexuality and the family became nearly interchangeable with that of religion and politics. Such interchangeability is a direct concern of the early American novel. While concentrating on gothic sensationalism and sentimental seduction, the novel in the early republic displays contemporary social and political anxiety about the stability of the family and its freedom from unfaithfulness, often figured as the contamination of the outside world.

In *God's Revenge Against Adultery* (1815), Weems presents two exemplary cases of the dangers of infidelity: the "accomplished Dr. Theodore Wilson, (*Delaware*) who for seducing Mrs. Nancy Wiley, had his brains blown out by her husband," and the "elegant Mr. James O'Neale, Esq. (*North Carolina*) who for seducing the beautiful Miss Matilda d'Estrange, was killed by her brother."[2] At first glance, the moral for adulterers is to stay clear of family members; at second, to beware women with disturbing names. But, as Weems unfolds them, the crucial problem with these scenes is that neither seducer has been educated to control his excessive desires. One professes himself a deist, and the other joins in religious revivals; both transgress the controlled confines of religious thought while violating the confines of the family. And despite the specifics of geography in Weems's account, it also becomes clear that this problem of uncontrolled desire is national, and that this pamphlet is finally as much about political and religious education in the new republic as about adultery.

Dr. Theodore Wilson deceives his wife because "He was infected with that most shameful and uneasy of all diseases, an incurable lust or itching after strange women." His "disease" is not from natural causes, however: "this elegant young man owed his early downfal to reading 'PAINE'S AGE OF REASON'" (146). This "libertine publication" sets loose Wilson's "boundless ardor for animal pleasures" and encourages him with "bold slanders of the bible"; Wilson "threw aside his father's good old family bible, and for a surer guide to pleasure took up the AGE OF REASON!" Paine's incitement to deism has not been uniformly treated as a "guide to pleasure," but religious infidelity becomes more than metaphorical as Wilson's disease spreads.

Wilson begins a liaison with the wife of a tavern-keeper. Nancy Wiley has been poorly educated; she overvalues her own beauty and "neglect[s] those immortal beauties of the mind WISDOM and PIETY" (150). They seem well matched, until her husband finds them together and kills Wilson, whereupon Wilson's wife dies of grief. The only beneficiary in Weems's account is Wilson's younger brother who forsakes the "*strenuous idleness*" of a study of the law to study divinity "and is now the pastor of the first Presbyterian church in Philadelphia" (166).

The lesson here—that religion provides surety against Paine's dangerous excesses—is countered by "Case the Second" in which a "rich old gentleman, whose name was L'Estrange," has found wealth but not happiness: "In spite of my money, I find I am growing old and crazy . . . I'll go to the BIBLE and see if I can find happiness there." He learns, curiously enough, that "religion, properly defined, is only the ART OF HAPPINESS," and therefore opens his home to religious revivalists, especially embracing young Mr. O'Neale, who "professed himself a CONVERT!" (169). Unfortunately, young O'Neale's education, like that of Nancy Wiley, has been "worldly minded" and he has sought "his happiness in the concupiscences of the FLESH, the chief among which is the appetite for SEX" (170). Looking for this happiness, in spite of his "conversion," O'Neale attempts to seduce Miss Matilda L'Estrange, "but her natural modesty, strengthened by education" helps her resist him until she too experiences a religious conversion. She reaches a "transport" of "convulsive joy, her breasts heaving and panting—her color alternately coming and going, now crimsoned with joy and delight and now pale and exhausted as if near overcome with fatigue" (172). In this sexual "holy extacy," Matilda finds O'Neale and throws "her arms around his neck," "fondly pressing him to her swelling breasts." These "virgin caresses" "served to kindle higher the fever of brutal passion"; O'Neale takes advantage of the moment, and "Miss L'Estrange was ruined . . . by a villain under the sacred garb of religion" (173). Inevitably she becomes pregnant and her family casts her out. Her brother shoots O'Neale, who laments, "Oh had I been but early brought up to religion and some good trade, I had never come to this miserable end!" (187).

O'Neale's lame regrets, and these case histories generally, emphasize the importance of a careful upbringing, safe from the introduction of false texts and the introduction of desires that exceed the bounds of marriage and the family. Purportedly a pamphlet about the dangers of adulterous sex, this turns out to be a tract that insists on a concept of education conservatively cordoned off from either deism or revivalism. Why are both extremes of religious discourse linked with illicit sexual desire? Put another way, why did post-Revolutionary writers see both religious and political excesses as threats to the family?

The most notorious deist was Thomas Paine, whose *Age of Reason* was vilified for making religious infidelity accessible through straightforward language and low price (Paine subsidized its publication).[3] Thirty-five replies to Paine's *Age of Reason* were published within a decade of its appearance (1794–1796), suggesting the alarm with which it was received.[4] Far more than the document itself, these replies link an "infidelity" of religious thought with infidelity in the family and, by implication, the state. Timothy Dwight, the conservative New England minister and Yale president, mounted several prominent attacks on Paine and other deists with his satirical "The Triumph of Infidelity" and sermons like "A Discourse on Some Events of the Last Century" (1801). In the latter, Dwight attacks infidelity as a composite of *"opposition to Christianity, devotion to sin and lust,* and a *pompous profession of love to Liberty."* Deism as a threat to institutionalized Christianity here becomes inseparable from a sexuality that erodes the boundaries of the family and a version of democracy that endangers the state.

If the exponents of deism had presented a "candid and logical opposition to Christianity," Dwight claims, "no reasonable objection [could] be made." But they insist on insidious rhetoric: the "infidels have neither labored, nor wished, to convince the understanding, but have bent all their efforts to engross the heart." The reader, "engaged by the ingenuity of the writer, is lost in a mist of doubtful expressions and unsettled sentiments. His faith is constantly solicited to gravely described dreams; and his eye is required to fix on the form of a cloud." Like Weems, Dwight appears to describe a process of seduction. The "ingenuity of the writer" is focused on the method rather than the matter of persuasion, and "From the highway of common sense [the reader] is invited into bypaths."[5] Implicitly, Dwight suggests that if Paine had stuck with "Common Sense," he would find no fault with his "ingenuity." But Paine and other deists have strayed "into bypaths" and the former efficacy of attempts to "convince the understanding" is now channelled into "engrossing the heart."

The dangerous character of infidels manifests itself in their talents and the diversity of their application: "Their writings have assumed every form, and treated every subject of thought." From "lofty philosophical discourse," they have "descended . . . to the newspaper paragraph . . . from regular history to the anecdote; from the epic poem to the song." The influence of deism is everywhere: "in a note subjoined to a paper on criticism or politics; in a hint in a book of travels." What is most insidious about deism is its omnipresence and the hapless plight of the reader who must assent despite himself, "to yield his judgment before he was aware that he was being called to judge."[6] Since infidelity may be at work in the most innocuous writing, all forms of writing become suspect.

The nervousness that Dwight displays about the omnipresence and diversity of deistic writings may help explain why he finds infidelity a political as well as a sexual and religious threat. The notion of infidelity penetrated political disputes in several ways. Religious boundaries were patrolled by the politically and professionally dominant Federalists who claimed a monopoly on religion and opposed what they saw as Democratic deism. Subsequently, as the historian Clifford Griffin has shown, many so-called benevolent associations that appeared during the early nineteenth century—the Bible Society, for example, or the American Tract Society, which distributed almost two million pamphlets in the first half of the century—were Federalist-inspired attempts to maintain social order. These associations saw the Bible as a "moral police" that kept "guard over property and life" and was "better than every measure of secret espionage to which a Napoleon or a Nicholas might resort." Finally, claimed the Home Missionary Society, *The Gospel is the most economical police on earth.*"[7] The Bible was unabashedly the most visible symbol of a conservative political order.

The policing that was carried out in the name of the Bible extended from the benevolent societies to other institutions like schools, and particularly to the new American institution of literature. At the heart of these gestures of containment was a model of social control that took the form of a clearly defined family order. Since the French Revolution had introduced a model of Revolution that undermined this order, writers of the period frequently worked to keep the notion of Revolution contained politically, and even metaphorically as a "family affair," a process that became linked with the desire to confine and institutionalize the family.[8]

Even such apparently innocuous terms as the "sacred honor" of the nation point to the conjunction of religious and sexual beliefs at the heart of national and familial identity. They may also shed a new light on the literature of the early Republic. Novels like Charles Brockden Brown's *Wieland* in many ways *because* of their gothic concern with incest, repressed desires, and lurid crimes, successfully "make the picture of a single family a model from which to sketch the condition of a nation."[9] By so luridly displaying the threat posed to the family by the outside world, these novels encouraged and promoted a conservative, closed model of the family, though at the same time, in the closed circle of incestuous violence of *Wieland*, we can see that concentration on the family produces its own threats. The representative family-as-nation that was portrayed in political pamphlets of the Revolutionary War found a fictional form in novels of the early Republic. National concerns were portrayed as domestic dilemmas, since to preserve the nation it was conceived necessary to preserve the family as a carefully constituted supporting unit. Therefore the sexual infidelity that represented the greatest threat to the family was presented as a national threat, especially after the French Revolution when women were popularly understood to be the instigators of the dread mob that came to stand for democratic rule, and Liberty came to be depicted as a whore.

Further links among the dangers of democracy and the introduction of religious and familial infidelity were read into Paine's writings. When the "Common-Sense" and "Crisis" pamphlets appeared, metaphorical associations between the family and the state were an understandable part of the contemporary political rhetoric that sought to justify Britain's continuing domination of the American colonies as the natural prerogative of a parent. Paine's language in *The Rights of Man* and *The Age of Reason* made these associations more foreign and more threatening. Since the former was an attempt to justify the French Revolution (albeit before the Reign of Terror), it became associated with the dangers of the mob, especially a mob of woman. Federalists attacked the *Age of Reason* not only for making religious infidelity popular, but also because, as one noted, "Infidels in religion are apt to be democrats in politics."[10] The concept of freedom of religion may have seemed most dangerous because of the threat it appeared to pose to all institutions. Paine claimed that churches were merely artificial devices to "terrify and enslave mankind, and monopolize power and profit"; freedom from this institution would bring both personal and political liberation.[11]

In a more familiar call for freedom, the paper known as "Common-Sense," Paine had taken the terms of family relations that loyalists relied on and transformed them for the American cause: "Britain is the parent country, say some. Then the more shame upon her conduct. Even brutes do not devour their young, nor savages make war upon their families."[12] In fact, he proclaimed, Britain had no rights, since "Europe, and not England, is the parent country of America." Instead of the "mother country," England may be more accurately portrayed as a philanderer, faithful to neither familial nor marriage ties: "Can ye give to prostitution its former innocence? neither can ye reconcile Britain and America." It would be as easy for "the lover [to] forgive the ravisher of his mistress, as the continent forgive the murders of Britain."[13]

As a woman, England is an unnatural mother; as a man, England ravishes the innocence of America and even turns her into a prostitute. America, like the heroine of an eighteenth-century seduction novel, is helpless before the offers of Britain:

> We sometimes experience sensations to which language is not equal. The conception is too bulky to be born alive, and in the torture of thinking, we stand dumb. Our feelings, imprisoned by their magnitude, find no way out—and, in the struggle of expression, every finger tries to be a tongue. The machinery of the body seems too little for the mind, and we look about for helps to show our thoughts by. Such must be the sensation of America, when Britain, teeming with corruption, shall propose to her to sacrifice her faith.

America's sensations are those of a woman in childbirth, but the child is already doomed ("too bulky to be born alive") and even that emergence seems questionable as "feelings, imprisoned by their magnitude, find no way out." With the phrase "sacrifice her faith," Paine completes the conflation of national honor, religious beliefs, and sexual chastity. Worse than the proposals of corruption, however, is the implicit judgment of America:

> No man attempts to seduce the truly honest woman. It is the supposed looseness of her mind that starts the thoughts of seduction, and he who offers it calls her a prostitute. Our pride is always hurt by the same propositions which offend our principles; for when we are shocked at the crime, we are wounded by the suspicion of our compliance.[14]

Britain has not only tried to seduce America, it has also, in the tradition of rape defenses, suggested that these advances were welcome. Paine suggests that Britain might have avoided these errors: "Had you studied only the domestic policies of a family, you would have learned how to govern the state." The "domestic policies of a family" are directly applicable to the political policies of the state; for a model of order and social control, the state should turn to the family.[15]

Once this model has been accepted, the sexual infidelity that represents the greatest threat to the family can be replicated on the level of the state.[16] The major conjunction of sexual, religious, and political upheavals was the French Revolution. As Timothy Dwight, among others, saw it, the French Revolution had unleashed Infidelity as the loose woman of the barricades:

> Emboldened beyond every fear by this astonishing event, Infidelity . . . walked forth in open day, and displayed her genuine features to the sun. Without a blush she now denied the existence of moral obligation, annihilated the distinction between virtue and vice, challenged and authorized the indulgence of every lust, trod down the barriers of truth [and] lifted up her front in the face of heaven.

In other words, Democracy appears as a bold prostitute. Dwight again conflates the abhorrent possibilities of allowing infidelity to have a recognized place in religious discourse, allowing "democracy" to control the affairs of state, and allowing the "genuine features" of prostitutes to be exposed "to the sun." Each act again involves the others; each spells out destruction to church, state, and family. What Dwight seemed to fear most was that the loose morals introduced by this loose woman might be accompanied by a dread contagion, perhaps venereal, and he preached against whatever would "spread the disease," suggesting that Jacobin democracy was a form of the yellow fever plague that had so terrorized Americans at the time of the Terror in France.[17]

Plague and Politics in 1793

"The cursed foul contagion of French principles has infected us" wrote Secretary of the Navy George Cabot in 1798. "They are more to be dreaded . . . than a thousand yellow fevers."[18] The fear of the French during the "undeclared war" with France was so strong that the Sedition Act of 1798 may have been enacted as a cure for the "infernal French disease," spread through the newspapers, but also through contact with the French themselves (hence the accompanying Alien Acts). This emerging American inclination to see the principles imported from France as a contagious disease was supported by an odd conjunction of events: "Jacobinism had first appeared in the United States," as John Miller has noted, "at almost the same time the country suffered its worst outbreak of yellow fever—the great epidemic of 1793."[19] The French Revolution and the plague equivalently represented threats to social order. Such a connection between plague and politics provides one indication of how Americans, and not merely conservative Federalists, began to abhor the revolutionary principles they had initially embraced. Proponents of the Alien and Sedition Acts feared that French immigrants would "contaminate" the American character; their "loose morals and irreligion threatened to infect Americans" caught in their "vile and loathsome embrace."[20] If Paine had called America's alliance with France "open, noble and generous," that alliance had turned into what one contemporary historian called the whining of "a weak dupe, who find[s] himself compelled to turn an unfaithful wench out of doors."[21]

The American novel that most nearly confronts this conflation of plague, politics, and sexual anxieties is Charles Brockden Brown's *Arthur Mervyn, or Memoirs of the Year 1793* (1798). *Arthur Mervyn* has only recently been studied in the context of its lurid setting, the yellow fever epidemic that devastated Philadelphia in 1793.[22] Less attention has been paid to the other major event of that year, the Reign of Terror that devastated Paris and flooded Philadelphia with refugees. What I want to suggest here is that Brown's novel addresses the same conjunction of contagion and politics that disturbed Cabot. Moreover, I want to suggest that the novel works to "treat" these linked infections by placing this conjunction in a third arena—that of the family. In brief, I want to argue that in bringing together these issues, *Arthur Mervyn* documents the rise of institutions of social order—and particularly the institution of the family—that counter the linked threats of revolution, contagion, and political and sexual infidelity.

I want further to suggest that the emergent institution of the American novel itself forms a part of this complex social reordering. In proposing to examine *Arthur Mervyn* at the nexus of these related concerns of 1793, I do not mean that the novel simply reproduces these historical circumstances, nor do I intend to read it simply as an historical document by which such circumstances may be elucidated. Instead, I wish to demonstate the ways in which the novel functions in a marked exchange with other discourses of the period. More precisely, I want to indicate how the novel itself may participate in the production of social regulation and the maintenance of order that it also represents—how the novel works as a social regulator and as part of a larger field of social discourses and practices. I want to argue that the critical tendency to set the literary text apart from or against nonliterary practices both obscures the novel's participation in these practices and facilitates it. I want implicitly to explore how the assumption that the novel stands apart from, criticizes, or ironizes social practices of regulation not only ignores the permeability of the novel to these practices but also provides a cover for the novel's relaying of such practices.[23] As we will see, *Arthur Mervyn*, like Arthur Mervyn, has an exemplary cover story for its interventions and regulatory actions. The novel tells a story of social regulation, but tells it by way of a proliferation of stories and narratives. While the first part of my treatment will be more concerned with the discourses that surround the novel, and the second part more focused on the novel itself, it is just such a sense of the relation between the surrounding discourses and practices and the "novel itself" that I want to consider here.

Because that weak dupe, Arthur Mervyn's father, fails to turn his unfaithful wench out of doors and instead marries her, Arthur feels an "alien and an enemy to the roof under which I was born."[24] Driven to find a new family and a new roof, Arthur comes to Philadelphia, the Revolutionary city and national capitol in which "strangers and newcomers were everywhere, especially displaced French escaping from the Reign of Terror."[25] Something of a refugee himself, Arthur wanders the city in picaresque fashion, joining various family groups, until, in the action described in the opening scenes of the novel, he is rescued from the streets and from the plague by Dr. Stevens, who narrates Arthur's story. The novel has many characteristics of a *bildungsroman*, but the story of Arthur's education is superimposed on the story of Revolution, the family, and the rise of institutions of social control. Specifically, the novel tells the story of Arthur's education in the family.

To concentrate on education and family in the novel is apparently to ignore an often sinister undercurrent of deception, seduction, and murder and omit what many consider the novel's core: the malignant agency of Welbeck.[26] I would like to argue that it is precisely through its focus on education and the place of the family that the novel gradually acts to control Welbeck, whose actions appear finally of a piece with those of the plague, which similarly infiltrates the city under many guises and acts to destroy families. Through its convoluted plot, embedded narratives, dissembling narrators, contradictory evidence, and confused identities, the novel traces a process of education and the desire for family that will bring order to apparent chaos.

The novel might be "about" the gradual containment and confinement of the "noxious vapors" associated with the plague. Implicitly inscribed in this quarantining, narrated first by the doctor and then by his apprentice, is a conjoining of political and medical practices. As Brown proclaims in the preface to the novel,

> The evils of pestilence by which this city has lately been afflicted will probably form an aera in its history. The schemes of reformation and improvement to which they will give birth . . . will be, in the highest degree, memorable. They have already supplied new and copious materials for reflection to the physician and the political economist. (AM, 3)

At first, the extent to which Brown finds "materials for reflection to the . . . political economist" in the Philadelphia plague seems obscure. A closer reading reveals them everywhere intertwined with the family, the prison, the "fever," and the hospital. The novel not only shows the failure of existing institutions to contain the contagion prevalent in the city, it also sets out a plan for profiting by those lapses. Importantly, Brown insists, one must glean from the "medical and political discussions afloat in the community relative to this topic" some version of instruction: "It is every one's duty to profit by all opportunities of inculcating on mankind the lessons of justice and humanity" (AM, 3). These lessons at once derive from and are applied to Arthur Mervyn.

Apparently resolved to "inculcate" lessons on everyone he meets, Arthur repeatedly echoes this combined sentiment of moral justification and a sense of profit. Although he claims to be grateful for his escape from the "perilous precincts of private property" in the early stages of the novel, he is equally "disposed to profit by every opportunity to survey the interior of dwellings and converse with their inhabitants" (AM, 45, 64). Without robbing houses, Arthur still wants to profit from them and this may explain why he is drawn to both the medical profession, where he can profit by surveying private interior spaces, and a kind of civic policing where he can treat the city as a body whose every space must be penetrated for proper diagnosis, treatment, and the eventual profit of both practitioner and patient. His apprenticeship under Dr. Stevens seems the perfect career choice.[27] Eager to study everyone he meets, Arthur is even grateful for his tutelage under Welbeck: "My knowledge of Welbeck has been useful to me" (AM, 357). Learning the "most secret transaction[s]" of Philadelphia's inhabitants, Arthur seeks at once to profit from and to correct their lives.

Arthur's sober examination of and attempt to benefit from the actions of people he encounters has led critics to compare him to Benjamin Franklin, though with the typical disclaimer that "Whereas Franklin demonstrated an uncanny ability for 'doing good' . . . Arthur repeatedly forces his good deeds upon the unsuspecting."[28] Arthur more closely resembles Franklin in his persistent attempts to be a "reasonable creature," a justification that similarly glosses over motive and action. He also follows Franklin's attention to civic details, his noticing of streets and houses, and his projects for the improvement of their inhabitants.

Franklin's 1754 pamphlet on the Philadelphia penitentiary and founding interest in the Pennsylvania hospital parallel Arthur's interests in reform, most explicit in his desire to administer the Bush-hill hospital, but his desire extends beyond the primary scene of contagion. His initial attraction to the horrors of the hospital is succeeded by his visit to the debtors prison, introduced late in the novel as a kind of last outpost of the plague: "The air is loaded with the exhalations of disease and the fumes of debauchery" (AM, 334). Dr. Stevens also visits the prison and, though presumably accustomed to disease, he complains that "the tainted breath of so promiscuous a crowd, loaded the stagnant atmosphere. At my first transition from the cold and pure air without, to this noxious element, I found it difficult to breathe" (AM, 254). Similarly, the imprisoned Carlton finds that "Impure airs . . . and perturbed thoughts" are an effect of prison "sufficient to generate disease and to deprive him of life" (AM, 254–55). But Arthur finds positive attributes in the prison: "Let me gain, from contemplation of thy misery, new motives to sincerity and rectitude" (AM, 334). Only Arthur can profit from the prison as a place of both correction and instruction. Such a relation between correction and instruction must be investigated.

Critical attention to the novel has focused on Arthur's psychological dilemmas rather than these aspects of profit and tutelage. Alan Axelrod proposes, for example, that an Oedipal conflict is central to the novel, a conflict resolved when "Arthur, by marrying his 'mamma' [Achsa Fielding], at last dethrones his own father."[29] Norman Grabo describes Dr. Stevens's treatment of Arthur as "almost a psychoanalytic strategy" in which Arthur "recounts his exposure to the moral disease of distrust." In other words, telling "the story of the progress of the disease" is a "therapeutic" exercise that Dr. Stevens imposes on Arthur.[30] Even if these accounts of familial conflict and therapeutic treatment are accurate, however, they do not articulate the more general functions of the familial and the therapeutic in the novel. On one hand, Axelrod's account ignores the social framework of the familial drama that Arthur is placed in: as we will see, Brown is more interested in a restored family as a restored form of institutional order. Without a family, Arthur is treated as a displaced person, a refugee without connections who can be fitted into any available slot. Not until he has carefully collected a father, a mother, and a sister, can he train for a career and take his place in a world now placed around him. The novel appears to enforce a notion that you only exist insofar as you have a family.[31] On the other hand, by finding a "moral disease of distrust" more important in *Arthur Mervyn* than the literal disease, Grabo implicitly points to an essential difficulty with accounts of the plague: its origins and character are so unclear that it can stand for almost anything that a person, a family, or a city might fear. However, Grabo undercuts the force of his observations by claiming not to "want to work this allegory or conceit too hard," and appears to overlook the literal possibilities it embodies. More than a literary conceit or allegory, the model of curing disease as a structuring principle for the reorganization of family and society acutely describes not only Arthur's story, but also the civic tale of Philadelphia and the plague—a tale told originally by an official representative of the committee of the sick that ruled the city during the crisis.[32]

Mathew Carey's *A Short Account of the Malignant Fever* was published just as the plague was beginning to die down in the late fall of 1793 and went through several expanded and revised editions in succeeding years. In Carey's account, as in Brown's, the plague travels so mysteriously it appears that merely talking about it spreads the contagion: "The hundred tongues of rumor were never more successfully employed," says Carey.[33] But such success bodes ill, since the "effect of fear in predisposing the body" for the disease "is well known" (SA, 76). Arthur notes that merely hearing the "rumour, which had gradually swelled to formidable dimensions" meant the "hearer grew pale, his breath was stifled by inquietudes, his blood was chilled and his stomach was bereaved of its usual energies," symptoms that frequently led to "lingering or mortal diseases" (AM, 128, 130). Writing about yellow fever to his brother James in 1796, Brown commented, "I cannot but admire the exaggerations of rumor." He continues, however: "Plague operates by invisible agents, and we know not in what quarter it is about to attack us. . . . We fear it as we are terrified by the dark . . . doubtless, owing to the influence of education." Philadelphians feared rumors of the plague because like communism in the 1950s, or Jacobinism in the 1790s, the plague could be anywhere and take any form. Brown admits that "I am not even wholly uninfected by the disease, because . . . in the dark . . . I find myself seized by unwelcome shrink-ings."[34] Instead of succumbing to this disease, however, Brown and Carey profit by the disorder they describe.

In fact, all three "authors" profit as they counter the effect of nonspecific rumors by inoculating themselves and their audiences with a carefully contrived narrative dose of the plague. Arthur initially embraces thoughts of the plague, claiming to be pleased to have "leisure to conjure up terrific images, and to personate the witnesses and sufferers of this calamity. This employment was not enjoined upon me by necessity, but was ardently pursued, and must therefore have been recommended by some nameless charm" (AM, 130). It appears that the "charm" of such an "employment" only lasts while Arthur lives outside the city besieged by the plague. But he does seem by his proto-novelizing to have successfully inoculated himself against a lethal dose. If the "influence of education" has caused a dangerous fear of the plague, perhaps the novel and the *Short Account* can re-educate. It may be to counter the malignant effects of rumor that Carey writes his *Short Account*, Brown writes a letter to his brother and a novel, and Arthur "conjure[s] up terrific images." Like Carey's "official" account of the control of a plague that still exists, Arthur's story creates as much as narrates order.

This order is achieved through acquiring a family, and significantly the novel is not directly narrated by Arthur until he has found his family, until, that is, Achsa has agreed to marry him. Both Arthur and Mathew Carey tell stories that describe the achievement of order through institutions of social control. As Carey describes it, before the plague Philadelphia was almost too prosperous; new houses were everywhere, but "something was wanting to humble the pride of a city, which was running on in full career, to the goal of prodigality and dissipation" (SA, 12). This "moral" account of the plague presents Philadelphia as a delinquent son whose outward show may be gaudy and convincing, but whose inner being needs correction. Although he introduces the dissipation of the city as one possible "cause" for the plague, Carey also explains that the "most probable and general opinion is, that the privateer Sans Coulottes . . . introduced the fever" (SA, 19). Whatever the basis of this "opinion," the Francophobic possibilities it suggests are difficult to ignore. Carey later comments that "the French settled in Philadelphia, have been in a very remarkable degree exempt" from the fever (SA, 75). Although he does not specifically draw the parallel, the context of the historical situation must suggest again the image of "French disease," a contagion introduced by the "Sans Coulottes" and particularly connected with the ravages of democracy during the Reign of Terror. The question for Americans was whether Philadelphia had brought the contagion on itself through the "prodigality and dissipation" that had become associated with welcoming displaced French, assumed to be sowing seeds of sedition in the city.[35]

Carey describes the civic response to the plague as the creation of new regulations and institutions. The cities and towns around Philadelphia enacted resolutions to keep out the Philadelphians, blocking ports, gates, roads, requiring all innkeepers to report the arrival of strangers, mandating all travelers to carry passes that proved their identity and place of origin. If they came from Philadelphia, they had to prove the length of their absence from that city. The alienation this quarantine produced echoes not only that of Arthur Mervyn, "made to feel an alien and an enemy under [his] own roof," but also that of the recent immigrants to America during the time Brown was writing the novel, when the Act Concerning Aliens (June 1798) and the Act Respecting Alien Enemies (July 1798)—passed because of the undeclared war with France—attempted to require all noncitizens to carry passes certifying that they were not dangerous.[36]

After the first lapse into chaos, the citizens of Philadelphia put out a call for volunteers to run the city, since the entire government had fled. These guardians of the sick controlled the city for the duration of the plague, forming a committee at City Hall (which Mathew Carey joined) to "receive applications for relief" (SA, 59). Among other concerns, the committee built an "orphan house," which "from the origin of the institution grew to hold 220 children, and instituted weekly public relief for 1200 families." (The plague removed poor people and was "equally fatal" to the *"filles de joie"* [SA, 74], a sinister version of urban renewal.) The committee borrowed $1500 because "the hospital was in very bad order and in want of almost everything" (SA, 56). This turns out to be an understatement. As Carey describes the hospital, it presented

> as wretched a picture of human misery as ever existed. A profligate, abandoned set of nurses and attendants . . . rioted on the provisions and comforts prepared for the sick who (unless at the hour the doctors attended) were left almost entirely destitute of any kind of assistance. The dying and dead were indiscriminately mixed together. The ordure and other evacuations of the sick were allowed to remain in the most offensive state imaginable. . . . It was, in fact, a great human slaughterhouse. . . . No wonder, then, that a general dread of the place prevailed in the city, and that a removal to it was considered as the seal of death . . . there were various instances of persons locking their rooms, and resisting every attempt to carry them away. (SA, 61–62)

The Bushhill hospital performs an inverted function as a "great human slaughterhouse." Its victims resist, but "the fear of the contagion was so prevalent, that . . . every effort was used to have the sick person carried off to Bushhill. . . . The cases of the persons forced in this way to that hospital, though laboring under only common colds . . . are numerous and afflicting" (SA, 62). Instead of curing these afflictions, the hospital more often pronounced a death sentence. Instead of providing a model for private emulation, the public institution of the hospital conveyed a threat and created the impression that private spaces, the home, the room, had to be protected against public violation.

An "extraordinary offer of humanity" came to set the scene in order when "a native of France . . . voluntarily and unexpectedly offered to superintend that hospital" (SA, 59). This of course mirrors Arthur's sudden desire to go and assume that office when he hears Wallace's descriptions of the miseries there. (But it is also curious that a Frenchman steps in to cure what might be called the "French disease." Was it because the French were assumed to be immune, like the African-Americans hired to collect the bodies?) The new administration reformed the institution so successfully that people began to desire the hospital, and had finally to certify that they were indeed suffering from the plague to be admitted there. Thus the measures enacted to stop the plague caused a shift in the values of public and private, opening private spaces, not by violently intruding into them, but by providing a better and more inviting model in the public realm. In other words, instead of shutting itself up against the threat of going to the hospital, the community now wanted to enter and make itself at home there.[37]

As a member of the committee of letters, a subset of the governing committee during the crisis, Carey wrote an account that was designedly therapeutic.
By tracing the progress and reporting the decline of the plague, he intended to
calm the fears of those who had fled Philadelphia, to encourage the lifting of
trade and travel sanctions against the city, and to reinvigorate business. The
publication of A Short Account was one of several institutionalized attempts to
cure the city and contain disorder. What Carey's account of the whole process, the drop into chaos and the creation of institutions to rectify that chaos,
finally accomplishes, however, is not so much a reassurance of order as a
reminder of the disorder that might follow from rejecting the institutions
created by the committee he represents. At the same time, the existence of
these institutions reminded the family that if it failed to maintain order,
institutional correctives would take over, supplementing if not supplanting
familial authority.

Social historians like Jacques Donzelot and David Rothman have traced
the changes in social control and the structure of the family during this period.
Jacques Donzelot's account of contract and tutelage as the basis of family
government helps explain the growth of institutional correctives to disorders
within the family. The notion of contract means that if the family maintained
itself, institutions would not interfere, while tutelage signifies what happens if
the family failed: it became subject to corrective measures from without,
measures that may be represented by the hospital attendants who broke down
doors to take patients from their homes. [38] Considering the city as a family that
had failed to keep order, we can see how the new tutelary state apparatus, the
committee that came to govern the city, prescribed new rules for the behavior
of the family and maintained them by creating new institutions, such as the
Bushhill hospital, the new orphanage, and public relief, to supplement the
family.

As David Rothman has described the rise of institutions in The Discovery of
the Asylum, it was not only that "the family was the model for institutional
organization," but also that "the family had to emulate the asylum as constituted." There was, according to contemporary proponents of the institution,
"no real divergence between the well-ordered asylum and the well-ordered
family." If the institution succeeded in "inspir[ing] private families to emulation," or, as the authors of reform literature saw it, "if they could define the
components of proper family government and persuade readers to adopt them,
then they would ensure the nation's stability": "They wished to bring the rules
of the asylum into the home, confident that as soon as parents became surrogate superintendents, the refuge, the penitentiary, and the rest could be eliminated. The well-ordered family would replace the well-ordered asylum." [39] In
other words, institutions were not conceived of as permanent adjuncts to or
replacements for the family; the committee at Philadelphia considered most of
its relief measures to be temporary. Rather, once the family had absorbed (or
re-absorbed) the principles and practices of the institution, the institution
would quietly leave the family in charge again.

In fact, however, as institutions proliferated, justifications for them took on a new twist. Instead of providing temporary stopgaps to transitory crises, the institution gradually became a permanent feature of the American landscape. While colonial jails and poorhouses were often just rooms in people's houses—a significant cohabitation of public and private spaces—the early republic saw an increasing concentration on the architecture of asylums and prisons as a visible emblem of the security and impenetrability of the institution. To convince the public of the need for these more permanent establishments, the architects of prison reform began to encourage a sense of the instability of the family as something for which the institution had to compensate. The family was still involved in a reciprocal relation with the institution, but the danger of family disorder that would bring the institution into play was kept continually present.

The Philadelphia plague was responsible for a great deal of disorder in family government. The picture of the family presented in both *Arthur Mervyn* and Carey is one of unnatural unconcern: "Terror had exterminated all the sentiments of nature. Wives were deserted by husbands, and children by parents" (AM, 129). Carey describes a "total dissolution in the bonds of society in the nearest and dearest connexions . . . a husband deserting his wife . . . a wife unfeelingly abandoning her husband on his deathbed— parents forsaking their only children without remorse—children ungratefully flying from their parents" (SA, 30–31). The destruction of the family becomes perhaps the most frightening effect of the plague, and both accounts of the contagion set out to restore order, whether through the supplemental support of institutions or through a concentration on the institution of the family itself. Indeed, as Ronald Takaki has suggested, the two come together in the treatments advocated by the most prominent physician of the day, Benjamin Rush:

> The method of social control, in which republican values were instilled into individuals, had two parts: the asylum and the family. In Dr. Rush's formulation, the two had a dialectical relationship. The first was public and curative, the second private and preventative. As institutions for cure were established, the educational function of the family was emphasized.[40]

Brown's concentration on education and the family may be seen to anticipate the focus on the family in succeeding American novels. The family becomes both the producer and the product of the education provided by the novel. The novel recounts and enacts a process of education, supplementing practices like Carey's but domesticating them; it at once produces a private discourse to be consumed in the home, presents the story of the family as a story of social and institutional reorganization, and functions as a lesson in social reordering. The novel operates more effectively as an educative and socializing project in that, unlike an account like Carey's, it does not appear overtly as such. The disguises and uncertainties of nested narratives, unreliability, ironies, and ambiguities both recount and enact a desire for discourse and order.

In the first pages of the novel, Dr. Stevens describes facing resistance from his neighbors for the "imprudence and rashness" of taking the plague-stricken Arthur in from the streets and making him part of the family. They argue that Arthur belongs in the public hospital rather than a private home, and in defying this (frequently fatal) edict Dr. Stevens acts in line with the contemporary attempt to collapse the difference between public institutions and the private home. Even Arthur initially suspects him, asking "What would you have?" "If we save your life, we shall have done you some service, and as for recompense, we will look to that," replies Stevens (AM, 7). The recompense turns out to be a recital of the lessons Arthur has learned. When Wortley protests to Dr. Stevens that Arthur is concealing a criminal connection with Welbeck—"No doubt the young villain is well instructed in his lesson" (14)— Stevens asks Arthur for the whole story. As recorded by Stevens, this is both a story of the family and a lesson about the need for a stable family, precisely as an alternative to Welbeckian criminality.

If *Arthur Mervyn* is centrally concerned with restoring families, this is in part because most of the families depicted in the novel are contaminated by infidelity or contagion. Forced out of his original family by sexual misconduct and deaths, Arthur moves in and out of other similarly contaminated family groups until he learns enough to create a family of his own. While I want to emphasize that the novel's quest for a family is political as well as social, I do not propose to settle the issue of family along political lines; instead I want to suggest that the focus and effects of either the conservative Federalist or "radical" Republican party's strategies were the same: to control the state, concentrate on the family; to control the family, concentrate on education; and, to contain disorder generally, emulate the family in structuring institutions, from the more abstract forms of government to the more concrete establishments of schools, hospitals, and prisons.[41] The novel repeatedly participates in this complex social reordering.

When Arthur first runs away to Philadelphia, he is covetously impressed by its dwellings—"The horses were here far more magnificently accommodated than I had been" (AM, 34)—and can scarcely believe his presence in them: other "miracles are contemptible when compared with that which placed me under this roof" (AM, 54). Although he is accused of criminal desires in his surreptitious comings and goings, Arthur does not wish to take anything from these houses. Instead, he wishes to leave himself; that is, he wants to be adopted into the family. He initially almost joins the Thetford family on the invitation of the apprentice Wallace, but manages to leave nothing but his shoes. As a prank, Wallace locks Arthur in his master's bedroom. Where Arthur goes in, however, a baby comes unexpectedly out, at least as Wallace retells the story: "A strange event had indeed taken place in their bed-chamber. They found an infant asleep in their bed." The almost laughable nonrecognition of what a "strange event" might be that leads to finding an "infant asleep in their bed" points to the unnatural constitution of this family group. Arthur's eavesdropping presence is blamed for the presence of the infant—"Some connection between these sounds and the foundling was naturally suspected"—although the child is apparently an illegitimate product of an affair of Mr. Thetford's (AM, 176). In any case, this family almost willfully refuses to recognize where babies come from. Neither the surreptitiously introduced Arthur nor the surreptitiously introduced baby "belongs" in the Thetford family, and it seems only chance that the baby is the one discovered and adopted into the family, while Arthur escapes to try his luck elsewhere with Welbeck.

Welbeck's "family" presents similar difficulties with the nature and legitimacy of its relations. After he has dressed himself in the clothes that Welbeck provides, Arthur comments that "I could scarcely recognize any lineaments of my own," while the "features" of Welbeck and his "daughter" become "fraught with a meaning that I was eager to interpret but unable" (AM, 51, 53). Unable to "interpret," Arthur is at no loss to fantasize: "Perhaps they discovered a remarkable resemblance between me and one who stood in the relation of son to Welbeck and of brother to the lady. This youth might have perished on the scaffold or in war. These, no doubt, were his clothes. This chamber might have been reserved for him, but his death left it to be appropriated to another." The "appropriation" of the family "relation" is the work of an instant for one so eager to find the slot vacant. Arthur finds no attachment to his own "lineaments" when the possibility of assuming another's presents itself. Although not "destitute of probability," as Arthur drily wishes, "these ideas were . . . powerfully enforced by inclination," an inclination he instantly traces back to "the death of my mother" (AM, 57). The loss of family has set the stage for the reassertion of family. And since Arthur "knew that the present was a period of revolution and hostility," he believes himself to be among "illustrious fugitives," implicitly French refugees, a condition that leaves them further open to appropriation (AM, 56).

Instead, Arthur is the one appropriated. Welbeck's "daughter" is in fact pregnant with his child, and while Arthur imagines that "Welbeck would adopt me for his own son," an occurrence, he imagines perversely, that would further his chances for marriage with Welbeck's "daughter," he is still imaginatively involved in incest ("but I was not her brother"), because he is threatening to supplant a "father" in a "mother's" affections (AM, 57, 58). As we learn later, Welbeck wants to be supplanted in Clemenza's affections, but although Arthur "laboured to invent some harmless explication of the scene," he cannot easily ignore Welbeck's nocturnal visit to her or the "marks of pregnancy" he detects. Arthur is forced to conclude that the "claims of a parent" had been part of Welbeck's seduction of Clemenza, another disturbing intrusion of sexuality into the family (AM, 77, 76).

The confusion of family resemblance and identity has been furthered by Welbeck's desire that Arthur "conceal" everything previous to "my being incorporated with his family." Cut off from his past self, Arthur reflects that the "mere physical relation of birth" must be suspect: "Identity itself frequently depends upon a casual likeness or an old nurse's imposture" (AM, 63, 57–58). Despite Arthur's recognition of the difficulties presented by illegitimacy and counterfeiting, he continues to try to establish identity in terms of the family. When he tries to find Wallace again, his first questions are: "Where was he born and educated? Has he parents or brothers?" (AM, 60). These are questions that seem unanswerable because of the changing relations of families in Philadelphia. Within a paragraph Arthur moves from the certainty that Clemenza is Welbeck's daughter to doubt: "What if this woman be not his child? How shall their relationship be ascertained?" (AM, 75). The intrusion of questionable sexual relations makes the ascertainment not only of family but also of the identity that family provides an illusory goal.

The suspicions of infidelity and incest make it unsurprising that Arthur rejects the model of the family that the city, "scene of ruin and blast," provides him, and leaves for the country, the home of "competence, fixed property and a settled abode, rural occupations and conjugal pleasures" (AM, 293).[42] Here he encounters a new though familiar family at Mr. Hadwin's: "Methought I could embrace him as a father, and entrance into his house, appeared like return to a long-lost and much-loved home" (AM, 123). Again, Arthur wants to become a permanent member of the family and thinks of marrying Eliza Hadwin to accomplish this, but stronger than his attraction to her is his attraction to remaining as a son in the family without marriage to the daughter. Even settled in the "rural occupations" of the country, Arthur is not free from scenes of "ruin and blast," which now intrude with the plague, and he finds himself returning to Philadelphia on a family errand. Everywhere he goes in the distraught city, he focuses on the dissolution of families, and this dissolution spreads; when he returns to Malverton, he finds the Hadwin family dissolved as well. Hadwin is dead, one of the sisters dies on Arthur's arrival, and Eliza, bereft of family and farm, loses some of her attraction for Arthur. His fraternal interest in her continues, but the charm of closer relations has disappeared with the disappearance of her family.

Arthur's "thoughts have ever hovered over the images of wife and children with more delight than over any other images" because of the power he associates with the family (AM, 291). An "alien" under his own roof, he makes himself at home under everyone else's: "I had opened doors without warning, and traversed passages without being noticed" (AM, 354–55). To foster the feeling of belonging, Arthur fantasizes himself a son to Welbeck, a brother to Eliza, a brother and a son to Achsa Fielding. "The first moment I engaged her attention," Arthur tells Achsa "the little story of my family." Arthur relates this "story" to present his credentials, the same action he performs for Stevens. As the first "moment" of engaged attention, the moment of the story of the family is also one that presents Arthur as without attachments, as available. Eliza is coopted in the service of Arthur's need for family; he won't marry her (to the regret of the Romantics), but he'll pass her along to Achsa as a "sister": "*That*, when there is no other relation, includes them all" (AM, 397, 398).

His desire to turn Eliza into his sister or daughter ("Would to heaven I were truly her father or brother") seems caused by a need to incorporate her into a family rather than by any disinterested benevolence or desire for incest, though the intensity of the focus on the family in Brown makes incest a virtual social analogue. That is, the desire for incest might be a consequence of the concentration on familial bonds as a locus of value in the nineteenth century, rather than a "psychological" or Oedipal theme. Achsa too seizes on the advantages of the family compact: "Are you willing to invest me with all the rights of an elder sister over this girl? . . . I will not be a nominal sister. I will not be a sister by halves. *All* the rights of that relation I will have." Not only does Achsa assume "*all* the rights" of her new relation with Eliza, she soon has Eliza calling her "mamma" as well. Having awarded her the power of the family relation with Eliza, Arthur takes back his own power: "I intended to kneel, as to my mother or my deity, but instead of that, I clasped her in my arms and kissed her lips fervently" (AM, 409). As soon as Achsa takes over as Eliza's mother and sister, Arthur claims her as his wife.

Apparently ending on a conventional note of closure through marriage, the novel presents the achievement of order as the triumph of institutions. Arthur finds in the family relation the most intimate form of knowledge as power, the culmination of his desire to "profit by every opportunity to survey the interior of dwellings" and his "eager[ness] after knowledge," which has led him to find out "the most secret transaction[s]" of the inhabitants while claiming disinterested benevolence (AM, 64, 39). To achieve this knowledge, Arthur has walked in without knocking, explored freely ("The satisfaction that I sought was only to be gained by searching [Mrs. Villars's] house"), intruded where he was unwelcome, then turned the undesirability of his presence into a charge against those whose privacy he is violating. These are finally not so much blunders as gestures of appropriation and mastery. As his behavior with Philip Hadwin demonstrates, Arthur is fascinated with the possibilities of control.

Expecting to be welcomed and to be at home everywhere, Arthur turns the hostility against him into a revealing vice. Like any form of publication (public action), he would not be turned away unless there were something to hide.[43] What must not be overlooked is the extent to which his sanctimonious ignorance is effective. In spite of (or because of) his intrusive bumbling, or "propensity to look into other people's concern" (AM, 332), Arthur acts as a normalizing force in the novel. But if his actions resemble those of Mathew Carey's Committee, they are also enacted with a certain indirection. Arthur attempts to make the private public, but he does so merely by acting as though there were no category of the private, no privacy anywhere. He claims to have no need to hide—"My behavior, I well know, was ambiguous . . . but my motives were unquestionably pure" (AM, 322)—and therefore refuses to understand the category of the hidden, a refusal that effectively demands exposure of all secrets.

Yet by the end of the novel, when Achsa has finally told him the story of *her* family, Arthur's confidence in his powers as a regulator has begun to fade. He entreats her to "be not a deceiver," and has a disturbing dream about the return of her former husband, who has run away with another woman, joined the French Revolution, and been killed in the Reign of Terror. This late introduction of the other great event of the year 1793 is also a sinister one. In Arthur's dream the husband stabs him. To counter that dream-knife, Arthur wields his pen, taking over the last quarter of the novel. After long stretches of embedded narratives, Arthur is at last speaking in his "own" voice, which may be taken as a sign that he has at last achieved control over his destiny as he enters the institutions of marriage and family. Carey similarly presents the plague as under control when he introduces a list of Philadelphia institutions; however, while a certain closure is possible for Carey, a different operation takes place in a novel, which finds certain uses for deferring closure.

The institutional control signalled by marriage and the family in *Arthur Mervyn* is at least partly undermined because Arthur's dream and his continued unease imply that these institutions are not firmly in control. His dream of the Frenchman points again to the way the French have come to stand for an American fear that its new institutions will be unable to maintain order. Arthur's "triumph" may be the accomplishment of the Federalist dream of order, but the danger of a new dissolution is kept alive. The city has been "managed," a professional career is in the works, and the family that Arthur has spent the entire novel in search of has finally been established. Institutions are functioning correctly, but the "world of revolutions and perils" remains, though Arthur claims wistfully that his "happiness depended not on . . . revolutions" (AM, 332, 312). And the love that he has found may be as dangerous as the fever he's recovered from: "All extremes are agonies." Writing the account only serves as a partial remedy: "I must continue at the pen, or shall immediately relapse" (AM, 414). Arthur establishes a precise equivalence here between ongoing narration and "treatment"; these remedies are effective as long as the novel continues, while, without it, both narrator and reader may "relapse."

For Arthur to cling to his pen is in part for him to defend himself against the sexual threat the small, dark Achsa embodies (he does, after all, meet her in a brothel), but the sexual threat resembles the same fear of loss of control that was induced by the plague and by Jacobin democracy in the late eighteenth century, an analogy furthered by Achsa's husband's connection with the French Revolution. Arthur values his projected marriage, and the "rights of the relation" the family confers, because he fears the intrusion of what is presented at once as sexual competition and political threat. But his dream affects him to the point that he feels compelled to put aside his pen "till all is settled with my love," announcing that the last words of the book, "THE END," will be his pen's "last office, till Mervyn has been made the happiest of men" (AM, 446). The apparent optimism of this ending is profoundly undercut by Arthur's repeated "till," a qualification that causes us to look for an epilogue not forthcoming and to become subject to the same "ominous misgiving" that has "infected" Arthur's anticipation of his marriage: "That time— may nothing happen to prevent it—but nothing can happen" (AM, 445). The nervous interjection is not reassuring. Instead, we are reminded again of the hazards of this "world of revolutions."

Arthur Mervyn, then, reflects a contemporary conjunction of a fear of sexuality and a fear of contagion. Sexuality was threatening because it involved the downfall of the family. This threat proved rhetorically effective in describing the danger to the institution of the state perceived in Jacobin democracy. The threat to the mutually dependent institutions of family and state was further seen as a contagious "disease" imported from France. The coincidence of a virulent yellow fever epidemic in Philadelphia the same year that the Terror ruled in Paris reinforced this metaphor in a politically convenient way, bringing home the Jacobin threat. And the response of early American novels was to domesticate the threat even more thoroughly. Brought into households as an educational tool, the novel taught Americans what to fear. Arthur's adventures teach him to desire home and family, while the uncertain threat of the novel's ending at once promotes a similar desire in the reader and reinvokes the threat presented to him by the outside world, an uncertainty and threat that itself, in the terms that the novel insists upon, produces a desire for continuing narrative "treatment," calling, in effect, for the institution of the novel.

2 ·

Wieland: Alien and Infidel

The Alien and Sedition Acts were a major late-eighteenth-century American attempt to maintain national insularity by promoting a sense of threat. Shortly before Congress was to vote on the measures, Senator Humphrey Marshall, who supported the Alien Act, turned to poetry to explain its necessity. Marshall begins "The Aliens, A Patriotic Poem," by praising the qualities of the United States that attract aliens. But the wrong aliens are attracted. A troop of "venal wretches," the French, have come to the United States because they were "At home involv'd in horrid war, / And all the vices, that curse the mind." The proper recourse:

> For Aliens, who've crossed the seas,
> In language strong, and firm accost them;
> The innocent—be they at ease,
> The guilty—make haste and arrest them.

Not surprisingly, the poem cordons off the "safe" alien from the potentially contagious one, but the paradox of America, epitomized by Philadelphia as the center of both government and aliens, is that its very order, especially its "laws, like those divine, / Calleth the Alien, from afar." Attracting those "Aliens" it wishes to repel, America must act to contain the threat of the Alien, perversely drawn by the order that his coming threatens to disrupt.[1]

Invoking the same model of attracting and even promoting disorder while producing a desire for familial and social order, Charles Brockden Brown's *Wieland, or The Transformation,* published the year the Alien and Sedition Acts were passed, might be read as their novelistic response, but also counterpart. There are also certain resemblances between Arthur's violation of the "perilous precincts of private property" in *Arthur Mervyn* and Carwin's penetration of private spaces in *Wieland.* Like the big houses that lure Arthur, and

44

the qualities of America that draw the "alien," the charm of the Wieland's idyllic community has attracted Carwin, the alien called from afar.[2] In each case, the attractiveness of order invites the intrusion of disorder. However, the novel does not unilaterally assign guilt to Carwin as the alien intruder, and indeed often questions whether we should instead blame, as the narrator, Clara, sometimes believes we should, the interior of the home itself, or, more particularly, "the immeasurable evils that flow from an erroneous or imperfect discipline" (W, 5). *Wieland* presents alternative versions of educational and religious beliefs, but frames the presentation with this announcement of a moral to be derived from the effects of such an "imperfect discipline": these "freedoms" of thought and belief may have caused the destruction of the Wieland family. Despite its gothic sensationalism, the novel, like Weems's pamphlet, often appears more significant as an educational tract, one that contains lessons about the contemporary disputes over religious infidelity, a strictly circumscribed education, the chastity of women, and the status of institutions, preeminently the institution of the family.

In its consideration of these debates, the novel sometimes appears as an allegory of America and the dangers that democracy poses. The elder Wieland resembles the typical immigrant: he rejects traditional religions when he comes to America, makes his living from the land, and preaches to the Indians. But he operates outside the sanctioned confines of the community and acts according to private rather than communal definitions of education, religion, and the family. In particular, Wieland's retreat from a social to a private definition of a deity appears to call forth his isolated death. That his children fail to heed the lesson and continue to segregate themselves from the community almost necessitates that they will suffer similar madness and destruction. Read as a history of America, *Wieland* encompasses the early Puritan sense of mission (where the Wielands' ideal temple is a "city on a hill"), and subsequent political, and religious upheavals, including and foregrounding the "crisis of infidelity" in a religious, political and sexual sense. The aim of the novel may be just what it disavows: to "make the picture of a single family a model from which to sketch the condition of a nation" (30).

Other critics have noted this possibility, but they have participated in attempts to contain political significance by emphasizing psychological or imaginary categories. Larzer Ziff mentions that Wieland's "fresh start" resembles that of the typical immigrant to America, and Michael Gilmore notes that Brown's subtitle, "An American Tale," suggests that he "saw in his central foursome a microcosm of the bourgeois American society that by 1798 stood in defiant opposition to the Puritan past," but neither sees any political significance in the conjunction of the historical setting with the subject of the novel. Michael Davitt Bell finds a contemporary political controversy in the novel insofar as a figure like Carwin is "linked with the excesses of revolution in France." But such figures "have little real political significance," since the "real threat" is "psychological rather than political": what "destroys the Wieland's idyllic American community is the force of the imagination." This collapse of the political into the psychological, of a "real threat" into an imaginary one, also informs William Hedges reading of *Wieland*'s religious commentary. He finds that the "novel reflects contemporary anxiety over religious skepticism. Brown even seems to be trying to make a statement on the problem but is unable to work it out in action because of the need to keep Clara in the foreground."[3] Instead of turning the crises of the novel into "imaginary" or psychological problems (frequently two ways of making the same point), I would like to argue that the metaphorical displacement of political and religious controversies or fears was an understood and necessary component of talking about them. Rather than making such issues marginal, Clara's centrality as narrator is essential to both a religious and a political interpretation of the novel: she may represent both the danger of infidelity and the ambiguous sexuality of the female figure of liberty in the mid and late eighteenth century.

The novel betrays, or indeed advertises, its susceptibility to both narrative and sexual ambiguity. Clara repeatedly questions her ability to narrate her own story and asks the reader to doubt her motives and desires: "What but ambiguities, abruptnesses, and dark transitions, can be expected from the historian who is, at the same time, the sufferer of these disasters?" (W, 147). Clara's attempt to narrate her own history is notoriously fraught with "ambiguities, abruptnesses and dark transitions." But more than emphasizing the impossibility of objectivity in narrating a "history" that has been personally experienced, her description of herself as a historian may explain how the issue of authorship and authority in the narrative appears as an issue of familial and national history: who will control the account of the past?[4]

In the novel, this struggle over presentation is foreshadowed by Wieland's interest in oration. Obsessed with a "scheme of pronunciation" of Cicero, he works at "embellishing his rhetoric with all the proprieties of gesticulation and utterance," seeking to imitate the original (W, 24). However, when his wife's voice is imitated, or "inexplicably and unwarrantably assumed" (W, 34), he becomes preternaturally upset. Carwin's assumption of Catherine's voice is of course what sets off the chain of disasters in *Wieland*. But Carwin's ability to project his voice and assume other voices may be even more disturbing for Wieland and Clara because his imitation of an original calls the original into question and disrupts understood patterns of authorship. Carwin's voice calls into question both the "evidence of the senses" by which Clara seeks to know the world and the "ground" of her brother's "belief." Having weakened the credibility of both written and spoken accounts of the world, the novel nonetheless produces a desire for static written renderings of the self, a desire promoted and (almost) satisfied by the novel itself, by Clara's diary, by her father's narrative, and by Wieland's legally inscribed self. Precisely because the narrative insists on its own unreliability, the reader wishes for resolution, as critical attempts to fix blame in the novel have repeatedly shown.[5] The novel's repeated, and repeatedly ineffective, recounting of and accounting for the past reflect the possible loss of control of origins in post-revolutionary

America. What was the authoritative account of self and history for Americans?[6] Taking this need into consideration, we may see the Sedition Act of 1798 as just such an attempt to ensure a politically authorized account of American revolutionary principles.

Clara's uncertain control over the narration of her family's story may especially appear as a parallel to the problem of the revolutionary historian because the Revolution was so frequently discussed as a familial confrontation that saw the overthrow of one "unnatural" parent and the ascension of a new one, George Washington. The story of the family was insistently the story of the state.[7] In an influential article for discussions of the historical change in political uses of family analogies, Edwin Burrows and Michael Wallace claim that, as colonials, Americans "tolerated prolonged subordination and dependency" because of a political rhetoric based on the notion that the "natural" patriarchal order of the family was akin to the "natural" order of government: "such analogies between family and polity . . . lay at the foundations of the English approach to problems of political power and liberty, authority and autonomy."[8] This patriarchal system of familial and state governments was challenged when the eighteenth century began to explain power in terms of the rights of all members of a family rather than justifying it, as in medieval times, by the divine right of kings, a nearly irrefutable buttress of the patriarchal system.

For both nations and families this change meant a new responsibility; that is, families were responsible for ensuring the education and eventual independence of their children as nations like Britain were responsible for the education and eventual independence of their colonies. Political discussion about the right of the colonies to rebel frequently used the same terms as discussions about the function of education in the early republic. Jay Fliegelman has argued that political and educational arguments were often indistinguishable in the eighteenth century, and that John Locke's *Education* (rather than his *Essay Concerning Human Understanding*) provided the terms for the Enlightenment versions of American political and familial, as well as educational, rhetoric and practice.[9] In the *Education*, Locke argued that paternal and political powers were distinct (a rebuttal of Filmer's *Patriarcha*) and claimed that consent and contract were the basis of the state. However, Locke's desire to halt the use of family analogies for political structures was subverted as his formulation of the rights of children within the family became the eighteenth-century justification for the rebellion of the colonies against their parent country. According to this argument, the most important familial obligation was not that of children toward their parents but that of parents toward their children.

Analogies or metaphors like these significantly *structured* and did not merely describe systems of government. Fliegelman claims that the "call for filial autonomy" was the "quintessential motif" of the Revolution. Focusing on this representation of political conflicts at the level of the family, Fliegelman attempts to show that shifts in attitudes toward the family were concurrent with shifts in political hierarchies. The American Revolution was most significantly, he argues, a "revolution in the nature of the understanding of authority."[10] Such a changed understanding of authority becomes most visible at the level of educational practices, and the late eighteenth century saw increasing emphasis on the importance of education in inculcating values.[11] As the disputes created by Rousseau's proposals demonstrate, however, the extent to which children should be educated to be independent remained controversial well into the nineteenth (if not the twentieth) century. In the 1790s, and in following decades, trends in education were mostly conservative and took their inspiration from paternalistic Federalist notions of order.

After the death of their parents, Clara and Wieland have a premature and, in Federalist terms, unnatural independence. They are "subjected to no unreasonable restraints," indeed are free from any external restraints, and are "saved from the corruption and tyranny of colleges and boarding schools," becoming "superintendants of [their own] education" (W, 20, 21). Clara's terms for her upbringing could have been taken from colonial pamphlets about the benefits of independence from Britain. The dangers of infidelity, however, would have been apparent to anxious contemporaries: "Our education had been modelled by no religious standard. We were left to the guidance of our own understanding and the casual impressions which society might make upon us. . . . We sought not a basis for our faith" (W, 22). In other words, the Wieland children are educated in the style of the Enlightenment, a style derived in the eighteenth century from the formulations of Locke and Rousseau. One purpose of the novel might be to question how successfully this style functions on American soil.

Clara's utopian upbringing has created a hazardous situation both because it has attracted Carwin and because it has not been supplemented by the institutions increasingly perceived as necessary in the young republic. Indeed, Clara judges that she has had a "perverse and vicious education," especially because she has not been "qualified by education or experience to encounter perils" (W, 80, 140). In *The Discovery of the Asylum*, David Rothman asserts that the late-eighteenth-century American fear of contamination by France was becoming a fear of contamination by anything in the "world"; to counter this fear, the family had to be at once protected and protective and "inoculate" the child against society. As we have seen, the rise of institutions of social control in this period, like the orphan asylum and even the school, is modeled on and supported by such an insular notion of the family. The institution compensated for the failure of the family, supplemented, and even instructed the family, from which it was presumed to have derived.[12] One of *Wieland*'s functions as a tutelary tract might be to prepare the way for the notion that institutions are a necessary supplement to the family. Without the formal institutions of education, religion, "benevolent societies," orphanages, or prisons, the new republic would be susceptible to the chaos unleashed within the Wieland family.[13]

In *Wieland*, that chaos is blamed on Carwin, whose intrusion has apparently roused sexual tensions in Clara and Pleyel, and an insane and murderous religious enthusiasm in Wieland. Published while the fear of contagion by the alien was at its height, the novel both blames Carwin for introducing sexuality, disorder, and violence into the Wieland family, and explains that introduction as nothing more than an enhancement of sexual and familial tensions already present.[14] Carwin is an intruder, an alien called "from afar" by what he perceives as the almost "divine" qualities of Clara and her brother. But he also embodies an instability already present in the Wieland family. Introduced as an external threat, the alien, Carwin, instead stands (in) for an internal one, the infidelity of religious and institutional beliefs that the novel at first appeared to celebrate.[15] If the family had been properly inoculated against him, he could have had no effect on them.

The extent to which the family can be seen as a haven from the outside world is made problematic on the historical front as well. Although *Wieland*'s action takes place "between the conclusion of the French and the beginning of the revolutionary war," Clara finds that "revolutions and battles, however calamitous to those who occupied the scene, contributed in some sort to our happiness, by agitating our minds with curiosity, and furnishing causes of patriotic exultation. Four children . . . exercised my brother's tenderness" (W, 3, 26). The unabashed segue from the "scene" of war to the family scene does not disturb Clara and would pass by the reader were it not that what seems continuous to her appears discontinuous to us. While Clara apparently intends that the violence outside should emphasize the harmony within the family, the introduction of the children is instead the introduction of violence: they are to be the object not of Wieland's "tenderness" but of violence "calamitous to those who occupied the scene." Both the absent battles and the present children mysteriously "contributed in some sort to our happiness," while both agitate minds with curiosity about violence.[16] If Clara conflates the revolutions of nations and the transformations of families, this conflation of national and familial violence further confirms the extent to which the novel registers contemporary national concerns in its portrayal of familial turmoil. The novel emphasizes the violence within the family while ascribing that violence to the intrusion of a violent force, but that very force seems immanent rather than intrusive and the efforts to name it as "alien" only emphasize its immanence.

The clearest instances of alien intrusion into the family may be the most explicit "otherworldly" experiences of the novel, the spontaneous combustion of the elder Wieland and the "inspiration" of the younger. While the younger Wieland begins by seeking a "ground of his belief" in the "history of religious opinions," Clara finds in the Calvinist "ground" her brother stands on nothing but "props" that can only be a temporary support: "Moral necessity, and calvinistic inspiration, were the props on which my brother thought proper to repose" (W, 23, 25). Unfortunately for Wieland, the shakiness of his "ground" points to an "obvious resemblance between him and my father" (W, 23). In other words, we are warned that his attempt to reason toward faith by combining "calvinistic inspiration" with the "history of religious opinion" will produce infidelity and madness. The conflation of Wieland's attempt to reason toward faith (apparently an oblique reference to Paine) and the horrific effects of his sudden access to God (reminiscent of some of the excesses of the Great Awakening) appears as a reference to the conflict earlier described between Timothy Dwight, the grandson of that arch-Calvinist Jonathan Edwards, and Thomas Paine, the arch-deist. Paralleling the twin downfalls of the Weems pamphlet, the novel shows the pitfalls of either position. Neither the inspired Wieland nor the rationalist Pleyel represents a form of belief that can effectively function against the hazards of the early Republic.[17] By demonstrating the weakness of either extreme, the novel enacts a desire for the norm. And the champion or hero of this enactment may finally be not the reasonable Pleyel or even Clara, but Carwin. His voice forces a questioning of perceived realities and underscores the abnormalities already present within the Wieland family. *Wieland* carries out many of the same moves of dissembling narrators, embedded narratives, confused identities, and an obsession with boundaries as *Arthur Mervyn*, and, like Arthur Mervyn, Carwin can be seen as an "alien" who introduces himself surreptitiously into households and exposes abnormalities as part of a regularizing or normalizing strategy.

Before examining further the effects of Carwin's presence in *Wieland*, I want to consider the context of this presence by returning to the terms established in Weems's pamphlet, where deism and revivalism were both excesses that led to disaster. In particular, I want to trace the religious, legal, and sexual implications of Wieland's destruction of his family by looking at the crime in the novel and in two possible sources for the novel. The novel's presentation of Wieland's brutal murders brings together, in the arena of the family, anxieties about law and religion. Set in a period when the nation was haunted alike by fears of the removal of an institutionalized God perceived in deism and of the direct access promised in the revivalism of the Great Awakening, the novel also works effectively to collapse the difference between these categories and to relocate the threat as an intrusive violation into the family.

When Clara reads Wieland's confession, which she transcribes as evidence within her own first-person narrative, she discovers his belief that in murdering his family he has obeyed a personal call to faith. Like the court he appears in, Wieland once wanted to "settle the relation between motive and actions, the criterion of merit, and the kinds and properties of evidence" (W, 23). Now he professes to be thankful for the chance "to testify my submission to thy will" (W, 165). Incongruously presenting a personal narrative of conversion in the world of the court, Wieland represents himself and his motives for the murder of his family in the terms of the conversion narrative that was required for admittance into the Puritan congregation.[18] But his story of conversion, instead of gaining him admittance into the "congregation," causes him to be cast out and emphasizes the conflict between "legal" and "religious" explanations that the novel examines.

Wieland's appeal to a transcendent deity was soon to become, in the eyes of the law, an insanity defense. Even in the 1790s, as the novel presents the case, Wieland's perceived madness saves him from the gallows, although not from institutionalization. David Brion Davis has discussed the change in the early republic from the Calvinist concentration on sin or sinful thought as worthy of punishment to the focus on crime and its origin in "parental neglect and faulty emotional growth [rather than] inherent depravity or a conscious choice of evil." According to this view, the early republic witnessed a basic change in notions of responsibility and communal legitimations and a shift in notions of character. The structure of social institutions, modeled on the family, becomes the locus of the moral and emotional "nurture" and formation of the subject: "there was a growing conviction that crime was a disease . . . to be prevented by improved education and social reform."[19] Adapting to this shift to the jurisdiction of the family, Timothy Dwight preached that "Murder in the proper sense is begun in . . . the early and unrestrained indulgence of human passions. This indulgence, therefore, Parents, and all other Guardians of children, are bound faithfully to restrain."[20] The conversion narrative has given way to the legal confession, innate character to education and growth, and penitence to the penitentiary. In one respect this transformation was itself dramatically ratified in the separation of church and state represented by the ratification of the Constitution and the dispersal of the authority of the church into the related institutions of education, law, and the family. The novel plays out the anxieties that this change in jurisdiction has produced.

More particularly, the novel dramatizes the change from judging Wieland's crime according to his faith (Wieland castigates his judges for their failure to recognize divine rather than legal jurisdiction: "Impious and rash! thus to usurp the prerogatives of your Maker!") to judging it according to a legal conception of sanity. Still the novel betrays an uncertain jurisdiction over the topic of madness. In part this results from the uncertainty of causal relations in a novel that foregrounds the problem of cause and effect.[21] The notion that madness is both motive and cause for Wieland's crime poses rather than solves the problem of motive, complicating what it means to have motives. Clara's uncle reassures her that "There could be no doubt as to the cause of these excesses. They originated in sudden madness, but that madness continues, and he is condemned to perpetual imprisonment" (W, 177). Instead of solving the crux of Wieland's motives, the weak causal links of this statement beg the question. What is the connection between the continuation of Wieland's madness ("but") and his imprisonment ("and")? If the "cause" or origin of Wieland's "excesses" is "madness," does his imprisonment represent an attempt to cure him or to contain the effects of his delusions? The notion that character can change is exhibited most problematically here: if Wieland's madness no longer continued, would he be freed?

An excess of belief has led to Wieland's crimes, but what may appear as a simple conflict between religious and legal explanations is further complicated by references to the family. Curiously, in his marked submission to a divine vision, Wieland appeals to the community, and he makes that appeal in terms that suggest he recognizes yet another version of the constituted self. Turning to the audience at his trial, he asks, "Who is there present a stranger to the character of Wieland? Who knows him not as an husband—as a father—as a friend?" (W, 164). His appeal to the community's "knowledge" of him in familial terms is at once an escape from the confines of legal and religious definitions of the citizen or congregant and a move to the heart of those definitions. If Wieland is "known" as a member of his family, he is placed safely in both legal and religious discourses. His actions in murdering his family have been as much a confirmation of his belief in the value of family as a denial.

Wieland contains a family destroyed from within, though agency is ascribed to outside forces. A similar displacement occurs in one of the presumed sources for *Wieland*. James Yates was sitting in front of his fire in 1781 reading the Bible when he suddenly heard a voice commanding him to destroy his idols. He threw his Bible into the fire; then, on further admonition from the voice, he killed his wife and four children. His next thought was to set the house on fire to make it appear that the Indians had done the deed ("I shall be called a murderer for destroying my idols—for obeying the mandate of my father—no, I will put all the dead in the house together, run to my sister's and say the Indians have done it!"),[22] but he was convinced that his actions were justified since they had been dictated by a divine voice and decided that it was better to have the deed known as a confirmation of his devoutness. Axelrod has argued that by taking "'communion' with the wilderness" Yates internalizes the threat of the Indians and acts as they would presumably have acted.[23] But if Yates, as a sort of afterthought, displaces his violence onto the Indians, his justifications for his actions—and indeed the acts themselves—explicitly invoke a different perspective. Yates's justifications, and his presentation of himself as wavering between a family of "idols" and "divine" injunctions to destroy them (reminiscent of Puritan iconoclasm), suggest that he has not so much incorporated the threat of the Indians as violently externalized the closely linked internal problems of belief and the family.

Another analogue for *Wieland* may be the *Narrative of the Life of William Beadle* (reprinted several times in the 1790s), which gives an account of a murder-suicide that took place in the last year of the American Revolution. This analogue has not been previously noted and may provide further clues about *Wieland*. Beadle was a retailer ruined because of the failure of continental specie toward the end of the war. One morning in 1782, he killed his wife and four children and then shot himself. Beadle left letters in which "he professes himself a deist" and claimed that "the deity would not willingly punish one who was impatient to visit his God and learn his will from his own mouth face to face": "That it is God himself who prompts and directs me . . . I really believe." Conflating the concepts of deism and revivalism, Beadle apparently meant that the promise of direct access to God enabled him to perceive his premeditated murders as righteous acts, and hence his mind, like Wieland's, "was contemplative" before the murders.[24]

The narrative of Beadle's life was presented by its editor as a testament to the "shocking effects of pride and false notions about religion," but it also and perhaps more strikingly shows the power of the unstable tension between family and world in the early Republic. When Beadle originally began to fail, "he adopted a plan of the most rigid family economy, but still kept up the outward appearance of his former affluence." More than an understandable attempt to retain status, Beadle's version of "family economy" is transformed into the necessity of family sacrifice. Beadle's family went hungry because "he was determined not to bear the mortification of being thought poor and dependent," but his considerateness did not stop there: "since it is a father's duty to prepare for his flock, he thought it better to consign them over to better hands." His wife had been having premonitory dreams of the murders, perhaps because Beadle had been in the habit of bringing a butcher knife and an axe to bed with him every night. Beadle wrote of her premonitions, but claimed that "heaven" thought "his purpose was right": God "now directs me and supports me." He wondered whether he could justify killing his wife; finally he decided that it "would be unmerciful to leave her behind to linger out a life in misery and wretchedness which must be the consequence of the surprising death of the rest of the family, and that since they had shared the smiles and frowns of fortune together, it would be cruelty to her, to be divided from them in death."[25]

Beadle's fear of alienation from the community, through poverty, or the family, through death, was dramatically realized when the community had to dispose of his body. No one wanted to be responsible: "at last it was performed by some Negroes, who threw him out of the window, with the bloody knife tied on his breast." Having found suitably marginal characters as undertakers and a thoroughly marginal means of egress, the community became perturbed about interring the body: "After some consultation, it was thought best to place it on the banks of the river between the high and low water mark; the body was . . . bound with cords upon a sled, with the clothes on it as it was found, and the bloody knife tied on his breast, without coffin or box, and the horse he usually rode was made fast to the sled." After a gruesome funeral procession, "the body was tumbled into a hole dug for the purpose like the carcase of a beast."[26] Despite the communal attempts to eliminate Beadle and even to eradicate his identity as a human being, the multiply outcast Beadle returned yet again: some children discovered his body washed up by the river, and it was reburied by a crossroads.

Finally, the difference that Beadle enforces between outward appearance and an inner "rigid family economy" sets up an unbearable distinction between the family and the world. Although Beadle's explanation of his actions invokes a peculiar form of deism, in fact the confusion of revivalism and deism he exhibits appears equivalently in the Weems pamphlet and other discussions of the early republic that create a striking correspondence between the effects of these religious excesses. The editor of Beadle's account, Stephen Mix Mitchell, asks, in terms reminiscent of *Wieland*, if it is possible that "a man could be transformed from an affectionate husband and an indulgent parent to a secret murderer, without some previous alteration, which must have been noticed by the family or acquaintance?"[27] The "previous alteration" that effected a transformation in Beadle seems again, as with Yates and Wieland, to have been caused by exposure to religious excess. What appears in these accounts to be on the one side an affirmation of devout Calvinist orthodoxy and on the other an affirmation of deistic reasoning that curiously allows for direct access to God turns out to be much the same when put into practice: deism and Calvinist revivalism are represented as significant, and significantly similar, threats to the family. What may be most disturbing, however, about these "alterations" is that they cannot finally be blamed on an alien intrusion; instead, the family-republic, like the Wieland family that serves as its "model," is caught in the grip of transformations in which it discovers that the alien is already within.

In *Wieland*, the direct result of excessive styles of belief is not only the violence we have been discussing, but also, and perhaps more significantly in terms of the scene of the family, irregular sexual desires. Specifically, as several critics have noted, incest appears almost unmistakable in both Wieland's actions and Clara's responses. In this final and most disturbing version of naming desires as alien to expel them, Clara performs a double action, at once projecting the violence of her brother's actions onto Carwin, and discovering Carwin in threatening scenes (with sexual overtones) where she has anticipated her brother.

Wieland and Carwin are repeatedly linked by Clara. Even the possible connection between the antinomian beliefs Wieland appeals to when he explains the murder of his family (grace may free one from moral law) and the Albigensian beliefs her father apparently held when he so spectacularly died (God and Satan manifest the same force) may link what Clara perceives as godlike qualities in Wieland and the apparently Satanic qualities of Carwin. Both Carwin and Wieland undergo "transformations," though their characters remain ambiguous and even interchangeable.[28] When Clara opens closets expecting to find her brother, or steps back from pits her brother has beckoned her toward, she finds Carwin. When she discovers the murders her brother has committed, she blames Carwin. Although she explains them as antipodes, the "virtues" of her brother may not finally be distinguishable from those of Carwin: the alien and the infidel are the same.

Further, Clara's obsessive concern with the placing of responsibility, the assumption of guilt, and the assignation of blame, her attempts to discover who is guilty and how that guilt shall be determined and judged, appear connected to her own displacement of a sense of guilt. Near the end of her narrative, Clara "acknowledge[s] that my guilt surpasses that of all mankind" (W, 223). One critic asserts plausibly that Clara's "repressed guilt and incestuous desires provide her with motivation" for the crimes that Wieland commits, and argues that she "writes our story with a pen sharpened by a knife steeped in her brother's blood."[29] Clara's fascination with Carwin as he interferes with her fantasy life, mingled with her immediate assumption of his agency in the destruction of her family, points to her desire to have a scapegoat for her own desires. She identifies with Wieland's "transformation" to the extent that she asks, "Was I not likewise transformed from rational and human into a creature of nameless and fearful attributes? Was I not transported to the brink of the same abyss? Ere a new day should come, my hands might be embrued in blood" (W, 179–80). Despite her attempt to maintain Carwin as a supernaturally gifted "double-tongued deceiver," Clara manages to castigate herself. Though she calls Carwin the "phantom that pursued my dreams," she suspects that he might be one of the "phantoms of my own creation" (W, 159, 83).

Clara responds immediately to Carwin's voice: her eyes fill with "unbidden tears" and are later "rivetted" on the portrait she makes of him (W, 52, 53). Though his features are "wide of beauty," the inversion of usual standards in the "inverted cone" of his face compels her to spend the day "consumed . . . in alternately looking out upon the storm and gazing at the picture" (W, 53, 54). She cannot "account for [her] devotion to this image"—though she allows the reader to suppose it a sign of the "first inroads of a passion incident to every female heart"—and similarly cannot explain why, although the outside storm passes, "thoughts ominous and dreary" overwhelm her as she continues to look at the picture (W, 54). Instead of pointing to a romantic infatuation, these signs indicate her participation in or even invocation of Carwin's existence at the same time as the associations she makes with him seem connected to her own desires. Looking at Carwin's portrait, she thinks of death, especially dwelling on the foreshadowed deaths of her brother and his children. This oscillation between the portrait and the storm is reiterated when, in her retrospective tracing of the events that led to the deaths of her brother's children, she remembers Carwin as "the intelligence that operated in this storm" (W, 190). The storm that raged outside has been internalized. Still, she does not finally know whether Carwin is "an object to be dreaded or adored" and moves to blame him with a tentative assertion: "Some relief is afforded in the midst of suffering, when its author is discovered or imagined" (W, 71, 190).

Indeed, Clara's attempts to "discover" or "imagine" (activities she appears to confuse in the novel) the "author" of the deeds she has been so appalled by seem finally disingenuous. Like Beadle, she has tried to separate the "inviolate asylum" of the home from the dangers of the world, and, like Beadle, she finds that the scene of the home is already the scene of destruction. (It seems revealing that Clara hears murderers in her closet.) While she claims that "That dwelling, which had hitherto been an inviolate asylum, was now beset with danger to my life," her mistake is to think that it has ever been an "inviolate asylum" (W, 60).[30]

Clara's efforts to fix blame and determine judgments are part and parcel of the attempts to maintain familial and social boundaries that may be seen to structure the action of *Wieland*. Although Clara and Wieland turn their father's restrictive and rigidly regulated retreat (the temple where he meets his demise) into a haven for free discourse (a new infidelity), it quickly becomes a place where transgressions are foregrounded. Carwin turns the temple into a zone of terror by his voice projections, but his intrusion should have been expected. Clara speaks of the meetings that take place there as free from interference and of Carwin as the destroyer of their peace, but more than the double-tongued deceiver she calls him, more than simply an intruder or foreign violator of the pastoral American scene, Carwin's very abnormalities expose the shaky underpinnings of the family "asylum." By his intrusion into what Clara has presented as normal domestic scenes, he emphasizes or highlights underlying incongruities and potent desires. As he systematically invades all Clara's retreats, including her body (albeit through the surrogate servant Judith, and through the ventriloquized sexual conversation that Pleyel "overhears"), Carwin may expose Clara's general policy of concealment. In her shaded retreat by the river, Clara dreams of terrifying incest; Carwin wakes her. Clara's bower already resembles a sexual recess; Carwin forces her to confront the mingled invitation and threat of her brother's and her own sexuality.

In *Wieland*, the family is initially presented as a retreat, or "sweet and tranquil asylum" (W, 193), from the intrusions of the outside world, but the distinction between home and world, radically personified by the figure of the intruding Carwin, gets blurred as the destruction seen to lurk without is discovered within. Clara concludes her account of her family with a typically mixed acknowledgment of this flaw: "the evils of which Carwin [was] the author, owed their existence to the errors of the sufferers." No violence could have been introduced into the family "if their own frailty had not seconded these efforts" (W, 244). What Clara still manages to assume in this statement is Carwin's "authorship" of an account she has written. Even as Clara cannot fully recognize the implications of her involvement as the author of the account of her family or see the family as the source of its own destruction, the novel presents her failed perceptions as part of a prevailing faulty perception in the early republic. For the family to keep its identity as an "asylum," the outside world must be posited as a threat. At the same time, the imitation of the family in social institutions designed to assume or supplement its functions provides a way out of the unbearable tension created between inside and outside by such an insular view of the family. *Wieland*'s message may finally be that for the family to be a haven from the excesses of radical democracy, deism, revivalism, it must be inoculated, through these social institutions, at once with and against the "outside" world. Following the lead of Charles Brockden Brown, the American novel continued to explore the boundaries of the family and to suggest styles of education that would appropriately maintain the family as the support for such an "outside" world, a world represented as alien to the tranquil space, the "inviolate asylum," of the family.

The Family in the Novel: Cooper and the Domestic Revolution

The people of America had been educated in an habitual affection for England, as their mother country. . . . But when they found her . . . willing like Lady Macbeth, to "dash their brains out," it is no wonder if their filial affections ceased.[1]

John Adams

Must I then, in order to be called a faithful subject, coolly, and philosophically say, it is necessary for the good of Britain, that my children's brains should be dashed against the walls of the house in which they were reared?[2]

Hector St. John de Crevecoeur

John Adams expresses a familiar version of the story of the American Revolution when he portrays England as the quintessential bad mother on the verge of murdering her children. Hector St. John de Crevecoeur, using the same analogy to describe the threat of the Indians, implies that England is guilty of malicious indifference rather than evil intent, but his language reveals a similar congruence of anxieties in the Revolutionary period. For both Adams and Crevecoeur the connection with the "mother country" has become a "habitual affection," a phrase that at once mitigates the loss of affection and emphasizes the frailty of an affection that would make familial violence seem "coolly, and philosophically" necessary.

And the violence of the literary allusion here—the short and bloody reign of Macbeth—also calls attention to a pronounced nervousness about the figure of the mother in times of revolution. If Lady Macbeth's response to the proposed assassination of a king who "looked so like my father" is to invoke the murder of children, what must colonists who saw themselves as the children of a similarly unnatural mother have feared as they set out on a regicidal mission that also involved patricide and fratricide? Images of England as a supportive mother, still relied on by loyalists, had been transformed by rebels into images of England as a child-murderer. Both contributing to and deriving from such a metaphorical transformation, as recent historians of the American Revolution have explained it, was a revolt against the authority of the parent. This revolt, in novels as well as political rhetoric, uses a changed language of parental responsibility that coincides with a perceived change in the structure of the family. Attention to the changing structure of the family develops concurrently with the new republic, and arguably produces the republican or bourgeois family, a more egalitarian family structure responsive to the new forms of industrialization and capitalism that accompanied the rise of the republic.[3] For purposes at once rhetorical and political, a new model of bourgeois family emerged, at least prescriptively designed to internalize and support the new democratic model of government.

Much of the rhetoric of the revolutionary period focused on the need to overthrow England as a bad mother, a focus that seemed to lead to the elision of mothers in novels that depict the American Revolution.[4] The women in these novels have been destroyed by revolutions: pushed aside as wives, abhorred as sexual objects, mistrusted as mothers. References to Lady Macbeth's attempt to share in her husband's bid for power, for instance, are to an event that destroys her; Crevecoeur imagines Indians destroying his wife and children; Adams imagines a murderous mother England destroying the colonies. Using such associations to portray a family in the midst of the American Revolution in *The Spy*, James Fenimore Cooper describes the outbreak of a revolutionary war that claims the life of the mother and the reason of the daughter.

The Discovery of the Family

The attempt to control the associations of revolution in the late eighteenth and early nineteenth century by keeping it "within the family"—that is, by writing historical novels where the nation is imagined as a family troubled with violence, disruptive incest, and infidelity—may profitably be viewed as part of a concentration on methods of fashioning and educating the family in the early republic. These methods include the creation of a corpus of domestic instruction manuals and the "elevation" of the hearth (or the "cult of domesticity") in the sentimental and domestic novels of mid-century. But in the historical fiction that precedes and prepares the way for this sentimental and domestic fiction, a rather different state of the family is depicted. The model of the family that previously explained political relations in terms of benevolent supervision was replaced by a concept of ineffectual and even malevolent parental interference. With mothers out of the way, and fathers already "imbecilic," the children, major figures of these Revolutionary novels, are left to fight over conflicting loyalties, struggles frequently caused by, then resolved in, the desire to marry and found new families. These figures of sibling strife are not just an uncanny anticipation of the Civil War, as they have been interpreted, but also and importantly an inheritance of the Revolutionary War, which similarly set members of families against one another and produced a violent separation within the country.[5] Writers sought repeatedly to show that the familial struggles they used to represent national conflicts were more than limited political figurations, that they involved broader issues than abolition or the inheritance of strife between landed holders of wealth and mobile upstarts that subsequent party battles emphasized, that they finally stood for the form of the nation that had been created. In short, these novels presented the fundamental question of what nation had arisen from the Revolution, a question they sought to answer by showing the development and resolution of familial conflicts. With these resolutions such novels produce, not always successfully, intimate identification with the nation.

The perceived corruption of the figure of the wife and mother when confronted by political strife—a corruption felt to be substantiated by the notorious behavior of women at the barricades of the French Revolution[6]—had initially led political writers to dissociate the state from women, emphasize paternalism, and establish a reliance on the figure of George Washington as an unshakeable father who combined benevolence with authority. (That Washington never became a biological father only strengthened his characterization as a metaphorical one.)[7] In terms of education and the rise of other institutions of social, political, and economic control in the early republic,[8] the transformation of George Washington into the father of the nation was an extremely effective way to inculcate national values. "Let the first lisps be Washington," proclaimed Rufus Choate, substituting Washington for the mother as the child's first words. But the infantilizing that such an association produced was apparent in political orations and other invocations of Washington.[9]

Tracing the influence of Weems's *Life of Washington* as an educational tool in nineteenth-century child rearing, the historian George Forgie has suggested that the mythologizing and, indeed, deifying process that presented George Washington as the "father" of his country had the somewhat hazardous side effect of inducing a sense of timelessness, "as if, for Americans, there was not yet a 'past' but only a continuous present" in which "the continuing presence of the fathers meant continuing dependence on the part of the sons."[10] The problem of the family that seemed to have been "resolved" in the eighteenth-century adoption of family contract rather than patriarchy as the basis for family government remained to plague nineteenth-century Americans, especially when they portrayed the American Revolution. They needed to represent their own succession from the "father" of the country, and to carry out an inheritance of paternal benevolence when patriarchy had been challenged and matriarchy dishonored by the revolution. As the very term "founding fathers" suggests, a curious metaphorical difficulty existed in carrying out the wishes of founding fathers, themselves previously sons who had wrested power from previous bad parents. In other words, there was a repeated debate in the early republic about the most faithful means of perpetuating an overthrow.[11] The recapitulations of the revolution embodied in sermons, orations, political pamphlets, and historical novels participate in not only a remembrance of the past, but also a continual and often fraught redefinition of that past.[12]

Attempting to cash in on a perceived inheritance of paternal benevolence, Andrew Jackson promoted himself as a second Washington, a "new" father to his country.[13] The American novels produced during this troubled succession (roughly the 1820s through the 1850s) achieved a further displacement, representing contemporary anxieties about the status of the nation and the problem of succession by focusing on a flawed family grouping that, in remarkably similar ways from one novel to the next, played out national conflicts as sexual competition among siblings aided poorly, if at all, by ineffectual fathers and essentially abandoned (whether by infidelity or desertion) by their mothers. In some cases, as in Cooper's 1821 novel, *The Spy*, the conflict is between daughters, whose choice of spouses and expressions of sexual interest prophesy their fates and political allegiances. In others, as in his *Lionel Lincoln* (1823), the conflict, at once domestic and political, is between brothers who fight each other on battlefields rather than in parlors.

The previous chapter's fictional and nonfictional accounts of literally bashing in the heads of children show the impetus for familial violence coming from the scene of the Revolution and from anxiety about the Revolution. Both Yates and Beadle massacre their families in the last year of the Revolutionary War. Such a combination of fear of revolution with anxiety about the family has been explored in psychological terms.[14] What has not been examined is how the combination of this fear and distrust of parental figures with a scenario of sibling rivalry informs the structures of the historical novels that treat the Revolutionary period. Novels that depict the American Revolution have often been read as Oedipal struggles (they are, to use Fliegelman's phrase, "against" patriarchal authority). These novels may instead show the rise of bourgeois marriage and the changes in the family caused by the promotion of affective individualism (they are "for" democratic marriage). Marriages in these novels are rarely influenced by parents; they are contracts between equals that claim to refuse or counter family ties, inherited wealth, tradition, and aristocratic forms. Such alliances repeatedly invoke a freedom of choice that involves the working out within a generation of the form of the family. That this form of marriage is entwined with the American Revolution suggests it is a democratic form, and even a functioning allegory for the nation. The dramatic action of the novels, often paralleling Revolutionary battles, is the frequently violent struggle for a democratic marriage.[15]

In 1821, when Cooper published *The Spy*, the United States was an audience receptive not only to the historical romances of Sir Walter Scott, but also—and perhaps more significant for the historicizing project of *The Spy*—

to a series of more locally nationalistic romances. Though typically presented in the form of election sermons, Fourth of July orations, and political broadsides, these romances had worked collectively since the American Revolution (and in an even more unified fashion since the death of George Washington) to produce an image of a country united under the benevolent paternal surveillance of the founding fathers.[16] Repeated appeals were made on behalf of the country's need to be sustained by a sense of familial continuity. The response in novels and political writing was to focus on relations within the family and emphasize the implications of the family relation for the larger politics of the state.

While the paternal nature of this sense of continuity has long been recognized,[17] what tends to be omitted is the conflicted image of family that the struggle over such a father figure must entail. Discussions of Oedipal conflicts focus on father-son relations at the expense of several other aspects of the family. Specifically, for example, the questions that seem to have been neglected in repeated discussions of founding fathers include: where does that leave founding mothers and what sort of family did they engender? What are the relations among siblings? Most important, what image of the family does early-nineteenth-century American discourse produce? How is that image genealogically connected with accounts of the American Revolution, and how does it function as a social, political, and literary mechanism in the early republic? By looking at the families presented in novels and other texts that portray the American Revolution, which remained for some time the dominant concern for national self-study, I want to consider the move to domesticity implicit in the focus on the family in these historical novels, as well as the rupturing of domesticity with the intrusion of revolutionary violence.[18] And I will turn finally to a consideration of the author's relation to profiting from the patriotic project.

Both Democrats and Whigs in the early republic linked fears about political legitimacy and inheritance with similar depictions of the nation as a member of an unnatural family. Cyrus Barton, for instance, concluded a Fourth of July address in 1828 by announcing that, just as Jefferson triumphed over John Adams, now Jackson must triumph over John Quincy Adams: "the election of Jackson *now*, as of Jefferson *then*, will restore the democratic party to its rightful inheritance, and the country to the arms of her legitimate sons."[19] The desire for legitimacy is combined with the suggestion of incest: the country is at once the desired object of a contest between legitimate and (implicitly) illegitimate sons, and a suspicious object, since she has both produced and apparently given her favors to illegitimate sons. Barton's address points to the connections among claims of political legitimacy and apparent fears of the consequences of an "unnatural" mother's behavior and the disruption of primogeniture her misbehavior might cause.

The family has always been used to explain the origin and structure of nations. But the family proved especially popular for explanations in the post-Revolutionary period. This popularity is due in part to an attempt to make authority seem "natural," which, it has been suggested, meant that the traditional form of patriarchal analogy was adapted to Enlightenment values: "authority in the family was so entangled with gentle affection that external control was imperceptibly transformed by love into self-control, making the line between paternalism and self-reliance impossible to draw."[20] The family continued to work as a model for government because, although it still contained as a central figure an authoritarian patriarch, the authority that patriarch wielded over its members could be traced to love. But if the "line between paternalism and self-reliance" was blurred by the entanglement of familial authority with "gentle affection," the possibilities for social control did not go unrecognized.

Revolution and Courtship

Catherine Sedgwick's 1835 historical novel, *The Linwoods*, announces the issues of familial and social control as the story of the American Revolution. After the hero of the novel, Eliot Lee, has saved George Washington from capture, the author comments, "Our revolutionary contest, by placing men in new relations, often exhibited in new force and beauty the ties that bind together the human family."[21] This passage appears striking not only because the revolutionary contest is said to exhibit "the ties that bind together the human family," explicitly linking a contest or breaking apart of ties with ties that bind, but also, and perhaps more significant, because it emphasizes a "new" exhibition of what might seem to be the same old ties. That is, the "new relations" men are placed in by the revolution do not seem to involve a new model of the family but a new exhibition of the family. What is crucially not new about the ties that bind together the human family is that they are used to exhibit the revolutionary contest and the state of the nation. Telling the story of revolution and political upheavals as the story of the family, historical novels of the early republic repeatedly make politics and domesticity the same story: that story may begin with what Catherine Sedgwick attempts in this novel when she presents the politics of family ties in "new force and beauty."

In her preface to the novel, subtitled *"Sixty Years Since" in America*, Sedgwick remarks that the title has been "chosen simply to mark the period of the story, and that period was selected as . . . affording a picturesque light for domestic features" (xi). If the American Revolution is notable for the "picturesque light" it sheds on "domestic features," the domestic revolutions that form the subject of her narrative become the central features of her American landscape. In exploring this landscape, Sedgwick explains that she seeks "to give her younger readers a true, if a slight, impression of the condition of their country . . . and by means of the impression to deepen their gratitude to their patriot-fathers; a sentiment that will tend to increase their fidelity to the free institutions transmitted to them" (xi–xii). This statement is perhaps Sedgwick's crudest polemicizing. To ask readers to combine gratitude to the patriot fathers with fidelity to institutions is at the simplest level to ask for an identification of the family with the state. Such an identification enforces the use of the family as not only a model for the state but also an instrument for relaying the practices and beliefs of the state.

While presenting the political controversies of the book as part of the problem of courtship, Sedgwick explains her procedure as a "feminine mode" of personifying or embodying political abstractions.[22] She announces, for example, that "a woman's political conclusions are rather sentiments than opinions" (II, 85). Isabella Linwood's rejected Tory lover complains similarly that "It is rather a feminine mode . . . of arriving at political abstractions through their incarnation in a favorite hero" (II, 16). While the use of political heroes as the incarnation of political abstractions is of course not limited to female authors—and is one of Cooper's favorite tactics—such a "feminine mode" involves a further congruence, or identification, between the domestic place of the family, a place marked in these novels by gestures of courtship and the forming of marriages, and the political place of the state, a place determined not only by battles, but also and especially by the virtually governmental endorsements of these marriages.[23] Although typically the action of these novels takes in specific battles, real prisons, and real historical figures such as Washington, the excitement or suspense is provided by obstacles to the marriages of their central characters. While it may be the formal requirement of the novel plot, resolution through marriage importantly represents the satisfactory conclusion of the revolutionary contest.

Binding marriage up with the fate of the country, both Linwood children marry politically. Herbert Linwood's marriage literally brings together national politics and domestic events when, taking over for the commander in chief as well as more intimate figures of authority, "Mrs. Washington, as the representative of the parents, pronounced a blessing on the bridal pair" (II, 266). Nation and family are so conflated that for Mrs. Washington to represent the parents becomes almost redundant. The new Mrs. Linwood seeks the "distinction" of "being a good wife and mother—the true *American order of merit*" (II, 275). Such an American order of merit is acquired through adopting a position within the family as well as the nation. It also necessitates the discovery of the self as political.

For Isabella Linwood to discover herself as an independent American involves overcoming prior attachments—in romance or politics. Isabella finds that "a new light had broken upon her, and she began to see old subjects in a fresh aspect" (I, 120). Of course, her rebel suitor, Eliot Lee becomes increasingly attracted to Isabella as her political allegiances change, since these changes are also linked with her renunciation of her former Tory lover. He declares himself to Isabella in a speech more political than personal: "I have seen your mind casting off the shackles of early prejudices, resisting the authority of opinion, self-rectified, and forming its independent judgments on those great interests in which the honour and prosperity of your country are involved" (II, 223). His insistence on a perfect identity of self, family, and state is reinforced by Isabella's first suitor, who, rejected, as Eliot Lee is accepted, on political grounds that subsume the personal, "felt, what was in truth quite evident, that Isabella Linwood was herself again" (II, 207). For Isabella to be "herself again" is very much like what is involved in placing men in new relations in order to exhibit in new force and beauty the ties that bind together the human family; that is, she has acquired "herself again" by forming "independent judgments on those great interests in which the honor and prosperity of [her] country are involved," interests the novel presents as identical to those of romantic choice. Isabella's marriage, like that of other characters in the novel, involves her discovery of self in a political world, a founding of the family that is a founding of the state.

A similar discovery takes place in other historical novels that treated similar problems in similar terms. Reviewing another historical novel by Sedgwick in 1822, Cooper argued that a novelist who wanted to write American fiction should avoid politics, education, and religion and concentrate on "our domestic manners, the social and the moral influences."[24] The point of concentrating on domestic manners in this fiction, however, is not to avoid issues of politics, education, and religion, but to look at their primary focus: the founding of the family. If one is substitutable for the other, the state for the family, the ideological work is successful. Although the historical novel stages American marriage as the "foundation of intellect and virtue" (I, 53) for the new republic, at the same time, the insistent rhetoric by which marriage and state are conflated in this fiction suggests a faltering of a sense of congruence between the government within self and family and that of the larger state. The very focus on the family may be a way of separating the family from the world; in other words, to focus on the family in the name of an alignment of the family with the state may paradoxically lead to what the authors of this literature apparently desire to work against: the separation of the family from the state.[25]

Revolution and the Republican Family

There is a strange connexion between Cupid and Mars, love and war.

Lionel Lincoln

A hesitation about the congruence between marriage and politics gets dramatically played out in James Fenimore Cooper's first "American" novel, *The Spy: A Tale of the Neutral Ground* (1821). *The Spy* was Cooper's first major success and filled a need that American reviewers had long been delineating: it was an explicitly American book, on an American theme, set in an American landscape, and focused on an American family. The dispute between England and the United States, Cooper announces in the preface, "though not strictly a family quarrel," still appears as one because it was a "war that partook so much of a domestic character" (3). In developing his story of this "quarrel," Cooper focuses on a family whose political identifications and loyalties repeatedly interrupt the progress of the Revolution. The marriage plot, the most prominent in the novel, presents the familiar scenario of marital choices that are identical to political choices—what I have been calling a congruence model.

But this plot is disrupted by another and rival set of concerns, concerns with the economic and commercial story of the new republican and bourgeois family that move the narration from the territory of the historical romance to that of the historical novel. This secondary plot presents the titular but also displaced subject of the novel, the peddler-spy marginalized in the neutral ground. Moreover, this secondary plot centrally places the figure of the American author and the critical problem of "profit" and "patriotism" at the heart of the novel. In brief, Cooper's "tale of the neutral ground" relates a transition from one model of family to another and a transition from one economic form to another, from an economy of landed aristocracy to an economy of portable bourgeois capitalism. Crucially, the divided loyalties that the novel portrays are recast in the divided form of the novel itself, and these divisions and tensions ultimately bring into focus the ways in which political, commercial, and familial divisions and tensions affect the problem of authorship and the uncertain status, and even loyalty, of the author of an American tale. In what follows I want to investigate these tensions, beginning with the marriage plot that forms the more traditional part of Cooper's story.

As in other revolutionary romances, much of the action of the novel revolves around the question of siblings and marriage. Frances and Sarah Wharton appear alike, but one loves her kinsman and countryman, the rebel Peyton Dunwoodie, and the other loves Colonel Wellmere, a Tory officer at once "outside" the family and the country. Their Tory brother, Captain Wharton, does not see their personal convictions as anything but political. He scoffs, "Women are but mirrors, which reflect the images before them. In Frances I see the picture of Major Dunwoodie, and in Sarah—" "Colonel Wellmere," she admits (49). Although their function in the novel appears to be simply to reflect the personal face each of the opposed political sides wears, the marriages in the novel invoke not only the political stance of the participants, but also their economic positions.

By concentrating on the marriages of the Wharton daughters, the novel presents at once the interpenetration of love and battle and an economic transition. A marked tension appears in Cooper between the family as an aristocratic form designed to carry on valuable ceremonies and traditions, and the family as a democratic form able to rescue valuable artifacts from the outmoded baggage of the past. Sarah Wharton's marriage with Colonel Wellmere appears at first as an attempt to reconcile a democratic family (she makes her own choice and proceeds without ceremony) with an aristocratic one (she marries a man she perceives to be a personification of landed, titled, inheritance and aristocratic attention to forms). When her sister, Frances, asks about Wellmere, Sarah's answer is simply that he is a "gentleman" (239). But the dramatic failure of this attempted reconciliation (and of the marriage) signals the failure of the aristocratic forms more generally; while patronage remains necessary to survival in the neutral ground, the Wharton family survives through an American version of patronage that involves contract and hidden agency rather than claims of title or wealth. The waning power of the old forms may be indicated by the faded Wharton arms on the carriage that will carry them away from the burned ruins of their home. Marriage in this novel will most importantly mean leaving the neutral ground, both literally and politically moving from a place of unfixed loyalties and futile attempts to hold onto property to a place of fixed loyalties and movable goods.

The patronage that protects the Whartons throughout the novel is provided by Harvey Birch, George Washington, and Major Dunwoodie, each of whom prods Frances, as the acting representative of the family throughout much of the novel, to give up the neutrality of her family's position and commit herself, politically and personally, by marrying Dunwoodie.[26] The equivocal nature of her family's neutrality means that Major Dunwoodie must work to reconcile familial tensions and duties with political tensions and duties. His position as a rebel soldier comes close to being compromised as he maneuvers to help the Whartons. Repeatedly, his orders from George Washington place him in proximity to the family, joining familial and political/military responsibilities. Indeed the passion that he shows on one front appears indistinguishable from that of the other. When he sees Frances Wharton watching from the window as he rides off to battle, "a flush of ardor began to show itself on his sunburned features; and his dragoons, who studied the face of their leader, as the best index to their own fates, saw again the wonted flashing of the eyes . . . which they had so often witnessed on the eve of battle" (76). As this juxtaposition shows, the main conflicts of the novel involve not only the battlefield and the trial for treason of Captain Wharton, but also the question of marriage that comes to subsume battles and treason alike.

The dramatic action of the novel revolves around interventions into the proposed marriage of Frances Wharton and Peyton Dunwoodie. First her brother's political loyalties threaten the union. When her rebel suitor must arrest the loyalist Captain Wharton, Frances finds herself in the difficult position of supporting both, wishing for "the safety of her brother and the protection of her lover" (71). Not only Wharton's captivity holds her back; she tells Dunwoodie she cannot marry him "so long as you are arrayed in arms against my only brother" (69), but she wants him to win. When she finally realizes that political loyalties must bring them into collision, "the appalled Frances shrank back from between her brother and her lover, where her ardent feelings had carried her" (72).[27] Her desires become contradictory; Frances's attempt to be loyal to both sides initially keeps her from her lover—"Do you think I can throw myself into the arms of a man whose hands are stained with the blood of my brother?" (70)—but ends by bringing them together. Her offer to marry Peyton if he will release her brother becomes an offer to marry him to slow his pursuit of her brother's escape. Captain Wharton has urged Peyton to become at once "brother, son and husband"; Peyton in turn presses Frances to turn the political controversy into a familial one: "Will you send me out this night to meet my own brother? or will it be the officer of Congress in quest of the officer of Britain?" (418)[28] While Peyton Dunwoodie insists on lining up the family and politics, Frances hesitates at such an involvement of politics with marriage. When Peyton asks her, "What will Washington think of me, should he learn that I ever became your husband?" she responds, "Are you not making us both of more consequence with Washington than the truth will justify?" (416) The novel insists on this sense of marital consequence: Washington hovers over the marriage and practically ordains it.

"You now have the fruits of rebellion brought home to you—a brother wounded and a prisoner" (149), Sarah Wharton says angrily to Frances when their brother is arrested. What gets brought home to Frances as a fruit of rebellion is sexual rivalry. She asks Isabella Singleton into her home when *her* brother is wounded and discovers that Isabella also loves Peyton Dunwoodie. Since Frances cannot be shown to be contaminated by her contact with revolution, Isabella must be. Because of her "wild" beauty and willingness to love unasked (the closest Cooper allows his "females" to approach to wantonness), Isabella represents the threat of licentiousness from the involvement of women in revolutions. Although "in her inmost heart she had personified her nation by the graceful image of Peyton Dunwoodie," Frances is curiously quick to resign her attachment and assign his marriage to the "ungovernable" Isabella, seeing in the wantonness of Isabella the spirit of revolution (83). She tells Dunwoodie that he should "soar" with Isabella since she envisions him (as the nation) wedded to Isabella (as the revolution), but Peyton has a more settled version of his prospects and sees in Frances the quiet domesticity that he associates with nationhood (222, 183).[29]

Frances Wharton's only competition in marriage, the female threat in the novel, is conveniently removed by a stray bullet. Almost literally felled by a broken heart, as she presses to her side a hand "dyed in blood," Isabella Singleton tells Frances that the "innocent, the justifiable cause" of her expressions of love for Dunwoodie (a love she apologizes for since it was "a love that was unsought") was that she was "motherless": "We are both motherless; but that aunt . . . has given you the victory. Oh! how much she loses, who loses a female guardian to her youth. I have exhibited those feelings which you have been taught to repress" (280). The real tragedy appears as one of education and family government. As a "female guardian," Frances's aunt has given her "countless lectures on genealogy," an education in the family that stands her in good stead. The prevailing motherlessness that hinders all the characters of *The Spy* again seems connected to American sensibilities generally: although Americans could rid themselves of their "bad" mother, they found no "good" one to take her place, until the call of "young America" for female guardianship was answered with the novel of domesticity. The loss of parental guardians results not (or not only) in substitutes but in the creation of new families through marriage.

When she finally marries her cousin, Peyton Dunwoodie, Frances acts "without the affectation of reserve" and "placed in his hand the wedding ring of her own mother" (364). But her older sister's earlier marriage to the British officer evokes very different behavior. At the last moment, it is discovered that the groom has no ring, and her aunt is troubled because "not for the world would she violate any of the observances of female etiquette" and interfere. In a simultaneous revelation, the sisters and the aunt remember the location of a ring: "It suggested itself to all the females, at the same moment, the wedding-ring of the late mother and sister was reposing peacefully . . . in a secret receptacle. . . . But it was the business of the bridegroom, from time immemorial to furnish this indispensable to wedlock, and on no account would Miss Peyton do anything that transcended the usual reserve of the sex on this occasion" (241). The marriage ceremony of Sarah Wharton is already bound up with the death of her mother and the violation of a sexual and familial order. No one ventures to disturb the peaceful repose of the ring in the "secret receptacle" of the mother.

At last the surgeon Sitgreaves sends for a ring that belonged to his sister and pronounces this benediction on it: "She for whom it was intended has long been in her grave . . . take it, madam, and God grant that it may be an instrument in making you as happy as you deserve!" (251). The question of what happiness Sarah may deserve is at once answered and left ambiguous: the wedding ring that seems to have been taken from a dead woman's hand heralds the destruction of her reason and the downfall of her family. Immediately after the wedding, Harvey Birch unceremoniously announces that Colonel Wellmere is a bigamist, having left a wife in England, and on the heels of Harvey Birch, the "Skinners," a band of outlaws, arrive to attack, plunder, and burn the Wharton house.

Colonel Wellmere's bigamy is "heinous" both because it destroys Sarah's reason and because it accords with royal treatments generally. The lament over Sarah's ensuing madness is appropriately political rather than personal: "It is in vain that we overcome our enemies, if, conquered, they can inflict such wounds as this" (267).[30] The threat of scandal is enough to unhinge her reason, and in this respect she acts not only as the sentimental heroine of romance, but also as the typical female instrument for measuring such political disturbances as revolution. The association of sexual unease with revolution that I have discussed with regard to the late eighteenth century was still potent in the nineteenth century as a fear of the processes of change: "In the nineteenth century any form of social change was tantamount to an attack on woman's virtue."[31] In The Spy, this social change has been tied back to the processes of the American Revolution. What the novel enforces as a safe social transition, however, often appears contradictory.

While marriage more than battle is the matter of The Spy, the form that marriage takes in the novel is intimately connected with an attempt to define what the battle stands for. Frances can use her mother's wedding ring without hesitation because she remains within the family and within the home. The doom that follows so swiftly on Sarah's marriage seems caused by her attempt to marry outside the family. Indeed, the immediate result of her marriage appears to be the destruction of the family home; not discriminating between the marriage and the attack of the Skinners, her aunt says, "There is a dreadful confusion in the house and there will be bloodshed in consequence of this affair" (260). The opposed accounts of these marriages point to the further importance of Peyton Dunwoodie's marriage to Frances: he is her "kinsman"— he is already within the family and can therefore save it. After her disastrous wedding, the deranged Sarah laments to Isabella, "Did you ever let a stranger steal your affections from father, and brother, and sister?" (262). In contrast, her brother repeatedly urges Dunwoodie to marry Frances: "become at once, brother, son and husband" (362). This quasi-incestuous pairing becomes the only possible solution to the dilemmas of the family (and the country).

If the marriage of Sarah and Colonel Wellmere fails partly because he is an outsider and partly because he stands for old aristocratic inherited forms, why does Cooper make Dunwoodie also appear to stand for old, aristocratic inherited forms? As a Virginia gentleman, Dunwoodie is both an outsider (to New England) and the scion of an aristocratic tradition of landed gentry. Indeed, as we learn from the last chapter, they have returned to live on the family estate. He appears to represent the compromise Cooper felt to be necessary between cherished Federalist ideals and the Democratic reality. More than that, he stands for free choice in marriage combined with the continuing potency of patriarchy. And, as we see in the final chapter, the son of this marriage gets presented as the embodiment of the new nation.

Fighting the War of 1812, announced as the final battle of the American Revolution, Wharton Dunwoodie effectively wraps up the loose ends of the novel. The son of Frances Wharton and Peyton Dunwoodie, his name combines the names of the novel's competing "brothers." He also merges male and female: his "proud expression was softened by the lines of a mouth around which there played a suppressed archness, that partook of feminine beauty. His hair shone in the setting sun like ringlets of gold, as the air from the falls gently moved the rich curls from a forehead whose whiteness showed that exposure and heat alone had given their darker hue to a face glowing with health" (395). The "feminine beauty" of this soldier is not a handicap in battle; indeed his "feminine" attributes may be designed to show the secure identification of the nation with the home, and even to show that women, or love, can now be safely equated with battle. The "glow" of this son of the Revolution, bedecked as he is with tributes of empire (ringlets of gold, rich curls) illuminates the secrets of the spy and makes his ambiguous acts clear: he discovers the note George Washington has written testifying to the peddler-spy Birch's "true" identity. But Wharton Dunwoodie not only combines male and female, not only links family names, he also displays family traits. Specifically, he reflects his mother as well as his father. When he begins to speak of his mother ("My mother was —"), the spy finishes for him: "An angel!" Cooper has apparently moved from the discredited mother to the Angel in the House, to a model of domestic bliss that has succeeded the burning of the house. A re-examination of the economic and political underpinnings of what appears as a satisfactory resolution through marriage reveals uncertainties in the perfect congruence Cooper establishes here.

The Peddler Spy

This disruptive secondary plotting and this second story of the Revolution may begin with the explanation one rustic character gives for the origins of the rebellion: "'Twas said the king wanted all the tea for his own family, at one time; and then again, that he meant the colonies should pay over to him all their earnings. Now this is matter enough to fight about—for I'm sure that no one . . . has a right to the hard earnings of another" (336). The "right to the hard earnings of another" is frequently asserted in the skirmishes that Cooper describes. Property is subject to confiscation, wages are seized, and the political allegiance, or "right," that covers for these actions is more frequently an appeal to power, or simple might. [32]

The territory of the novel's action is the neutral ground: "Its name, as a neutral ground, is unauthorized by law; it is an appellation that originates with the condition of the country" (345). The condition of the country is shown in the novel to be one in which neutrality is affected to protect property, and especially to protect it from marauding groups of "Skinners" and "Cowboys." Each group is nominally attached to the British or American forces, but each is depicted as equally out for profit: "The convenience, and perhaps the necessities, of the leaders of the American armies . . . had induced them to employ certain subordinate agents, of extremely irregular habits . . . whose sole occupation appears to have been that of relieving their fellow-citizens from any little excess of temporal prosperity they might be thought to enjoy, under the pretence of patriotism, and the love of liberty" (24). The irregularity of these "habits" seems at first to be symptomatic of a class warfare. Indeed, John McWilliams has argued that the "true significance of the Revolution," for Cooper, "is not the historical battles between British and Americans, but an interclass conflict in America."[33] But the "arbitrary distributions of worldly goods" that Cooper comments on are not the pre-existing conditions that cause Revolution; they are the irregular crimes of the war and Cooper calls them "unlicensed robbery" (24). This unfixing of the bounds of property does not result in a desirable change in class stratification. Instead, the mix of profit and patriotism is summed up in the stand of the leader of the Skinners, who boasts, "we shall have a free government, and we, who fight for it, will get our reward" (238). The desire for "reward" in a "free government" is at once a desire for free access to property and the insertion of a profit motive into patriotism. In its exploration of the neutral ground, the novel picks up on both options. [34]

In the neutral ground, the economy has been reduced to subsistence farming because the marauding Cowboys and Skinners will take any surplus. Currently, Mr. Wharton's land is mostly unoccupied, and his fields untenanted: "The proximity of the country to the contending armies had nearly banished the pursuits of agriculture from the land. It was useless for the husbandman to devote his time, and the labour of his hands, to obtain over-flowing garners, that the first foraging party would empty. None tilled the earth with any other view than to provide the scanty means of subsis-tence . . . limiting his attention to such articles as were soon to be con-sumed with his own walls" (139). The disruption of the economy described here is a failure of the possibility of either the landed gentry or the yeoman farmer. The economic disorder also anticipates the way in which a "free" capitalist government works for reward and profit. In short, the counterside of republican values and the republican family is irregular trade and the emer-gence of the bourgeois family.

The neutral ground is the space between two armies, but also the space where property is up for grabs precisely because of how political loyalties are concealed and do not count or count only as a matter of economic calcula-tion. The Wharton family attempts to remain neutral at once to avoid the question of patriotism and to confront it in these economic terms. Mr. Whar-ton wants "to maintain so strict a neutrality, as to ensure the safety of his large estate, which-ever party succeeded" and has come to his summer residence "in obedience to a constitutional prudence that pleaded loudly on behalf of his worldly goods" (28, 29). He dreads "the misrepresentations of my kind neigh-bors," whose motive for denouncing him would be "by getting my estate confiscated, to purchase good farms, at low prices" (36). These, as Sarah Wharton tells her sister Frances, are the "fruits of rebellion brought home": "your father distressed, his privacy interrupted, and not improbably his estates torn from him, on account of his loyalty to the king" (172–73). His estates are not "torn" from him, but when his house is burned, Mr. Wharton is reduced to "moveable goods" placed on a cart like that of a peddler (263–64). The "local color" figures of the novel, Betty Flanagan and Katy Hanes, think of plundering the "moveables on the ground"—Betty suggests that "the proper time for plunder had arrived"—but they are cautioned: "The time must arrive when Americans will learn to distinguish between a patriot and a robber" (268). That time has not arrived yet, though Katy "scrupulously" rescues only her own goods from the flames, loading them into a "bundle, that vied in size with the renowned pack of the peddler" (265).

The novel questions profit motives and political allegiances throughout, a questioning and a hesitation that centrally involve Harvey Birch as a spy who is also a peddler and whose skill at disguises makes his "true" position impene-trable for most of the characters in the novel.[35] The peddler Birch is an itinerant image of an itinerant economy of portable property, who dispenses news and information and acts as an operator for the plot of the novel. An in-between figure, the peddler appears at once as a hero and an anonymous agent of exchange, but in peddling news of the neutral ground, Birch reveals the author's ambivalence about making a profit from his own patriotism. Birch may be the only functional figure in the neutral ground, in effect peddling

Washington (as Mason Weems peddled his *Life of Washington*), and, in his interventions into the lives of the Whartons, mediating between Tory and rebel. As an itinerant peddler figure, he also mediates between aristocratic and bourgeois notions of value and between varying notions of identity and property, in part because he shifts his own property and identity so easily.

Harvey Birch does nothing to protect his property, although "those who closely studied him in his moments of traffic . . . thought his only purpose was the accumulation of gold" (141). It is commonly believed that "love of money is a stronger passion than love of his king," but Katy Hanes, his housekeeper, who wants to marry him for his money, has "kept her political feelings in a state of rigid neutrality" because she "never lost sight of that important moment, when . . . she might be required to sacrifice her love of country on the altar of domestic harmony" (140). She has her eye on the peddler because she knows about the British gold he hoards, but she cannot decide what side he supports: "the good woman had grievous doubts into which scale she ought to throw the weight of her eloquence, in order to be certain of supporting the cause favoured by the pedler" (140). She wishes that he would "leave off his uncertain courses and settle himself, handsomely, in life, like other men of his years and property" (14). The most puzzling feature of Harvey Birch, in the mercantile terms that most of the characters finally endorse, is his refusal to act for gain, a stand perceived to be precisely antithetical to his position as either a peddler or a spy. Katy complains that if he "did nothing but peddle, and would put his gains to use, and get married so that things at home could be kept within doors," he would be a successful and comprehensible figure (268). As it is, she says glumly, "Harvey is a man that no calculation can be made on" (337).

The "calculation" that Katy Hanes wants to make on Harvey is at once economic and marital, a question of money and of "love." That calculation gets repeated in terms of money and of patriotism by other figures in the novel. It is at first assumed that "The war did not interfere with the traffic of the pedler, who seized on the golden opportunity, which the interruption of the regular trade afforded, and appeared absorbed in the one grand object of amassing money" (35). Indeed, the war does provide "golden opportunity" for Birch as he piles up the gold the British have paid him. Because he works with moveable goods, he can profit from a time of shifting boundaries and portable property. But his repeated presence in compromising situations has led to the conclusion that "the truth has proved you to be an enemy too dangerous to the liberties of America to be suffered to live" (224). Condemned to death and chased through the neutral ground, Birch consoles himself with the thought that "Washington can see beyond the hollow views of pretend patriots" (224).[36] The novel puts into question these "hollow views," which oppose spying to serving "openly, manfully, and bravely" (337). Birch laments: "Such are their laws; the man who fights, and kills, and plunders, is honoured; but he who serves his country as a spy, no matter how faithfully, no matter how honestly, lives to be reviled, or dies like the vilest criminal!" (376) At the close of the novel, Washington does indeed recognize him: "To me, and to me only of all the world, you seem to have acted with a strong attachment to the liberties of America" (452). Washington treats him as a mercenary agent rather than a patriotic one, however, telling him, "It is now my duty to pay you for these services" and, when he refuses the money, asking him, "If not for money, what then?" (452) Even Washington seems unable to conceive of spying as something that involves patriotism without profit (452).[37]

Harvey Birch functions in the novel as a peddler both of domestic goods (laces and calico) and of national news (troop movements and strategies), trading innocuous secrets of rebel armies and positions for the British gold his housekeeper so covets while searching for ways to help the rebel cause (and the Whartons)—a chore for which he refuses payment.[38] Looking for news of the war, Sarah Wharton threatens, "I'll not buy even a pin, until you tell me all the news" (36, 37). Though a peddler is not an unusual purveyor of gossip, he is appropriately also George Washington's domestic agent, carrying out the business of the home as well as the domestic concerns of the country. And part of this business of home and country is the purveying of secret information. The news that Birch tells is cryptic and brief—he more frequently interrupts the action of the novel with missives scrawled in Bibles or delivered by nameless boys. These messages dramatically herald a major change in plot or character, such as his announcement of Colonel Wellmere's bigamy or warning of the attack on the Wharton home. As such a pivotal figure, Birch might be considered a novelistic agent, or even a figure of the novelist. Cooper, too, presents his political position ambiguously. And he writes anonymously, assuming a disguise at once as a gentleman and as an amateur (rather than as a mercantile agent and a professional).

The mercantile distribution of literature in the early republic was mostly carried out by figures like Harvey Birch, "peripatetic literary agents," or "hawkers," like "the peddler with his horse-drawn wagon [who] continued to ply his wares through rural post-Revolutionary America, often selling the occasional novel along with pots and pans, sometimes selling the occasional pot or pan along with his novels, Bibles, and other books."[39] What Cooper leaves out of his account of the peddler in *The Spy* is that his young ladies would have used novels to while away their time in the exile of the neutral ground. Even Cooper's novel would have been hawked in such a fashion. What good are Birch's laces and calico if he can't give them novels?[40] The wares which Cooper displays are as domestic as those of Harvey Birch; he lays out his laces and calico in the form of the marriage plot and the emphasis on dress and manners because the novel is read by women. The novel in nineteenth-century America will achieve prominence because of this audience of women.

The peddler in this early period was popular not only for books and goods, but also for news of events, fashions, and scandals in distant places. As we have seen with Harvey Birch, in transmitting the news, the peddler also produces news. An important precursor of Harvey Birch is Mason Locke Weems, who peddled books for Cooper's publisher, Mathew Carey: "Timing his appearances to coincide with country fairs, elections, market days or other local events, Weems would enter onto the scene crying out 'Seduction! Revolution! Murder!'"[41] Weems wrote several of the books that he peddled, including a *Life of Washington* that initiated the famous cherry tree. Cooper may also use the spy-peddler to sell his life of Washington. Like Weems and Birch, Cooper profits from his tale of revolution. And this profiting invokes as well the question of motive. Again, like both Weems and Birch, although Cooper profits from his tales of revolution, seduction, and murder, he insists that he is acting out of patriotism. The infection of the profit motive is presented as the disease of spying—the heroism of Harvey Birch is that he is free of this disease since he does not care about money.[42] The peddler-spy engaged in an uncertain relation with the contest between Britain and America is also the author-spy, the author who spies out the neutral ground to see if he can make his own profit there, and who writes at the close of a trade war with England about a war from which he is profiting.

Finally, the peddler-spy invokes at once the method of book distribution and a professional author in disguise as an amateur. The peddler is a conjuror, a master of disguise, and his career as a peddler-spy fits with the image of the author as a mercantile agent in disguise as a landed aristocrat (the genteel man of letters) and an amateur. I would like to close by looking more closely at Cooper's analysis of his own role as the author of this novel of problematic patriotism. In the preface to the first edition of *The Spy*, Cooper notes that "There are several reasons why an American, who writes a novel, should choose his own country for the scene of his story, and there are more against it" (1).[43] Cooper hopes that "the patriotic ardor of the country will insure a sale to the most humble attempts to give notoriety to anything national, as we have the strongest assurances our publisher's account of profit and loss will speedily show." Despite these assurances, he wonders whether the production of nationalism will be profitable and he professes to be anxious because, "although the English critics not only desire, but invite works that will give an account of American manners, we are sadly afraid they . . . will revolt at descriptions here, that portray love as any thing but a brutal passion—patriotism as more than money making" (1). The American author must continually take his loyalties into account when he considers his profits: he must at once be measured against the standards of literary excellence that belong to England and the standards of homespun nationalism that belong to his own land.[44]

In the prefaces he wrote to succeeding editions of *The Spy*, Cooper moved from optimism to pessimism in his assertions about patriotism. In 1831 he announced, "Of all the generous sentiments, that of love of country is the most universal," and claimed that "A brighter prospect is beginning to dawn on the republic which is about to assume that rank among the nations of the earth which nature has designed her to fill, and to which her institutions inevitably tend" (9). American institutions work harmoniously with nature here to ensure the fulfillment of America's destiny. In 1842, Cooper still asserts that "There is a purity in real patriotism which elevates its subject above all the grosser motives of selfishness, and which, in the nature of things, can never distinguish services to mere kindred and family" (5). Patriotism is etherealized in this view (one the novel has attempted to enforce) and can work above the "grosser" profit motive. And like John Adams, who finds "all the sympathies of domestic life and kindred blood" combined in "the tie that binds us to our country," Cooper asserts here a patriotism that absorbs not only the profit motive but also familial relationships. In putting together these domestic and financial concerns, Cooper finds finally that the profit motive has taken over from the familial one to produce the republican or bourgeois family.

In 1849, Cooper replaced the 1831 closing paragraph about "brighter prospects" dawning on the republic with a curious injunction: "There is now no enemy to fear, but the one that resides within. By accustoming ourselves to regard even the people as erring beings, and by using the restraints that wisdom has adduced from experience there is much reason to hope that the same Providence which has so well aided us in our infancy, may continue to smile on our manhood" (7). The enemy which at the time of the Revolution was a visible antagonist, even when in disguise, has become an internal danger, to be warded off through suspicious vigilance, apparently a vigilance against democracy in the form of "the people." Although the timing of this preface suggests that the new revolutions in Europe in 1848 have brought new fears, the fear of the enemy that resides within the economic story told by the novel indicates as well the fear of a profit motive stronger than patriotism. The Revolutionary War has resulted in a commercial victory antithetical to patriotism, but Cooper's novel dramatizes, in the Skinners who want their "reward" from a "free government," precisely the origins of such a commercialized family and state. While Cooper ended his first preface in 1821 by giving "our compliments to those who read our pages—and love to those who buy them" (4), the economic and social transformations that his novel heralds will make the conjunction of love and money, of profit and patriotism, ever more difficult to enforce. The neutral ground will never be a "common ground"; instead it will remain open for speculation.

Monuments and Hearths

Children of the Present

Nineteenth-century fiction that makes the story of the American Revolution into a story of courtship or family romance repeatedly derails narrative attention from the central story of historical romance to the at once peripheral and destabilizing business of how profit and patriotism collaborate to keep the story available. That is, the political story ostensibly bound up with the romantic or familial story becomes "quilted" with an additional question of who will benefit from the successful deployment of a patriotic sensibility.[1] The stress of such a deployment and the violence it unsuccessfully defers emerge vividly in Nathaniel Hawthorne's early series of short stories, "Legends of the Province House." The focus on the location of these tales—the one-time residence of royal governors and hence a space maintained simultaneously as home and as political stage—keeps Hawthorne's narrator oscillating between the private space of patriotism and the public matter of profit. This chapter considers what happens when such plots announce that they will manage the business of patriotism. Beginning with Hawthorne's splicing of public and private spaces, I move to the endangered families of Cooper's *Lionel Lincoln* and other contemporary revolutionary novels before engaging the bloody ruptures of George Lippard's revolution.

The traditional understanding of a Hawthorne who escapes through ambiguity from the awful inevitability of the political may be refigured by considering how, as a "spy" in the "neutral ground" of the romance, Hawthorne presents such ambivalence as itself a political move.[2] Like the house, combining private ceremonies and public consequences, these four short stories repeatedly establish orthodox representations of national destiny and then shift their terms to domestic transactions, arguably and paradoxically to assert national identities even more fixedly. In "Legends," violence is located in the background of the Province House—or, better, identified in the foregrounded procedure of interpreting domestic objects. Although Hawthorne's investigation of political trauma through the haunted founding of a house has more typically been located in works like *The House of the Seven Gables*,[3] "The Legends of the Province House" presents such hauntings in disturbing tableaux leading up to the transfer of power of the American Revolution.[4] Particular elements—a political house, an embroidered mantle, a murky painting, an obscuring mirror—serve to simultaneously hide and reveal political moments, highlight and trouble particular decisions about political identifications.

At the end of the last tale, the new American governor of Massachusetts receives the key to the Province House from the bewildered loyalist Esther Dudley (who has long bewitched children with her stories of British rulers), and announces that "We are no longer children of the past!"[5] This call for "filial autonomy," as we have seen, was the "quintessential motif of the Revolution,"[6] and colonialists portrayed themselves in pamphlets and orations as overgrown children kept unnaturally under the dominion of mother England and father George, but Hawthorne's stories reveal ambivalent attempts to reassert those ties with England. Fifty years after the Revolution, fictional treatments of the family had changed: in familial terms (signalled by the unchanged portrait that hangs in front of the inn in Washington Irving's "Rip van Winkle") the father was still George, but he had a new surname, and no one was quite sure about the mother's identity.[7] Among the radical Democrats, the so-called "Young America" movement that appeared during Jackson's administration worked the hardest to create a "Democratic literature."[8] Their most significant platform, the *United States Magazine and Democratic Review*, published in the national capital, flourished between 1837 and about 1850. Martin van Buren helped found this nationalistic Locofoco Democratic review; Andrew Jackson was its first subscriber. Early issues of the *Democratic Review* contained fictional and historical accounts of the American Revolution and sought to relate contemporary political events to the principles of the founding fathers.

Hawthorne published about fifteen pieces in the *Democratic Review*; the four "Legends of the Province House" appeared sequentially between May 1838 and January 1839.[9] Certainly John O'Sullivan, the editor of the *Democratic Review*, promised Hawthorne more money than he had received elsewhere, but he also assured him a prominent place in a new "democratic literature," which would provide "proofs of the dissemination of the democratic spirit." Writing pre-Revolutionary tales, Hawthorne set out to "prove" a "new" spirit, but one in marked tension with the magazine's usual Revolutionary tales, written to show how "Our national birth was the beginning of a new history . . . which separates us from the past and connects us with the future only."[10] For the new governor of Massachusetts to assert that "we are no longer children of the past" at the end of a series of stories haunted by the past, presents an ironic counterpoint to the magazine's sense of itself as connected "with the future only." Hawthorne's stories reveal the anxiety about origins and family connections that such metaphorical reshaping of a birth story produces. The asexuality of Hawthorne's account appears in the bachelors and old maids who obsess about children and their own place in history. Instead of "natural" reproduction, the stories are full of objects and architectures that absorb identities and the function of identities.[11] The relation of reproduction to historical production and the economics of possession and loss structure Hawthorne's politico-historical rendering of Boston's self-conceptions.

That neither Revolutionaries nor loyalists prevail may make these stories even more exemplary of contemporary attitudes toward the Revolution. The ambivalent record of past heroism suggests that to celebrate the past produces a stressful uncertainty about origins.[12] The narrator's mediating presence in the frame tale (a frame often omitted in reprinting the stories) emphasizes the difficulty of an encounter with the traces of the past. Stumbling on the Province House, he alternately boasts about the increased business that his tale-telling has brought the place and stays away as much as possible, finally "being resolved not to show my face in the Province-House for a good while hence—if ever" (303). Barely successful in its current incarnation as a bar with rooms to let, the Province House "force[s the narrator] to draw strenuously upon my imagination" (241) in order to do away with the banality of its present appearance. The "arched passage, which penetrated through the middle of a brick row of shops," brings him from the "busy heart of modern Boston, into a small and secluded courtyard" (239). Penetrating through shops to sell wares of the past at the Province House that once ruled the political decisions of the colonies, he finds the return to an imagined pre-economic and pre-natal state alluring and, finally, disappointing. The reception area has become a bar, where the bartender, Mr. Thomas Waite, is a "worthy successor and representative of . . . many historic personages" (241). For this bartender to follow and "represent" the services of a series of royal governors suggests "waiting" rather than acting; Mr. Waite's rule has become commercial, in a space that is now for rent.

The narrator seeks to rescue the Province House from its obscure position; in the past, "the front of the Province-House looked upon the street. . . . Now, the old aristocratic edifice hides its time-worn visage behind an upstart modern building" (242). The "visage" of an aristocratic past, eclipsed by "upstart modern[s]," will be revealed in these tales, but the nostalgia for an "aristocratic" past seems incongruously evoked when the glorification of the republican present is the project of the narrator self-identified as "thorough-going democrat" (291). In the past, before the Revolution, the "buildings stood insulated and independent" (256) with the "whole presenting a pictur-esque irregularity" (257); they were "not, as now, merging their separate existences into connected ranges, with a front of tiresome identity" (256). The "tiresome identity" of the present seems caused by crowding out the indepen-dent past; that is, the "picturesque" colonial past allows a differentiation impossible in the democratic present. The tales repeatedly align accounts of the architecture of Boston with a telling commentary on the social profile of its inhabitants. What appears contradictory, if the Revolution was a War for Independence, is that buildings then rather than now "stood insulated and independent." In this Tocquevillean rendering, the result of the war was to merge or even to dissolve identities.

Such anxiety about the location of identity appears in "Howe's Masquerade," the first of the "Legends," which presents an orthodox history of the American colonies: the Revolution marks the end of a parade of British oppressors and a decisive break with the past. The masquerade takes place in Boston during the siege of 1770, where the last British governor of the Massachusetts Bay province is giving a celebratory masked ball.[13] Unable to control his circumstances, Howe controls the narration of his circumstances; he demonstrates control by hosting caricatured "guests" such as George Washington in rags. Suddenly the festivities are interrupted: the masked images of the deceased previous rulers of Massachusetts tramp down the stairs and disappear to the muffled beat of a martial/funeral drum. At the end of the procession, Howe confronts his own image and is overcome by the face the cloaked figure reveals. By Howe's reaction, the usurpation of the masquerade foreshadows the usurpation of British authority by the colonists; also suggested, however, is a peculiar kind of identity crisis, where Howe's terror at confronting the image of himself is the terror of not knowing which of the images has priority. For a nationalistic resuscitation, the project appears ambiguous: historical events are pervaded with a "nebulous obscurity," and while the narrator is conscious of a "thrill of awe" as he leaves the Province House after this visit, he complains that it has been "desperately hard work" to produce such a happy sensation (255).[14]

Months later the narrator returns to try the trade of the Province House again, "hoping to deserve well of my country by snatching from oblivion some else unheard-of fact of history" (256). Snatched from no oblivion, "Edward Randolph's Portrait" narrates the well-known surrendering of Castle William in Boston to a British contingent.[15] The darkened painting of the title, presented as emblematic of the decision, is rumored to be an "original and authentic portait of the Evil One, taken at a witch meeting near Salem" (260). Although "one of the wildest," this invocation of a bloody judgment sanctioned by the state is at the same time the "best accredited" account. Or it may be a portrait of the original governor of the Massachusetts colony, Edward Randolph, seen as a betrayer of the colony's independence because he gave up the original charter. Competing attempts to identify the portrait link fears about national upheavals with tales of the devil and prophecies about unnatural deaths and final judgments. At the same time, such competing accounts of historical and national identity make the matter of identity a matter of narrative control over national and political destiny.

The story again turns to historical representation, introducing the "Selectmen of Boston," the redundantly "patriarchal fathers of the people, excellent representatives of the old puritanical founders" (264). These fathers appeal to the current governor of the Massachusetts colony, the man still known for his history of the colony, Thomas Hutchinson: "You, sir, have written with an able pen the deeds of your forefathers. The more to be desired is it, therefore, that yourself should deserve honorable mention . . . when your own doings shall be written down in history." Hutchinson resists such a desire to be placed in a narrative (and familial) history: neither the lesson of the portrait nor the lesson of historical annals will sway him. His mismatch between knowledge and interpretation is seen within the story to be demonic. The British claim that the mobs have "raised the devil" and that they will "exorcize him, in God's name and the King's" (265). The Selectmen answer that they will "submit to whatever lot a wise Providence may send us—always, after our own best exertions to amend it." "And there peep forth the devil's claws!" responds Hutchinson (266).

What is devilish is the attempt of the Selectmen to say "amen" while they are amending or emending royal proclamations. They claim to be acting according to Providence, but leave room for interpretation and amendment. That "[t]he king is my master" is Hutchinson's justification for ignoring further interpretation (266). He denies choice by appealing to an external authority that determines actions and makes choosing unnecessary. Signing his name to the document, he fixes himself in history. What Hutchinson sees as demonic is the emendation of interpretation under the cover of a "submission" to authority. What the story, in contrast, sees as "demonic" is the disavowal of such interpretation. The fable/story/portrait is the motivating force of Hutchinson's decision *in his refusal of this motive.* In the story's focus on emblem and interpretation, the bloody consequences of putting pen to paper become not only subsumed under but translated into the demonic possibilities of interpretation.

We have already seen that to make the nation into an intimate category, to tell the story of the nation as the story of romance and family tensions, is to make romantic choices have political consequences.[16] Other intimate dimensions—a haunted house, a key, a mantle, a painting—are here invested with fraught decisions about national identity. Once these decisions are made, the stories are emptied out. To make the tension of these almost vacant allegories palpable, it is important to think about what they refuse. These accounts of historical choice insist on commemorating the revolution in a bloodless way—or they make the shedding of blood itself allegorical— derealized. I am not simply arguing that the instability of decisions about identity and narrative control can be compared to bloodshed; there is an easily overlooked relation in Hawthorne between such narrative instability and the shedding of blood.[17] That is, while these moments call attention to themselves as decisions about political identity, and locate such decisions as a contest between democracy and aristocracy, the stories tend to mask the violent consequences, the literal shedding of blood, connected to such decisions. The possible exception is "Lady Eleanore's Mantle."

In "Lady Eleanore's Mantle," a more domesticated artistic symbol of political change fatally galvanizes an earlier conflict between loyalists and colonials.[18] As an "emblem of aristocracy and hereditary pride, trampling on human sympathies" (276), the arrogant Lady Eleanore represents the pamphleteer's version of the evil of British oppression.[19] The relation between the mantle and the woman who wears it becomes repeatedly confused in the story, especially when Lady Eleanore refuses to remove her embroidered mantle. The strange powers with which she is invested when she wears it appear to represent those of the British crown. This embroidered mantle, created in London by a diseased seamstress, is blamed for a smallpox epidemic that "left its traces—its pit-marks, to use an appropriate figure—on the history of the country, the affairs of which were thrown into confusion by its ravages" (282).

Lady Eleanore brings contagious democracy to the colonies even though she is an aristocrat. Her disease spreads through the streets (reminiscent of the nightmare fear of the mob that Federalists invoked after the Revolution and that was called back into play with the election of Jackson, or "King Mob"). "Lady Eleanore's Mantle" shows democracy as contagion, something that creates both a sexual risk and a mortal one. The contagion she spreads first kills the aristocratic suitors who have surrounded her. In the process of becoming an emblem of the aristocracy, Lady Eleanore introduces a contagion that destroys the aristocracy and gives rise to democracy. Within the threads of the embroidered mantle of royal government is the germ of contagious democracy. It may be too easy here to line up aristocracy and democracy. That they cannot be untangled seems the point and there is something dizzying in the attempt. Such irresistible and relentless attraction and repulsion leads in Hawthorne to a sort of problematics of representation, and to violence in the other narratives I examine here, but I want to suggest provisionally that these are the same story.

The story combines an argument for inoculation with a diatribe against the infidelity of England. In the anecdote that has been taken as the source of the tale, however, the exhuming of a grave releases the smallpox that had killed the corpses and kills the exhumers.[20] More important analogues for the tale seem to be anecdotes and metaphors propagated by political pamphlets around the time of the Revolution. In one, Benedict Arnold was thought to have spread smallpox among the rebel army by sending infected women of less than perfect morals out of the city and into the camps to spread the contagion. Several treat the "loose" quality of the female figure of Liberty and suggest that the "infernal French disease" (by implication gonorrhea, though explicitly "Democracy") may be caught by too intimate contact with her. The eighteenth century is not alone in speaking of undesirable political viewpoints as "contagious," though, in a time of both widespread pamphlet reading and widespread smallpox, the analogy may have had the most force. Lady Eleanore may therefore be viewed as a representative not only of a heedless aristocracy, but of an aristocracy with loose morals that spreads democracy unwittingly.

The last story in the series, "Old Esther Dudley," is told by an "old loyalist" (288) instead of an "old toper" and the narrator comments that the "sentiment and tone" of the story "may have undergone some slight, or perchance more than slight, metamorphosis, in its transmission to the reader through the medium of a thorough-going democrat" (291).[21] The issue of narrative control has become increasingly important and the sense of strain that underlies this final "metamorphosis" (again, an artistic and political manipulation masquerading as a natural event) is almost palpable. When Howe, the last British governor, must leave Boston, he entrusts the aged Esther, whose "presence seemed as inseparable from it as the recollections of its history" (292), with the keys to the Province House. "So perfect a representative of the decayed past" (294), Esther seems well suited to maintaining the forlorn hopes of the British. The "new authorities" (295) think she is harmless and even exemplary, and are happy to have her "still haunt the palace of ruined pride and overthrown power, the symbol of a departed system, embodying a history in her person" (296). As a living representative of both a dead cause and the dead themselves, Esther spends her time telling tales about the past to the local children. When she reenacts these legends, Esther "bribes" them with domestic currency, "gingerbread of her own making, stamped with a royal crown" (297). The beguiled "little boys and girls" leave the Province House "bewildered," "rubbing their eyes at the world around them as if they had gone astray into ancient times, and become children of the past" (297).

With the collapse of Esther on the threshold of the Province House as the new governor arrives, the repudiation of the decayed system seems complete. Hancock calls her a "symbol of the past," and, seeming to conflate the potent attractiveness of Lady Eleanore with Esther's tattered form, proposes to "reverence, for the last time, the stately and gorgeous prejudices of the tottering Past" (301). He claims to "represent a new race of men, living no longer in the past, scarcely in the present—but projecting our lives forward into the future" (301) and concludes that "We are no longer Children of the Past!" (302). Hancock's triumph on behalf of the new order and his account of being without origins sound temptingly and appropriately American, like that of the *Democratic Review* of 1842 that boasted: "No other civilized nation has at any period of its history so completely thrown off its allegiance to the past."[22] The narrator would like to believe him, would like also to be a "child of the future," if not of the present. But he sounds nostalgic and plaintive when he asserts that the "glory of the ancient system vanished from the Province-House, when the spirit of old Esther Dudley took its flight" (302), and claims that he would not be surprised if her "phantom" appeared and told him to "leave the historic precincts to herself and her kindred shades" (303). Disowning the past and, at the same time, recreating the power of the past in order to "sell" it: the reader's "profit and delight" may be derived from the ghost that still haunts the Province House.

What does the representation of the Revolution as a national death accomplish for Hawthorne? Hawthorne's "ambiguity" may be seen as a political strategy for coping with this artistic difficulty. The ease in representation provided by an aristocracy must not be explicitly preferred to the confusing looseness of representation in a democracy. But by interposing a frame tale and several narrators, including a drunken loyalist, Hawthorne can represent the difficulties of the present without having to confront it face to face. Such representation and interpretation may be said to fail in both directions as the anguished symbolism of these sometimes pallid sketches seems categorically to be the exhaustion of binarisms that are repeatedly reinstated and repeatedly fail. And these exhaustions of identity may appear as violent as the more graphic spilling of blood in the writings of Hawthorne's contemporaries.

The Marriage of *Lionel Lincoln*

Figures whose ambivalence about national values overwhelms any celebration of them preoccupy Hawthorne's fiction. Hawthorne's stories appeared when debate over public figures like Jackson focused on politicians at once as family figures in national stories and as afflicted with particular scandals. Joining the condition of the family to the condition of the nation and representing threats to the family as threats to the nation continued throughout the Jacksonian era. In many cases, personal attacks on Jackson stood in for political diatribe. Such an attack appears, for instance, in the scurrilous *Reign of Reform, or The Yankee Doodle Court* (1829) by "A Lady." The *Reign of Reform* begins by reproaching Jackson for ignoring the work of the founding fathers, but proceeds from that reproach to launch more scathing accusations. Proclaiming her affinity with the Revolutionary spirit, the author presents her work as a "Dialogue between Col. Hardfare and Major Dauntless (two Revolutionary patriots)." They declare Jackson's presidency a "Reign of Terror," in which "His 'Hickory' Majesty [uses] Parisian mirrors to reflect himself and his troop." Linking Jackson's presidency with the terrors of the French Revolution, they reinvoke the threat of the French that so appalled the Federalists. The "patriots" combine the political dangers present in such a "mirroring" of American politics by French principles with the familial and sexual dangers that were also still associated with the French. In particular, alluding to Jackson's infamous extramarital relationship with Mrs. Peggy Eaton, the two soldiers speak euphemistically of the "bone of contention" that has caused conflict within the presidency.[23]

To locate the relation between sexual mores and political positions similarly appears as the major preoccupation of Cooper's *Lionel Lincoln* (1825), which takes many of the themes of *The Spy*—love and battle, the rivalry of siblings, resolution through marriage—and undermines them. At the same time, the novel works like *The Spy*, and like many later Cooper novels, to achieve closure—albeit a violent and disturbed closure—through the discovery that all of the characters are related. Where *The Spy* achieves a peculiarly happy blend of incestuous resolution, *Lionel Lincoln*, written only two years later, sounds a note of despair and helplessness on the same themes. The mother in *The Spy* dies patriotically out of grief that her son has joined the British army; here the mother's death is surrounded with accusations of infidelity that destroy her husband's reason. Cooper inverts the usual nationalist image of a hero born in England who finds a home in America to create a British soldier who, though born in America, fights his American father and his brother, and then goes "home" to England after his marriage. Cooper's first title, "Lionel, or Boston Beleaguered," identifies Boston with the hero of the novel: "possessed" by the British, but "beleaguered" by the Americans. Contemporaries noted a certain ambivalence on Cooper's part: "Mr. Cooper, in this work as well as in a former one—*The Spy*—has made his most accomplished and fascinating gentlemen the enemies of republican liberty and strenuous supporters of the oppressive and wicked war waged upon the American Colonists."[24] A tale of the Revolutionary War proposed to initiate a series of thirteen novels on the Revolution to be called "Legends of the Republic," the fighting appears incongruously from the viewpoint of the British and the story trails off before the war officially begins.[25]

Returning to the colonies after years in England, soldier Lionel has been pursued during the passage by a man known to him as Ralph. Ralph wants to educate him to find himself at home in Boston, an education Lionel resists. Although he is mysteriously drawn to Ralph ("I not only venerate but love you!" [15]), Lionel Lincoln is astonishingly inept at interpreting the characters and events that surround him on his return to his home town. In particular, he is obtuse in matters of family. Although his father's identity seems obvious to everyone else, Lionel does not listen when Ralph cries, "Accursed be the birth, and neglected the education, which would teach a child to forget its parentage!" (12)

Not only his father has vanished from his familial landscape. As soon as they land in Boston, Lionel Lincoln discovers a dishevelled figure named Job Pray being beaten by British soldiers. He rescues him and employs him as a guide, a service at which Job appears singularly misleading. When Lionel threatens to punish him for disloyalty (for remarks about the Province House), their father intercedes: "The young man knows the ties of blood and country . . . and I honor him!" (21) After Lionel protests that "we are the subjects of one king; children who own a common parent," Ralph returns, "He has proved himself an unnatural father" (45). Now, England's "offspring is able to go alone" (69).

In a curious mixing of these signals, Lionel's father hopes that he "will not disregard the natural ties of country and kindred" and asks, "Is it in nature to love any as we love a parent?" (76, 141)—but these directives could as easily bind Lionel Lincoln to England as to America, and Lionel repeatedly claims England as his home. The underlying irony of Ralph's comments on the disagreement between Job Pray and Lionel stems from the fact that the two are brothers ("children who [don't know how to] own a common parent"). To know "the ties of blood and country" is to find an "unnatural father." Certainly there can be no Oedipal struggle with a father who has no strength. And even the feeling of sibling rivalry is disabled because Job Pray, though he shows moments of efficient and deadly consciousness, such as when he shoots the British soldier, is repeatedly identified as an "ideot."

Everyone has family secrets, nearly every familial relation is kept secret, and the strain of these secrets is repeatedly explained as political. The French and Indian War, for example, coincided with the death of Lionel's mother and brought his father back to Boston from England where he had gone to claim his inheritance. In his family, "There is a strange connexion between Cupid and Mars, love and war" (141), and this connection serves to bring together Lionel and his bride. When the Battle of Bunker Hill commences, Lionel rushes into the fray and is seriously wounded. Reviving after seven months of unconsciousness, he determines to marry the woman who has nursed him.

While he makes his marriage plans, Lionel Lincoln begs Ralph for "that sad tale of my own domestic sorrows" (143). For all the suspicions he expresses, he seems not to notice the clues dropped, for instance, when Job Pray says, "Major Lincoln is to be married, and he asks Job to the wedding! . . . blood is blood, and flesh is flesh, for all [his mother's] sayings!" (239) Immediately after the ceremony, Lionel Lincoln is kidnapped from his bride by his father who wants to show him his mother's grave. This dangerous foray behind enemy lines has been repeatedly foreshadowed—as Ralph promises to tell Lionel Lincoln the "secret" of both of their lives. His wife follows him behind "enemy" lines and finds him with Ralph, who tries to persuade him to join the rebels. At the moment when his "sacrilegious foot treads on [his] mother's grave" (335), Lionel learns her "secret" from Ralph, though his wife protests against his listening to "the sorrows of my family" (336). "'My wife,'" says Lionel, turning to her in apparent obedience. "'Thy mother!' interrupted Ralph, pointing . . . to the grave" (337). In the competition set up between mother and wife, the mother's story wins; Lionel listens to the story of her supposed adultery and jumps up "with a violence that cast the tender figure that still clung to him, aside, like a worthless toy" (340). The story of the abused mother is presented again as the story of Britain's abuse of America. Ralph promises to go on with the story "provided thou wilt swear eternal hatred to that country and those laws." Lionel is ready to promise "More than that . . . I will league with this rebellion" (340).

Ralph asks Lionel Lincoln to live up to both his family and his country, as Job Pray curiously does, but to renounce his title and the English identity that comes with it proves too much for him. The three escape pursuit and return to Boston, where they receive a series of further revelations. As they visit the dying Job Pray, they learn, in rapid succession, that the story of Lionel's mother's infidelity is a hoax, that "Ralph" is Sir Lionel, Lionel Lincoln's father, and that Lionel Lincoln and Job Pray are brothers ("Job is your brother" [352]). When Sir Lionel's keeper rushes in, Sir Lionel attempts to kill him, and is killed himself. Making no attempt to defend his father or succor his brother, Lionel Lincoln "looked upon the savage fray with a vacant eye"

(356). The story ends swiftly with the return of Lionel Lincoln and Cecil to England and the remark that the current heir probably "never knew the secret history of his family, while it sojourned in a remote province of the British Empire" (365). The climactic scene of the deaths of his brother and his father effectively severs any family ties that might have kept him in Boston. The relief of returning to aristocratic forms, to primogeniture (only possible after Job Pray dies), the release from the strain of infidelity and illegitimacy, is only provided by a return to England with his bride.

To educate Lionel Lincoln about his family is to educate him about his country: they occupy an inseparable place in Ralph's mind. He urges Lionel to risk death for his country because his mother has died dishonored. That the story of adultery Ralph imagines will drive Lionel to "league with this rebellion" turns out to be a fabrication casts into doubt Ralph's motives for fighting on the American side, as well as making it even more difficult to determine Cooper's view of the "rebellion" celebrated as the American Revolution. If the only proponents of rebellion Lionel knows are mad relatives, what surprise can it be that he wants to return to England? In striking contrast to *The Spy*, which ends on a note of family reunion, *Lionel Lincoln* presents the failure of the family to contain the violence of revolution. Although the suspected infidelity of the wife and mother has been falsely blamed, only with the return to England can the family be considered saved. America becomes, in the closing words of the novel, "a remote province of the British empire" (365). As part of a projected series of novels on American colonies during the American Revolution—there were to have been thirteen volumes, or one for each of the original thirteen colonies—the book reveals Cooper's misgivings about the values of the American victory as well as of the American way of life that succeeded it. The story told by an imbecilic brother and a crazed father about a mother's infidelity becomes the story of national betrayals, masquerades, and illusions.

Love and Battle in the Early American Historical Novel

Fraught with ambivalence about the price of liberty (and about the heterosexual family plots they ostensibly support), the actions of characters who inhabit revolutionary battlefields repeatedly merge sexuality and bloodletting. Ranging from the stereotypical to the lurid, they show the dynamics of revolution in terms of family violence, most often played out as a contest between brothers and sisters. The bloody confrontations of revolutionary war novels are often "offstage," or conducted in family dramas. In Lydia Maria Child's *The Rebels, or Boston Before the Revolution* (1825), for instance, two girls who regard each other as sisters are at odds, both over loyalty to Hutchinson's regime and over the question of a suitable partner for marriage, a question presented as inextricably connected to political loyalties.[26] An 1850 reviewer of *The Rebels* asserted that the "great defect of this, as of most historical novels, is that the historical events which are brought before the reader's attention are not connected with those of a domestic nature to which he is expected to give his attention. . . . To combine these elements, the historical and the domestic interest . . . is no easy task."[27] The historical novelists of this period frequently glide over historical accounts and concentrate on the "domestic interests," or give up in frustration, leaving the story of battle to concentrate on that of love. Readers expect (and are expected) to bring their attention to bear in the domestic sphere; the historical realm appears subordinate to, or merely illustrative of, conflicts within the home. Yet they have a reciprocal relation in these novels: the historical aspects support domestic ideologies; the domestic details clarify historical change.

While the chiasmus created in *The Spy* by the loves of Frances and Sarah Wharton for a rebel and a Tory officer does appear "excessively neat,"[28] that chiasmic neatness and the violence that seems endemic to it were repeated obsessively in other historical novels. The problem was in part one of representing the succession from England not as a violent overthrow, as children deposing parents, but as a struggle between children about their marriages. As we have seen, this problem was crucial to the early republic because they had to represent their own succession. Yet the merging of marriage and the matter of succession repeatedly gives way to a bloody competition that casts doubt on the inheritance.

A representative American "John" is the main character of James Kirk Paulding's *Old Continental, or The Price of Liberty* (1850). A rebel soldier, John is imprisoned in a British prison ship, escapes to become involved in the capture of Major Andre, and finally gets tried for treason himself. Set in Westchester County, a "sort of neutral ground," the novel retells several of the themes of *The Spy*: sons and daughters must act in the face of absent mothers and vacillating fathers; they know they will achieve freedom, however, because "God and Washington are on our side."[29] The colonies are looked on as "ungrateful and rebellious children rising against the sacred authority of the parent" (II, 4), but the thematics of the novel explain that as a misconception. John fights for an often confused and confusing combination of his country and his sweetheart, Jane: "He had two mistresses, his country and Jane, who, so far from dividing, concentrated his heart on one and the same object" (I, 85). That object often appears to be death, but a series of obfuscating substitutions where his sweetheart is not equivalent to his nation allows for the possibility that money is not equivalent to a patriotic death.

The Old Continental, Jane's father, charges John with the task of winning Jane by doing well in battle. He thinks that John "wants the one thing needful, without which a man is no better than an empty purse, or a pocket turned inside out" (I, 23). Without money, John must go for glory: "He loved his country and his mistress, and all his hopes of possessing the one, were founded on serving the other" (I, 19). The substitutions of money and glory here suggest that the war is fought so that men with empty purses can marry. When the Old Continental catches them in an embrace, he admonishes, "Remember, there never has been a lie told in my family since the declaration of independence. Do you love him, I say?" Ignoring the ambiguities present in her father's statement, Jane is not shy to affirm her affection, and John responds, "My twin darlings, equally dear, liberty and my Jane" (I, 22). Basing the history of love declarations on the short period since the Declaration of Independence presents an unenviable foundation for the family.

After John returns from his first skirmish expecting to be able to claim his bride, the Old Continental, a veteran of the French and Indian War whose tattered scarlet uniform nearly gets him killed by the rebels, explains the task more explicitly. It is only a "pretty good beginning" to have "Six Yagers killed, two wounded prisoners, and a fine horse, all at the expense of a cut over the eye . . . such things as these happen every day in war-time and are never recorded in history. You must be in the chronicles."[30] Jane initially protests the price that has been placed on her, but John responds, "The contract is made, and shall be fulfilled. . . . I mean to strive for you and my country, and if I fall, I shall die for love and liberty!" (I, 70) Though the underlying motive for John's participation in battle is frequently alluded to, the novel also presents the "spreading" of familial and national ties. Because he loves Jane, John loves his country and seeks the "approbation" of Washington. His father is killed in battle ("another item in the price of liberty!") and his need to establish a new family by winning Jane is thereby strengthened. But the strong connection between love and liberty also sexualizes battle. And the mounting body count of the ledger that these battlefields seem to stand in for may indicate how to purchase domestic security through the sacrifice of members of your family.

Two brothers seek to marry two sisters in John Neal's *Seventy-Six—"Our Country, Right or Wrong"* (1823; published in England as *Love and Battle*). The narrator, the elder brother who marries the elder sister, begins with a promise to tell the "truth" about the American Revolution, but detours into romance with the excuse that he finds his younger brother more "interesting." Rather than a substantive deviation from his original promise, the narrator implicitly argues that the "true" story of the Revolution is the story of his brother, and particularly of his brother's courtship. More than an indiscriminate combination of the genres of historical fiction and the sentimental novel, *Seventy-Six*, or *Love and Battle*, presents the conflicts I have been describing (of succession, of the place of the woman) on a familial and marital stage. To give an absurdly condensed account of the plot: the mother of the Oadley brothers dies after she has been raped and their house burned in a Hessian raid. Then the younger sister, Lucia Arnauld, betrays the younger brother, Archibald Oadley, for the Tory Colonel Clinton. Archibald kills Clinton in a duel and cannot forgive himself, wasting away in grief until he dies—at the moment of his marriage to Lucia ("His wife was a widow!"). The question of the "battle" or of revolution is everywhere and always the question of "love." Jonathan resigns his attempt to stay with battles with the remark: "The war, and the men of the revolution . . . the army—my country; all are forgotten, or remembered, as a matter subordinate to the sorrow of Archibald and Lucia."[31] Such sorrow, I would argue, instead of obliterating the griefs of the national contest, becomes a memory device for keeping that national struggle personal.

Robert Montgomery Bird again presents the Revolution as the backdrop for a story of courtship in *The Hawks of Hawk-Hollow* (1835). The novel focuses on the oldest and youngest of seven sons whose sister has been violated. Oran Gilbert and his five wild Tory brothers, known as the "Hawks," have, years before the time of the story, saved the life of Colonel Falconer. They take him to their home to convalesce and he ungratefully seduces their sister. In a characterization typical to the point of stereotype in these works, their father has proved ineffectual and their mother is dead. The oldest son leads a band of Tory marauders; the youngest son, with rebel sympathies, returns to his father's home (which has been purchased—in the also typically dense and incestuous plotting of these novels—by his sister's violator) and becomes involved in a struggle for the daughter of the current tenant. Because his brothers have been fighting for the Tory cause, the name of Gilbert is dangerous, so he calls himself Herman Hunter. The names of hunter and hunted are thereby inverted: Colonel Falconer has ruined the Hawks, but the Hunter will now ruin him. His family has been "ruined" because of its Tory sympathies, but political and personal sympathies are shown to be inextricable in this tale of seduction and political violence.[32]

Falsely imprisoned for the murder of Colonel Falconer's son, Herman could, if he signed a commission as a British officer, be tried under the more lenient terms of a prisoner of war, but he refuses to "avow myself the enemy of my native land" (II, 253). The woman who Herman has revered as a dishonored sister turns out instead to be his mother. This revelation means that when Colonel Falconer "ask[s] for the blood of your son's murderer . . . it is the blood of your own son": "The brother kills the brother, and the father kills the son—ay, as he before killed the mother" (II, 208).[33] Still believing "Herman Hunter" guilty, Colonel Falconer cries "Alas, wretched boy, you have killed your father's son" (II, 213). It can be difficult to untangle how this language of family killing stands in for revolutionary violence. A simple way to ask this may be to pose the question of who gets killed in such stories of the revolution. The brother who, in this riddle-like formulation, has been killed seems as easily to be the killer. At the least, to kill your father's son puts your identity—and your familial affiliations—in question. The resolution of this family muddle—and of the unpleasant discovery that his father is his enemy—occurs immediately. Herman has asked his "brother" Oran to shoot him before he can be hanged for the murder for which he has just been convicted. Firing into Herman's cell, Oran instead kills Herman's father, Colonel Falconer.

In this family romance, to discover "his real parentage" (II, 237) is not to find a restored family. Mother, father, and brother are dead, and his sister dies shortly afterward. The book ends with a somber moral: "The retribution which so often visits the sins of the fathers upon the heads of his children" (II, 238) is a lesson the narrator does not expect will be heeded: "Americans are a race of Utilitarians—all busied in the acquisition of profitable knowledge, and just as ready . . . to forget all lore of a useless character" (II, 255). Such novels, it might be noted, fail to present successful resolutions of heterosexual plot dynamics. Always tinged with regret about the *price* of liberty, they end up promoting violence—most often against the family. In the case of George Lippard, on the other hand, even the most symbolic violence appears to be committed just for the sake of blood.

Patriotic Gore

In his influential *Life of Washington* (1809), Mason Weems narrates the battles of the American Revolution in conventionally romantic terms. The farmers of Lexington and Concord in his account are not only shepherds but lovers: "Never before had the bosoms of the swains experienced such a tumult of heroic passions. . . . they flew to their houses, snatched up their arms, and bursting from their wild shrieking wives and children, hasted to the glorious field where LIBERTY, heaven-born goddess, was to be bought for blood." Reminiscent of another sort of tryst, the prospect of an encounter with this goddess finds the "sturdy peasants, with *flushed cheeks* and *flaming eyes*, eager for battle!" Their aroused features emphasize the sexual implications of both the confrontation and the prize. Looking on are "thousands of tender females, with panting bosoms and watery eyes." Their presence adds to the confusion of reference; is the "equal ardour" of these patriots directed toward "that glorious inheritance, liberty, which they received from their gallant fathers; and now owe to their own dear children," a more traditional story of inheritance and succession? Or is this a battle over women, specifically over the sexual right to women? Weems subsequently recounts in detail the triumphal entry of Washington into Trenton in 1789, after he has been elected president. Hundreds of young girls in white dresses, backed by their mothers, sing him a welcome as he passes under an arch that proclaims: "THE HERO WHO DEFENDED THE MOTHERS, WILL ALSO PROTECT THE DAUGHTERS."[34] Defending national honor and national purity, Washington's heroism becomes a sexual safeguard and the Revolution becomes a story of sexual contests. But while women are the usual beneficiaries of narrative violence, their association with "LIBERTY, that heaven-born goddess" suggests another kind of displacement. What I want to argue is that the familiar sexual emphasis here might be a cover for the excitation of violence itself.

One of the most jarring moments in George Lippard's *Blanche of Brandywine* (1846), a "porno-gothic" celebration of sexualized violence not incidentally set in the American Revolution, is a ritual of fraternal initiation staged around a corpse.[35] The blackened body of the schoolmaster Jacob Mayland, burned alive in a haystack by the British, is presented to the circle of the assembled "Men of Brandywine" with the cry, "Behold the mercy of the Briton—the justice of King George!"[36] In making this corpse the center of a political drama rather than the personal one it really is (Mayland has been set up for revenge and for access to his daughter, pretty Polly), the rebels enact a ritual that treats the burned body as a totem of national victimization and, more extravagantly, an altar of national brotherhood.

Gathering for political union as the British threaten to invade their valley, the men are confronted with the corpse and cut open their arms. One after another, they let blood drip onto Mayland's skull. The pace and repetition of the passage secure the sexual meaning of the scene: "The warm blood spurting from the wound, fell, drop by drop, on the skull of Jacob Mayland . . . the warm blood fell, drop by drop, on the skull . . . and in a moment, the mingling blood-drops fell in a shower . . . their arms were bared, and their blood mingled . . . pattering down upon the skull" (115). The phallic exhibitionism of this patriot band who each bare a "right arm of iron muscle" (115) links masculine sexuality and patriotic passion. The blood dripping on the skull appears as at once violent and regenerative, a sexual consummation and collective ejaculation. This homosocial procreation, it appears, will fertilize Mayland's body and give birth to a new nation: "A Republic has sprung into birth, from the gory sea of revolution" (159). The bloody fraternal family gives birth to national collectivity. Here the desire for a consummate union between the idealized male and female protagonists of so many previous novels of the American Revolution gives way to the fundamentally homosocial union of Brotherhood. (And Lippard, of course, wrote similar fraternal initiation rites with symbolic blood drinking for his "Brotherhood of the Union," founded in 1850.)

Renouncing familial blood-ties, these men literally cut their newfound fraternity into their own bodies. As Elaine Scarry has observed, blood brothers open their bodies and mix blood in order to transcend biological relations.[37] Lippard's construction of national identity in this scene involves the exchange of a potentially divisive loyalty to class and race—one emphasizing familial lineage—for an affiliative bonding of national "Brotherhood." In a ritual entry into a masculinized family, each man is "reborn into his fraternal family,"[38] an affective bond that establishes George Washington as the common father. The homoerotics of the scene emerge as Lippard celebrates the "figures of the troopers" that make "the heart of an admirer of manly proportion, and muscular power, warm and throb to look upon" (84). In his influential *Nationalism and Sexuality*, George Mosse has noted that the "national stereotype" of the male body poised for battle may project homoerotic desire onto the "figure of the nation."[39] The male readers of *Blanche of Brandywine* are taught both to admire and desire the troopers even as the troopers learn to desire union with Washington.

A more disturbing form of such a bloody brotherhood appears later in the novel. As the men who have staged this ritual prepare for the battle in which they will act their violence out on British bodies instead of their own, there is a curious interjection from the narrator. Preparing the reader for bloodshed on a somewhat larger scale, he muses:

> Dark and mysterious are the instincts of man, dark and foul is that instinct
> of lust, which grapples with womanly beauty, like a beast gorging his
> bleeding food; dark and dread is that instinct of Hunger, which has put
> such fire in a Mother's veins, such agony in her heart, that she has
> devoured her own babe, tearing it to gory fragments as it hung smiling on
> her wasted bosom; dark and horrible is that instinct of Life, which makes a
> man forget honor, forswear his own father, and give his dearest friend to
> death, in order that he may prolong a few hours of ignominious existence;
> but darker and more dread and most horrible of all, is the instinct of
> Carnage! Yes, that Instinct which makes a man thirst for blood, which
> makes him mad with joy, when he steeps his arms to the elbows in his
> foeman's gore, which makes him shout and halloo, and laugh, as he goes
> murdering on over piles of dead! (223)

The phallic forearms that once spurted their regenerating fluid are now thrust
to the elbows in the foeman's "gore."

The movement in this parenthesis between what (anticipating Freud) are
literally characterized as the instincts of Life and Death, enacted in a series of
horrific attacks (allegories of familial betrayal not related to actual incidents in
the novel), is strangely counterposed to the unspecified violence about to take
place on the battlefield. Lust, hunger, and life—each is transformed into
violent death. Womanly beauty rouses an appetite for murder (whose satisfaction appears as a beast devouring a bleeding body); the starving mother devours
the child she should have suckled. And the instinct of self-preservation causes
a man to betray both father and friend. "Most horrible of all" is the desire to
kill, animated not by patriotism nor even a particular desire for revenge, but by
the "instinct for carnage," a manic yearning for blood that powers its way
across the field of battle.

In her *Reflections on Political Identity*, Anne Norton argues that "violence
is the most important means available to a political group to inscribe meaning
upon the world," yet "those passions, appetites, and institutions that bind the
individual to politics" develop from "sexuality."[40] What I am arguing is that
those passions, appetites, and institutions of revolutionary violence are
scarcely to be distinguished from sexuality. That is, while I do not mean to
conflate physical and metaphorical bodies, fraught attempts to embody the
revolution accompany an excited disembodying (or disembowelling) of combatants.

The pornography of violence in this excitation of blood appears endemic to
the repeated rhythms of this novel that lead to an ejaculation of bloodletting.
The increasing demands for a variety of release suggest a Sadean aesthetics of
murderous pleasure. This bloody violence is acted out not as a dissolution that
makes the republic impossible but as a fusion of aggressive instincts, of variously racial, national, and gendered antagonisms. Such generative violence,
which founds the republic, reflects the integrative opposites of Lippard's parenthesis. As Laplanche and Pontalis observe of the relation between life and
death instincts: "Destructive tendencies are accorded the same force as sexu-

ality" in which "libido and aggressiveness are not in fact to be looked upon as two diametrically opposed component elements."[41] The coordination of these elements, in Lippard's fusion of sexuality, infanticide, and patricide, produces the fuel for revolutionary violence.

Before developing further the aggression and violence of the male family story, I want briefly to examine the courtship and heterosexual family alternatives in this novel. In *Blanche of Brandywine* two cousins, Blanche and Rose, are each courted by rival brothers, one rebel and one Tory.[42] The hypersymmetrical structure is typical of the historical romance's schematic plotting of the conflict between forces that will inherit the nation, and yet wildly at odds with the novel's chaotic violence. Blanche, the eponymous heroine, has an American suitor who functions as the emotional and political center of the novel, the locus of attraction for both men and women. The abandoned son of an English earl and an Indian princess, Randulph spends much of the novel in a murderous rivalry with the man later revealed to be his half-brother Percy, the earl's acknowledged heir, and Blanche's English suitor.

Blanche has been raised by an uncle and knows nothing of her parents. She calls her uncle "father," but muses, "The word has ever been a strange sound to me . . . Father! mother! Ah, me!—the meaning of the words is all unknown to me!" (28). To learn "the meaning of the words" is to learn the horrors of her origins. Her uncle tells her finally that he and her mother survived a political massacre in Scotland, in which men "murdered my father, butchered my brothers, and . . . outraged the mother of my birth" (30). The surviving children escaped to the colonies and settled near Brandywine, where her mother was wooed by the Walford brothers. The Walfords are "a CURSED, a DOOMED family" in which "generation after generation . . . quarrel for the undivided possession of five hundred broad acres of Rock Farm" (31, 32). The struggle for succession, the desire for an undivided inheritance, has led to "Dark tales of murder . . . by the hoary father" and "tales of parricide, of fracticide [fratricide?]" (31).[43]

Walter and Dave Walford, sons and nephews of the brothers who fought over Blanche's mother, themselves fight over their cousin Rose. Their father, in turn, threatens to shoot whichever of them should kill the other: "Will I, your father, shoot the brother-murderer" (73). Doing so, he will become a "son-murderer"—which happens soon afterward as he kills his son, and is in turn killed by his own brother, Blanche's father (106). In short, the major activity of families in this novel is internecine murder. Murder between unwitting relations—relations that the action of the novel sometimes reveals fatally late—and between knowing brothers, parents, and children.

Much of the violence proceeds as a peculiar form of courtship: the desirable women characters (with the exception of the hideous battlefield scavenger, the aptly named Death) tend to be threatened with kidnapping, rape, and murder rather than marriage. Blanche is both the heroine of the novel and its prize, the spur to the action of the opposed half-brothers, Randulph and Percy. "Let Blanche be the prize!" shouts Percy as he rides to battle Randulph

(228). Like Blanche, Randulph has grown up fatherless, his Indian mother abandoned by his aristocratic English father (80). He fights initially for "one terrible idea—the idea of a wronged mother, and a treacherous father" (81). This motto changes after he meets Blanche. His comrades shout "Forward! For Washington!" Randulph instead says "WASHINGTON—BLANCHE!" (242, 243).[44] Heterosexual desire becomes displaced onto the male figure symbolic of the nation, the father who is not treacherous.

After several encounters with his brother in which he finds his hand stayed by some mysterious force, Randulph kills Percy in the very graveyard where so much of the novel's killing conveniently takes place. When he learns that his victim was his half-brother, Randulph breaks his sword in remorse and informs the "father" Washington that "every tie that bound me to your race is rent asunder." The bewildered Commander asks, "Do you not belong to the white race? Are you not an American?" "I am an Indian!" is the reply. Randulph adopts the name of his mother's tribe, Wyamoke, before going to England to tell his father that he has killed his brother: "the curse of the orphan who became a fratricide for you!" (344, 350). Although he is now entitled to his father's English inheritance, "Wyamoke" chooses the American style of self-reliance and renewal through marriage: "For you the Earl of Monthermer forsakes his princely home, his lands, the smile of Royalty, the pomp of power—Blanche I come!" (351). For Randulph to kill Percy is a "foundational fratricide" that lets him inherit both Blanche and, by implication, the nation. But the withdrawal of his affiliation to Washington that accompanies this fratricide suggests that the novel's generative violence, its repeated spilling of blood, must be disowned as a national inheritance attached to both homoerotics and the white race.

After a fantasy that Washington is tempted to betray the colonies for a Dukedom (a fantasy explicitly compared to the temptation of Christ), the narrator imagines Washington's body dismembered and the pieces scattered around the colonies after he loses the war: the "ghastly fragment of a human body, hung on high, for public scorn; a festering limb, or an arm, or a trunk, that bleeds in the hot sunshine. On the State House in Philadelphia, over the very door of the Hall of Independence, is nailed a human head; green with corruption, clammy with decay . . . the head of Washington" (171). The imagined dismembering of even this sacred body, the body of the father, both brings home the erotics and violence of this national inheritance and anticipates the most horrific dismemberment of the novel. The body of Gilbert Gates, who betrayed Jacob Mayland to his fiery death in the haystack, is hoisted up between two trees that have been forcibly tied together. After his arms and legs are attached to the ropes, the knot that holds the ropes together is shattered by a bullet. The man firing the gun that bursts knot and man is spattered with the final bloody ejaculation of the novel, ending the bonds of brotherhood and setting the scene for Randulph's killing his brother Percy and his subsequent marriage to Blanche.

This is, in short, not just a story in which the homosocial or homoerotic founding family is opposed to the heterosexual, since the procreation imagined for either is a heritage of violence. To attach erotics and politics is to find both subsumed in the violence of a national identity. A patriotic education is at once an education in ambivalent identifications—the problem of the household—and one of violent dismemberings of the families that might inhabit the national house.

Generation Through Violence:
The Making of Americans

An early analogue to the slaughter of women and children in *The Last of the Mohicans* is the surprising sacrifice of the colt, who "gliding like a fallow deer" follows its mother into the forest. [1] The colt's resemblance to a deer turns out to be ominous: the first deer that appears in the novel has a knife passed "across its throat," after which it is proposed to "cut our steaks, and let the carcass drive down the stream" (35, 51). When Natty Bumppo decrees, "That colt, at least, must die," Chingachgook's "knife passed across its throat quicker than thought, and . . . he dashed it into the river, down whose stream it glided away" (47). Such killings in Cooper, acts of violence "quicker than thought," have traditionally been seen in mythic and sacrificial terms. [2] This way of reading emphasizes the ritualistic character of these frontier rites of passage, mythologizing the act of entering the wilderness, but it also, perhaps inevitably, ignores the specific transformations of identity involved in such violence. In *The Last of the Mohicans*, these killings conflate domestic and wild, suggesting the conflations of animals and humans throughout the novel; beyond that, the explanations given for them point to the renegotiations of the racial and sexual identities of Indian and white, male and female.

Responding to the threat to his colt, David Gamut confers on it almost human status: "Spare the foal of Miriam! It is the comely offspring of a faithful dam" (47). Natty Bumppo accuses him of betraying his species: "It wont be long afore he submits to the rationality of killing a four-footed beast, to save the lives of human men" (51). The "rationality" of killing the colt to save the lives of "human men," however, does not seem as significant as the attempt to specify discriminations that the novel repeatedly transgresses and reasserts, a transgression and reassertion that in its very restlessness raises the question of what recognition is being enforced, or what difference is being asserted between, it would seem, nonhuman and human men, or human men and women. The animal's death appears logically unnecessary, but thematically significant in initiating a series of lessons in categorical distinctions—"human men," "four-footed beast"—in which physical embodiments become emblematic and the emblematic gets embodied.

Natty Bumppo first contrasts and then conflates the value of life for animals and the value of life for humans; he notes both the difference between beasts and men and the danger of losing "moments that are as precious as the heart's blood to a stricken deer" (46), and in doing so he makes unsteady declarations of species. While on the one hand he calls for the sacrifice of the colt for the survival of humans, on the other he equates the "heart's blood" of the deer with the precious moments of the hunter. Arguing further about the need to kill the colt, he asserts, "When men struggle for the single life God has given them . . . even their own kind seem no more than the beasts of the wood" (47). This analogy may be designed to justify the (forthcoming) killing of humans as though they were animals, but its implicit contradiction emphasizes how much the struggle in the woods becomes a struggle to stabilize identities rather than to respect already stable distinctions of "kind."[3] These instabilities are registered, for instance, in the name given to Uncas, "le cerf agile" or "the nimble deer" (91), a name ironically juxtaposed to one of Natty's alternate identities as the deerslayer or, again, to the name he calls his rifle, "kill-deer." Alternately personifying and dehumanizing, these names point to the violent struggle in the novel to locate personhood.

Hence if there appears to be something gratuitous about killing "Miriam's foal," then the motivating of such a gratuitous act entails comparisons that call attention to the formation of a peculiarly elusive species identity. If killing the foal appears neither necessary for their escape nor sufficiently motivated as a mythic sacrifice to enter the wilderness, it seems rather to force the fundamental question of how the crossings of animals, humans, and landscapes produce identity. Leslie Fiedler has perceptively identified miscegenation as the "secret theme" of the Leatherstocking series.[4] In *The Last of the Mohicans*, frontier transactions involving animals and humans produce a radically crossed or miscegenated identity, causing, in effect, a miscegenation between nature and culture.[5]

One of the Indian legends Cooper may be drawing on—the Lenni-Lenape myth about the origin of human beings, their emergence from a dark and pre-cultural underworld—involves a hunter encountering and killing a deer. Emerging from the underworld to the earth's surface, the hunter chases the deer into the wilderness and returns to his people with the meat. They follow the hunter out into the world.[6] In this Indian legend, the drawing of human beings into culture is accomplished by the pursuit and consumption of the natural. The killing and eating of the animal explicitly lead the hunter to a sort of nature worship, a worship of a personified Mother Earth. The emergence of persons is thus linked to the marking of the difference between what's natural and what's cultural: nature worship only becomes possible once the separation between persons and nature has been violently effected.

What occupies the position of the natural and what occupies the position of the cultural in this narrative are violently shifted, however, by Cooper's anthropology. Rewriting the Indian legend, he substitutes the Indian for the deer followed into the forest, and traces a rather different genealogy of the origin of human civilization. And while it has been argued that the elegiac heroicizing of "the Indian" as natural man is only possible once his disappearance has been assured (the *last* of the Mohicans), in Cooper this means that the difference between human men and what appear as nonhuman men gets violently effected.

Translating the tense negotiations about persons and places into the "hard facts" of Indian removal and massacre, Philip Fisher's account of Cooper in effect tends to ratify such an elegiac inevitability of "the last" of the Mohicans.[7] In contrast, Richard Slotkin has suggested, about Cooper's Leatherstocking novels, that "as we cross the border between civilization and wilderness the 'normal' order of sexual and social values begins to be inverted."[8] I would argue instead that it is just the location of these borders that is in question, or rather that setting and demarcating such borders is precisely what these crossings aim to accomplish. Such crossings affect not only how landscapes are figured but also how the making of persons gets figured, and it is just the violent relation between the national landscape and the making of persons that I want to look at next.

II.

The first person to become visible in the novel, David Gamut, displays a body and an identity that seem barely held together:

> He had all the bones and joints of other men, without any of their proportions. . . . His head was large; his shoulders narrow; his arms long and dangling; while his hands were small, if not delicate. His legs and thighs were thin nearly to emaciation, but of extraordinary length; and his knees would have been considered tremendous, had they not been outdone by the broader foundations on which this false superstructure of blended human orders, was so profanely reared. (16)[9]

Gamut's lack of proportion is traced to a "false" and profane mixture of "blended human orders," a miscegenation that seems to place him in opposition to the often advertised "unmixed" blood of Chingachgook or Natty Bumppo, the "man without a cross." But also and more basically, the strange relations of his large head, narrow shoulders, and tremendous knees, the apparently borrowed "bones and joints of other men," show up here as a problem about how to put the body together; and the architectural language of "superstructure" or "reared" suggests that the novel is returning to a primal scene of the emergence of persons or the taking apart of persons.

Gamut's opening remarks on Duncan Heyward's horse similarly treat the production and genealogy of bodies. As the first character to speak in the novel, Gamut sings "forth the language of the holy book" to celebrate a "beast," whom he loudly declares to be "not of home raising." He claims that the "barter and traffic in four-footed animals" would not include this animal, who seems to have "descended to our own time" "from the stock of the horse of Israel" (17). To use the "language of the holy book" to celebrate the genealogy of a horse perhaps suggests an ironization of the familiar conceit that America has "descended" from Jerusalem; but Gamut's genealogy also shows again how comments on generation and questions of descent and origin get almost reflexively affiliated with questions of identity in animals and humans. After these remarks, Gamut leans on his "low, gaunt, switch-tailed mare," "while a foal was quietly making its morning repast, on the opposite side of the same animal" (18), as though the mare fed both. In what looks like an attempt to establish new forms of bodies, the novel repeatedly calls attention to Gamut in terms of a suspicious questioning of generation and descent.

The apparently artificial construction of Gamut's body gets emphasized again when he rides into the forest: his body unsurprisingly "possessed the power to arrest any wandering eye," since it appears as an "optical illusion"; "the undue elongation of his legs" produces "such sudden growths and diminishings of his stature as baffled every conjecture that might be made as to his dimensions" (22, 23). The problem of the unnaturally growing and diminishing dimensions of David's body calls attention to its production as an unsolvable question in geometry. Duncan Heyward asks if he is "one who draws lines and angles, under the pretence of expounding the mathematics" (24)—but it is the lines and angles of Gamut's body that produce mathematical explanation. While he claims to "understand not your allusions about lines and angles," such allusions line up with the artificial production of humans in the wilderness, and may even be seen to produce the intersection between human beings and the forest as a geometrical matter of lines, angles, and figures in the wilderness space. This geometry appears as "an inhabitant of the forest" "traced the route" of

> the light and graceful forms of the females waving among the trees, in the curvatures of their path, followed at each bend by the manly figure of Heyward, until, finally, the shapeless person of the singing master was concealed behind the numberless trunks of trees, that rose in dark lines in the intermediate space. (27)

To describe "females" as "forms," or "numberless trunks of trees" as "dark lines" presents the elements of the wilderness that might appear most natural as an entirely unnatural matter of forms, numbers, "curvatures," and bends. This attention to proportion, geometry, and measure suggests, one might say, an artifactual and almost technological landscape.

And appropriately at home in this landscape is the perpetually discursive Natty Bumppo, who stops dangerously during the suspense of a gunfight to give a lecture about his rifle: "'Of all we'pons,' he commenced, 'the long barrelled, true grooved, soft metalled rifle, is the most dangerous in skillful hands, though it wants a strong arm, a quick eye and great judgment in charging to put forth all its beauties'" (70). His elaborate attention to the proportions and dimensions of the killing machine in the wilderness suggests the technology of the machinery of death generally in the novel. Such a mechanics of death appears, for instance, as "the tomahawk of Heyward, and the rifle of Hawk-eye, descended on the skull of the Huron, at the same moment that the knife of Uncas reached his heart" (113). Again, this over-kill indicates the emblematic status of a dehumanized violence that Natty Bumppo presents with an affection for the personified machinery of that violence. "'I have got back my old companion, "kill-deer,"'" he added, striking his hand on the breech of his rifle" (116).

A different loss of distinction between animal and human, which takes the form of an "unfitness between sound and sense" (27), is exacerbated when the inhabitants of the cave at Glenn's Falls listen to the screams of the frightened horses and think they hear something supernatural—or, almost equivalently, Indians—or "a sort of unhuman sound." "I did believe there was no cry that Indian or beast could make, that my ears had not heard," comments Natty (59). "I have listened to all the sounds of the woods for thirty years. . . . There is no whine of the panther; no whistle of the cat-bird; nor any invention of the devilish Mingoes, that can cheat me! I have heard the forest moan like mortal men in their affliction" (62). Bringing together animals, forest, inven-tion, and "mortal men," Natty Bumppo calls attention to the possibility of a "cheat," or of the artificial construction of identity in the wilderness. The blurring of boundaries between animal and human in this wilderness comes increasingly to accompany such artifice or cheating, especially through dis-guise, and specifically through the taking on of animal identities. These deliberate transgressions at once infuse agency into the inanimate (the forest can "moan like mortal men") and withdraw agency from inhabitants of the forest, such that, whether made by "Indian or beast," what Natty Bumppo listens for is the "sounds of the woods."

III.

The novel's merging of persons and landscapes first appears when the travelers enter the woods through a "blind path [that] became visible" (21).[10] Although the immediate question for the travelers is whether they can see the path, the play on blindness and visibility, and the suggestion that the natural world might be able to see them as well, if it were not "blind," is part of the more general animism that appears in Cooper's landscapes. Such a possibility is raised repeatedly about inanimate objects in the woods, and consequently problems about animation and agency in the novel tend to be correlated with problems of vision and visibility. Duncan Heyward, for example, looking about him after he has led them into this blind path, "believed he had mistaken some shining berry of the woods, for the glistening eyeballs of a prowling savage" (27). But eyes are often taken for unseeing things in the forest. In making berries and "eyeballs" appear the same, the passage both removes agency from the "prowling savage" by seeing an eyeball as a "shining berry" and ascribes agency to the woods by imagining its shining berries capable of vigilance. A perhaps more conventional example of Heyward's deluded sight occurs as,

> Glancing his eyes around, with a vain attempt to pierce the gloom that was thickening beneath the leafy arches of the forest, he felt as if, cut off from human aid, his unresisting companions would soon lie at the entire mercy of those barbarous enemies, who, like beasts of prey, only waited till the gathering darkness. . . . His awakened imagination, deluded by the deceptive light, converted each wavering bush, or the fragment of some fallen tree, into human forms (45).

Although Duncan converts bushes and trees into human form, the "human forms" he imagines are "like beasts of prey." These distinctions among human, animal, and vegetable "forms" become critically difficult to maintain as he produces a radically animated landscape.

And this uncertain crossing of human and nonhuman elements of the landscape produces other difficulties with identification. When Duncan, hiding near the Indian camp later in the novel, sees a clearing where a "hundred earthen dwellings stood on the margin of the lake," he thinks that their "rounded roofs . . . denoted more of industry and foresight than the natives were wont to bestow on their regular habitations." Looking out for the "natives" who inhabit the landscape, he finds himself surprised by their unnatural industry: "In short, the whole village, or town, which ever it might be termed, possessed more of method and neatness of execution, than the white men had been accustomed to believe belonged, ordinarily, to the Indian habits." The "method and neatness" that determine the outlines of the "town" are not the only aesthetic features of the landscape that surprise this white man; the houses are beneath a "cataract so regular and gentle, that it appeared rather to be the work of human hands, than fashioned by nature" (218). Even to see a waterfall as "fashioned by nature" comes close to presenting it as an unnatural construction, but to see it as the "work of human hands" leads to a further blunder about the native builders who construct the landscape. Although Duncan "fancied he discovered several human forms, advancing towards him on all fours" until "the place seemed suddenly alive with beings" (219), he is startled to discover at last that these "forms" or "beings" are industrious beavers.

Almost as revealing as Duncan's failure to see, or failure to distinguish, the difference between "human forms" and animal, between the safe site of a beaver dam and the dangerous homes of Indians, is his subsequent racial identification of a human form, which continues this series of generic mislabelings. Near the beaver dam, he sees a "stranger Indian" whose facial features cannot be discovered "through the grotesque masque of paint, under which they were concealed" (219). Completing a series of transformations among animal, human, and Indian, this form is unmasked as David Gamut, whose mask has been painted on by the Hurons holding him captive. Duncan's superficial scrutiny appears as an almost willful refusal to distinguish between forms and disguises: "His lurking Indians were suddenly converted into four-footed beasts; his lake into a beaver pond; his cataract into a dam . . . and a suspected enemy into his tried friend" (222). To convert Indians into "four-footed beasts," and confuse the boundaries between human and nonhuman constructions, or to transpose animal identities with human ones becomes continuous with substituting Indian for white identities. In addition, for Duncan to see Gamut as an Indian suggests that all the white man needs to take on an Indian identity is to be painted, as though the capacity of whites to improvise a racial identity consisting of superficial marks and remaining at the surface of the skin were set in contrast with the fixed racial identity of the Indian. And indeed Duncan himself gets painted as an Indian and follows Gamut back to the Indian camp after this lesson in how to change racial identity.[11]

Leaving behind the beaver dam with "those little huts, that he knew were so abundantly peopled," and coming to the "margin of another opening, that bore all the signs of having been also made by the beavers," Duncan discovers "some fifty or sixty lodges, rudely fabricated of logs, brush, and earth":

> They were arranged without any order, and seemed to be constructed with very little attention to neatness or beauty. Indeed, so very inferior were they, in the latter two particulars, to the village Duncan had just seen, that he began to expect a second surprise, no less astonishing than the former. This expectation was in no degree diminished, when, by the doubtful twilight, he beheld twenty or thirty forms, rising alternately from the cover of the tall, coarse grass in front of the lodges, and then sinking again from the sight, as it were to burrow in the earth. (230)

This "second surprise" does seem rather "less astonishing" than the first because it involves what would no longer be surprising, and indeed has become an "expectation": seeing animals where Indians were anticipated, or, in this case, viewing an Indian camp as inferior to a beaver's. This expectation is enhanced by the materials with which both Indians and beavers build their villages: both have "earthen dwellings" as though the natural shelter or burrow of both these forms were the earth itself, or even as though little distinction could be made between earth and the "forms" that burrowed in it, whether human or animal. Watching the "juvenile pack" of the Indian camp, for example, Duncan finds that the "naked, tawny bodies of the crouching urchins, blended so nicely, at that hour, with the withered herbiage, that at first it seemed as if the earth had, in truth, swallowed up their forms" (232). But of course a distinction is made: the artistic deficiencies of the Indian village, where Duncan looks for arrangement and human "order," "neatness," and "beauty," are presented as "inferior" to the "method and neatness of execution" of the beaver dam. Such distinctions are certainly part of a familiar scheme in which a white author both mythologizes and denigrates Native Americans, but they also work to produce an emphatically uncertain relation between human and nonhuman, the cultural and the natural.

The identities of Indian and beaver are collapsed again when Chingach-gook improbably disguises himself as a beaver and hides from the Hurons in the same beaver dam that has just confused Duncan Heyward. The beaver has a particular symbolic resonance for the Hurons in this novel. Magua, for example, uses the beaver to initiate a hierarchy of discriminations between humans and animals, Indians and white, by claiming that "wisdom" is the quality that provides the "great point of difference between the beaver and other brutes; between brutes and men; and, finally, between the Hurons, in particular, and the rest of the human race" (282). When the Hurons pass Chingachgook's hiding place, the beavers are addressed by "one chief of the party who carried the beaver as his particular symbol, or 'totem' [and] called the animals his cousins" (284).[12] The Hurons take it as a sign of "gratifying the family affection of the warrior" when they see the "head of a large bea-ver . . . thrust from the door of a lodge." But the family affection that the Huron warrior experiences with the beaver's head turns out to be an identifica-tion with a human interloper. A transmutation occurs when the warriors leave: "Had any of the Hurons turned to look behind them, they would have seen . . . the entire animal issue from the lodge, uncasing, by the act, the grave features of Chingachgook from his mask of fur" (285). Changing species identity by donning a fur mask, Chingachgook seems perversely to enforce the associations that Duncan makes between Indians and animals. More signifi-cant, for Indians as well as whites in this novel, identity can appear a matter of surface and artifice.

The effects of looking for identity on the surface of the skin are displayed when Duncan, disguised as an Indian healer and searching for Alice in an Indian cave, confronts what he believes to be a bear. The "fierce and dan-gerous brute . . . turned and came waddling up to Duncan, before whom it seated itself, in its natural attitude, erect like a man" (256). The reason why the "natural attitude" of the bear includes erect posture "like a man" may well be because it *is* a man, dressed as a bear, so that it is at once "natural" for it to sit "erect like a man," and a sign of good artifice that a man dressed as a bear can appear as "natural" as the bear who sits "like a man." Cooper's apparent source for this scene, John Heckewelder, writes similarly about a conjurer disguised as a bear: "'a human being to transform himself so as to be taken for a bear walking on his hind legs?' . . . the more he went on with his perfor-mance, the more I was at a loss to decide, whether he was a human being or a bear; for he imitated that animal in the greatest perfection, walking upright on his hind legs as I have often seen it do. . . . he assured me that although outside it had the appearance of a bear, yet inside there was a man."[13] Heckewelder needs assurance to keep the distinction between the outside appearance of the bear and the inside presence of the man. His anxiety suggests that the problem of "imitating that animal to perfection" is the "loss" of the presence of the human being, such that imitation *becomes* transformation, and the outside "appearance" displaces the "inside" man.[14]

When Natty Bumppo unmasks himself, Duncan compliments him on his performance: "The animal itself might have been shamed by the representation" (257). The "scout" happily explicates:

> Had it now been a catamount, or even a full-sized painter, I would have embellished a performance, for you, worth regarding! But it is no such marvellous feat to exhibit the feats of so dull a beast; though, for that matter too, a bear may be over acted! Yes, yes; it is not every imitator that knows natur may be outdone easier than she is equalled. (257–58)

Natty Bumppo's skill in embellishing the performance of the bear, the restraint he announces in equalling but not exceeding "natur," calls attention to the bear's identity *as* a performance. In Duncan's suggestion that Natty's representation would shame the "animal itself," however, Cooper seems to propose that the observing bear, "erect like a man," would, like the observing human, be "at a loss to decide, whether he was a human being or a bear." Like Chingachgook, Natty Bumppo transforms himself with the skin of another species in a manner that challenges the integrity of species distinctions. Taking the skin of another species to save his own skin challenges natural and cultural distinctions in such a way that the idea of the natural becomes bound up with representation, acting, and imitation.

These artificial transformations between human and animal states may stand in for the struggle between Indians and whites over land and identity, and in the next section I will consider how the crossings of racial and human boundaries get affiliated with a specifically racialized and gendered formation of national culture. For now I want to focus on how the novel makes it obtrusively difficult to decipher or classify identity—a difficulty appearing most obviously in the multiple disguises of characters—and how it insistently refuses to assign precise racial, national, or biological identity. It can even paradoxically seem that the novel's very insistence on rigid categories and classifications, or on actions justified by such categories, calls them into question.

In her discussion of *The Last of the Mohicans*, Jane Tompkins claims that by "putting on a disguise none of the characters risks his or her own identity." That is, she finds identity, finally, a determinate property. But the disguises and substitutions of the novel indicate a rather more fundamental uneasiness about the constructedness of identity, or about whether the body is more than a theater for the performance of identity. Instead of showing, as Tompkins argues, a "proper respect for the 'natural' divisions that separate tribe from tribe and nation from nation," *The Last of the Mohicans* repeatedly makes such divisions at once unnatural and violently contested. Tompkins astutely suggests that the novel's "subject is cultural miscegenation," but insists at the same time that the novel works to restore order by working against that miscegenation, since "what is to be avoided, in short, is . . . the confusion of

mutually exclusive systems of classification, which is what occurs when disparate cultures collide with one another."[15] As we have seen, however, rather
than working to avoid "mutually exclusive systems of classification," the novel
obsessively reiterates such collisions and confusions in its very production of
identity, and, further, produces identities by a miscegenation of animal and
human, natural and cultural.

Disguises in the novel involve a cultural miscegenation or blending of
human and animal orders through elaborate and even farcical concealments
of the human body—in a bear costume, say, or in a beaver dam—as a
biological fact.[16] The pathos of being born into a racially hierarchized culture
is played out and ratified through disguise and substitution and through shifting biological or racial identities within that culture. When, for example,
Duncan Heyward and Natty Bumppo, disguised respectively as an Indian
healer and a bear, go into the Indian cave to rescue Alice, they must first
confront an ill Huron woman they have ostensibly come to cure. The Indian
woman "lay in a sort of paralysis . . . happily unconscious of suffering," and
Duncan finds that his "slight qualm of conscience" about the "deception" of
being a "pretended leech" is "instantly appeased" by her unconsciousness
(253). They carry Alice out of the cave disguised as the Indian woman, who,
left alone in the cave, dies. Natty Bumppo instructs Duncan to "wrap [Alice]
in them Indian cloths. Conceal all of her little form. Nay, that foot has no
fellow in the wilderness; it will betray her. All, every part" (259). To rescue
Alice, they wrap her in "them Indian cloths," another version of giving her the
skin of a different identity. The rescue of the white woman is made possible by
and even seems to be paid for by the death of the Indian woman they leave
behind in the cave. The novel might be said to locate the future of national
culture in the wrapping of Alice's body—and in the activities of Duncan
Heyward and Natty Bumppo who literally wear the skins of another race but
act in that guise to valorize and rescue their own race. Although characters
clearly engage in such disguises and transformations to save their own skins,
the proliferation of these acts troubles the presumed integrity of human or
racial identity. Moreover, in the death of the ill, and apparently irrelevant,
Indian woman abandoned in the cave, and in the saving of Alice, or in the
transfer of generative power from the Indian woman to Alice, we may locate
the question of how both history and generation are acted out on the bodies of
women—that is, those who can transmit identity; and it is this enactment of
generational and historical continuity to which I want to turn.

IV.

In the 1826 preface to the novel, Cooper refuses pleasure to the "reader, who
takes up these volumes, in expectation of finding an imaginary and romantic
picture" (1). Insisting on the conventional disclaimer of the novelist that his
"narrative" is based on facts, and demanding that his reader work from the first
page to understand the "obscurities of the historical allusions," he warns off

those who are "under the impression that it is a fiction" (1). More significant for our purposes, his rigorous segregation of readers of fact and fiction depends on an opposition between male and female readers, between the facts fit for the male audience of the historian and the desires of the "more imaginative sex, some of whom, under the impression that it is a fiction, may be induced to buy the book" (1). Cooper wants to "advise all young ladies,"[17] "if they have the volumes in hand, with intent to read them, to abandon the design" because they "will surely pronounce it shocking" (4).

What is the shock that the "more imaginative sex" will experience as a result of reading *The Last of the Mohicans?* Perhaps it is the shock that William Cobbett so graphically described a few years earlier in the preface to his political pamphlet *A Bone to Gnaw for the Democrats:* "If you are of that sex, vulgarly called the fair . . . let me beseech you, if you value your charms, to proceed no further." Warning women to desist from reading (and writing), he presents a fearful precedent: "Have we not a terrible example of recent, very recent date? I mean that of the unfortunate *Mary Wollstoncraft*. It is a well known fact, that, when that political lady began *The Rights of Women*, she had as fine black hair as you would wish to see, and that, before the second sheet of her work went to the press, it was turned as white, and a great deal whiter than her skin." Thus, comparing Mary Wollstonecraft, whose hair turns whiter than her skin, and, perhaps, as white as the "sheet of her work" from writing about the politics of women's rights, with the reader who will lose her "charms" from reading about politics, Cobbett concedes that "It is a little singular for an author to write a Preface to hinder his work from being read; but this is not my intention; all I wish to do, is, to confine it within its proper sphere."[18] His separation of reading spheres, like Cooper's, becomes a separation of gender spheres. As women are warned not to read Cobbett's political work since it will cause their bodies to change unnaturally, so are they also warned from inhabiting Cooper's historical space. And this political and historical exclusion of women as writers and readers may relate to the novel's representation of women as characters, and, beyond that, the novel's elimination of women, and women's bodies, from the sphere of history and its making.

Warding off women readers generally, the novel more specifically displays an anxiety about mothers, and what appears, finally, as an anxiety about natural reproduction as such. For one thing, there is the notion popularized during the American Revolution that England, as a mother, has failed the colonies, as children. National identity in the newly formed United States is built on at once emphasizing and repudiating England's role as a mother.[19] In the historical explanation with which he opens the novel, Cooper presents what has already become a national mythology when he states that the colonies have been "reverencing" England "as a mother" they "had blindly believed invincible" (13). To see England as a mother who is now "vincible" is to see motherhood, at least that nation as mother, as something that can be overcome. By this reading, the birth of a nation comes not from recognizing but from repudiating that mother, or from repudiating the nation-as-mother in order to produce a kind of self-making appropriate in a nation of self-made and celibate men, men such as Natty Bumppo. Looking to England for protection, the colonies find that she has failed to provide for their safety. On the frontier, "mothers cast anxious glances" at their children (13). Their glances are anxious because of the Indian threat, a threat that England is supposed to be protecting them from. But they should perhaps be more anxious about the violence the novel has in store for them. Indeed, *all* mothers are eliminated from the novel, or, as with the mothers of Cora and Alice and Uncas, dispatched beforehand.

And such violence against mothers is part of the violence against natural reproduction or against the natural family. The violence that the novel directs against Cora and Alice and Uncas, for example, seems motivated by their status as children. As the "last of the Mohicans," Uncas is at once the last child and the last possibility of a new generation. The attempts Alice and Cora make to get to their father are thwarted because Magua sees them as standing in for their father. (And it is, of course, the thwarted journey of daughters to their father or, in the second half of the novel, of father to daughters, that makes for the novel's plot.) When Magua proposes to Cora, he does not address her by name, but calls her "the daughter of the English chief" and "the daughter of Munro" (104).[20] Such a relation to the identity of the parent reminds us that, as a female child, Cora has inherited at once a racial and a national identity and can transmit these identities. "Like thee and thine," says Cora to the old Indian chief Tamenund, "the curse of my ancestors has fallen heavily on their child!" (305) The novel repeatedly links an inherited identity with the violence directed against its biological carriers: women and children.[21]

These links appear vividly in Horace Greenough's "Rescue Group" (1853) (Fig.6), a statue that stood on the front steps of the national Capitol well into the twentieth century. Here a mother and child cower beneath the raised tomahawk of a fierce Indian. Behind him a gigantic frontiersman grasps the Indian's tomahawk-wielding hand. In part, the story seems a painfully clear version of how the woodsman must kill the Indian because of the threat the Indian poses to mother and child, and it presents an all too familiar justification for exterminating the Indian because he threatens the white family. But while the frontiersman looks down into the eyes of the Indian who looks back up at him, the extended line of sight of the frontiersman suggests that his eyes gaze ominously down at the mother huddled over her child.[22] In consequence, the towering figure of the frontiersman also seems to threaten the woman and the child, expressing a violence at once mediated and displaced by the violence between men. In this alternate scenario, the frontiersman's threatened violence toward the mother and child is inextricable from the violence directed toward the Indian who threatens them, and the Indian

Figure 6. Horace Greenough, "Rescue Group" (1853). *Courtesy of the Library of Congress.*

seems almost a surrogate victim, at once a threat to, and a substitute for, the family.

In the massacre scene at the middle of *The Last of the Mohicans,* no rescuing hand stays the Indian tomahawk and the mother and child are killed. Although his sources for the massacre emphasize that the Indians initially killed wounded soldiers, Cooper chooses instead to focus on a "mass of women and children" that he compares to "alarmed and fluttering birds."[23] Specifically, in a scene that mimics the more involved kidnappings of the novel, a "wild and untutored Huron" offers to trade a woman's baby for her worldly goods. When she does not adequately meet his ransom demands, the "savage" "dashed the head of the infant against a rock" and "mercifully drove his tomahawk into her own brain" (175).[24] Initiating a massacre by killing a mother and child, he kills both the next generation and the source of that generation.

Because Magua has other designs on Cora and Alice, he saves them from the subsequent slaughter of women and children. Renewing his proposal to Cora, he announces, "The wigwam of the Huron is still open. Is it not better than this place?" (177) In offering Cora his "soiled hand," Magua gives her the chance to escape being sacrificed because of her sex and race. But his offer is inseparable from a violence at once racial and sexual. When Cora repulses Magua, he confronts her with his bloody, "reeking hand," and boasts that "It is red, but it comes from white veins!" (178) The gruesome mixture he invokes of red skin, red blood, and "white veins" appears as a miscegenation made visible, a violent mingling of red skin and white blood. And the choice Magua offers Cora between "this place," a battlefield turned killing field where such miscegenation of red and white occurs, and the "wigwam of the Huron" appears as a choice between rival forms of racial and sexual violence.

Violent miscegenation, or mixing of blood, takes an even more startling form on the battlefield: "The flow of blood might be likened to the outbreaking of a torrent; and as the natives became heatened and maddened by the sight, many among them even kneeled to the earth, and drank freely, exultingly, hellishly, of the crimson tide" (176). Kneeling to the earth and drinking blood, the savages treat the "crimson tide" of the female bodies they have killed as though it were a wilderness stream that nourished them: a hellish generation through violence. The bloodbath moves beyond graphic descriptions of battles into an emblematic and terrifying fantasy of the "unnatural" mixing of blood in which the Indians violently reproduce miscegenation by killing. In this last and most appalling version of miscegenation we can locate the extreme form that the fear of women and natural reproduction takes in this novel: the crossing of white and red bodies in a nonsexual miscegenation, a drinking of blood. And this unnatural mixing of blood provides a final instance of the crossing of boundaries that the novel proposes, a crossing located, even if only by denial, in the bodies of women.

V.

The killing of women and children during the massacre, like the killing of the deer and the colt with which the novel begins, seems insufficiently motivated as either Indian revenge or as a sacrifice to the wilderness. Although Cooper tends to bring women and children to the frontier and then violently eliminate them, their deaths do not just mark a ritual sacrifice of or for civilization. Rather, these deaths operate as a kind of generation through violence of relations among landscapes, races, and genders. More specifically, they mark a conflict about what makes up a person, or how persons are made, a conflict played out on the frontier between civilization and wilderness, culture and nature, white and red. This conflict appears most dramatically in the anxious representations of women, and of the female body, as conflicted signs of culture and of nature.

The crossing of the cultural and the natural appears, for instance, in Cora, who wears a veil to hide both her "not brown" face and the "colour of the rich blood, that seemed ready to burst its bounds." Yet "her veil also was allowed to open its folds, and betrayed an indescribable look" when she first sees Magua (19). When Cora blushes, she betrays her "blood," a blood her veil does not conceal and her apparently white skin can scarcely contain. Cora's "indescribable look" has been traced to an instinctive racial affinity with Magua, an affinity with the native body that her "tell-tale blood" (67) repeatedly reveals. Beyond this, the revelation of her "rich blood" at once establishes Cora's racial identity in terms of her blood and brings that racial embodiment together with the female blush. Her blush, that is, brings together her race and her sex, the racial body and the gendered body.

Instead of concealing her identity, Cora's veil, like her blush, reveals her gender and her race. Her veil arouses attention in the forest, enabling Uncas and the others to track her from the massacre scene when they notice she has dropped "the rag she wore to hide a face that all did love to look upon" (185). For Cora to hide her face seems another version of the concealments and disguises that proliferate in the novel. But if her veil fails to "hide a face that all did love to look upon," as her skin barely contains her blood, both female face and racial blood are paradoxically revealed through and by means of veil and skin. By this means, veil and skin, artifact and body, work together as the nature and culture of Cora's racial and sexual identity.

Cora's veil, left behind in the forest, echoes "those dense shadows, that seemed to draw an impenetrable veil before the bosom of the forest" (47). Moreover, the veil that "covers" for her identity permits a chain of relations between landscapes and the female body that returns us to the question of the relation between the female body and the nature of the native American. Gendered by veil and bosom both, the forest appears female and even maternal, yet the "impenetrable veil" that the shadows draw across that bosom suggests also an uneasy relation between such a maternal personification of the forest and the threat its dense shadows pose. The threat behind the veil appears dramatically when the travelers initially enter the woods and the "forest at length appeared to swallow up the living mass which had slowly entered its bosom" (15). Converting people into a "living mass," and the bosom of the forest into a kind of mouth that swallows them, this passage makes the female or maternal forest into an ominous consumer of humans.

Such a contradictory or conflicted image of the female body draws gender, race, and landscape into contested relation. Cooper's presentation of the forest as a maternal body that swallows rather than delivers human bodies inverts the more familiar relation between the maternal earth and Indian bodies that his sources depicted. "The Indians consider the earth as their universal mother," notes Heckewelder. "They believe that they were created within its bosom." Before their birth from the bosom of the earth, they "contend that their existence was in the form of certain terrestrial animals." The genealogy of this earlier animal embodiment and this relationship to a personified mother earth produces a belief in the "intimate ties of connexion and relationship" that exist "between man and the brute creation." The Indians, according to Heckewelder, do not classify the difference between animals and human in the way that whites do, because in personifying the earth as their mother they include "terrestrial animals" in a family relation.

To structure the genealogy of human identity in this way, to find human identity continuous with identity as an animal, affects or even structures the grammar of the Indian language, according to Heckewelder. Specifically, rather than differentiating in terms of gender, the Indians Heckewelder describes discriminate by the animate and the inanimate: "Hence, in their languages, these inflections of their nouns which we call *genders*, are not, as with us, descriptive of the *masculine* and *feminine* species, but of the *animate* and *inanimate* kinds."[25] For the grammar of the presumably white "us" that Heckewelder addresses, gender discriminations exist as species discriminations, and it seems almost as though to have a masculine or feminine identity is to belong to a distinct species. In contrast, the discrimination between the animate and the inanimate not only softens distinctions of gender but also aligns animate "kinds," suggesting a continuity among human, wilderness, and animal identities.

These complicated relationships among, for example, veil and blood as signs of female and racial identity, and the uneasy tensions among landscapes, animals, and persons in the novel, reappear in the novel as a problem of language, and specifically as the problematic involvement of women with reading and writing. Natty Bumppo resentfully notes that "a man who is too conscientious to spend his days among the women, in learning the names of black marks, may never hear of the deeds of his fathers" (31). In this association between women and language, women are the source of "the names of black marks" that carry "the deeds of his fathers." Natty resists women, in this view, both as linguistic transmitters of a patriarchal identity and as biological carriers of that identity.

The relation between women and language appears in yet another guise in Cooper's preface: he describes how the Lenape, laying aside their arms, become "in the figurative language of the natives, 'women'" (3). Natty Bumppo notes, "I have heard that the Delawares have laid aside the hatchet, and are content to be called women!" (50). In the sources Cooper drew on, to be called women is to have stopped fighting and to act as negotiators for peace. The Delaware are pressured "to assume that station by which they would be the means, and the only means, of . . . saving the Indian race from utter extirpation." Faced with such pressure to save the race by changing gender, "to become *the woman* in name . . . they gave their consent and agreed to become *women*."[26] Like the taking on of animal identities, this transmutation involves both imitation and a kind of transformation. To become nominally a woman is a choice made in the name of or in order to rescue racial and national identity, but, at least for the white observer, it also implicates the Indian nation in a suspicious identification with female gender. [27] And it raises again the question of how national identity gets transmitted: through blood or through the name, through deeds of the fathers or women's naming of the fathers.

In a recent and influential account of national identities, Benedict Anderson argues that "from the start the nation was conceived in language, not in blood." That is, ostensibly natural elements like race and gender get subsumed under the cultural element of language so that "one could be invited into the imagined community. Thus today, even the most insular nations accept the principle of *naturalization.*" Language makes it possible to produce artificially a national identity that seems natural. [28] But Cooper's account indicates a tenser relation between the natural and linguistic "conceptions" of the nation and indicates further, through the chain of associations among genders and races, and how they are mapped onto landscapes and languages, that the project of national formation cannot be separated from these competing forms of bodily and linguistic ways of conceiving a national self. For Cora, for example, to have "a blood purer and richer than the rest of her nation" (343) indicates the uncertain crossings of gender, race, and nation. The links between violence against women and violence against Indians, as Greenough's "Rescue Group" suggests, crucially involve relations between national landscapes and the female body, and between the female body and the native race.

It may finally be that the danger for women in *The Last of the Mohicans* is that the novel's violence involves, after all, not quite killing a man, but killing a woman, or a man seen in female terms, those who have become woman. Such a reading indicates not just the crossing of racial and female identities, but the elimination or replacement of both by a fantasy of national identity. For Natty Bumppo to be "a man without a cross" in a novel where everything seems to be a matter of crossing the natural and the cultural may even be for him to be a man not born of woman. And in Cooper's American project of settling and founding nature, we find such an identity at once naturalized and nationalized.

6 ·

The Identity of Slavery

The uncertain status of the body in slavery discourse may be evoked by two images from the cultural history of slavery. First, the female "topsy-turvy doll" popular in the nineteenth-century American South (and still produced). Held one way, the doll appears as a white woman with long skirts. Flipping over her skirts does not reveal her legs, but rather exposes another racial identity: the head of a black woman, whose long skirts now cover the head of the white woman.[1] This visual and physical change from white to black and black to white appears also in a second form of popular representation, Lydia Maria Child's 1831 children's story, "Mary French and Susan Easton," in which two little girls, one white, one black, are kidnapped and sold into slavery. The white girl has been disguised; she appears black, but her tears gradually dissolve this surface identity, revealing the white body beneath the black surface, and she is restored to her family. Her friend's tears cannot accomplish a similar miracle: because they do not change her surface identity, she is left in slavery.[2]

The tears that mark the formation of a sentimental subject here crucially reveal that subject as white, and such an identification of sentimental subjects and white bodies, or, more exactly, white interiors, appears in both pro- and anti-slavery literature in the early republic.[3] And the double gesture of at once presenting and refusing a reversibility of identity—the topsy-turvy doll can be only one color at a time; Mary French can appear black, but Susan Easton cannot appear white—shows up repeatedly as white and black are paired and set in opposition. Such an opposition of white and black, an opposition that keeps them together but insists that they cannot mix, is insistently mapped onto national oppositions by nineteenth-century American writers whose opposition of North and South correlates individual and national bodies.

Representing slavery in nineteenth-century America involved either fixing the slave's identity in the body, as a matter of "blood" or of "skin," or unfixing the identity of slavery by understanding identity as transcending the body.[4] I want to focus here on how such uncertain locations of identity function across rival accounts of slavery, both the justification of it and the opposition to it, and I want to examine as well how these configurations of the body and identity, of exteriors and interiors, bring together an apparently incongruous range of concerns, including abolition, the "science" of phrenology, and the "woman question." These diverse concerns raise the problem of the families that produce and reproduce bodies and identities. Hence in what follows I will explore appeals to families as "nurseries of the state" in slavery discourse and will further investigate how the intense concentration on the family as the locus or warrant of identity makes visible matters of miscegenation and incest that threaten to undo that very identity.[5]

Racial, gender, and national problems of identity appear provocatively in the following different yet representative texts: *The Devil in America*, a pro-slavery epic written just before the Civil War by a Southern minister; *The Slave's Friend*, an abolition journal for children published in the 1830s; and *The Romance of the Republic*, an abolitionist novel written just after the Civil War by Lydia Maria Child. I will look at how such texts constitute their readers and their characters as subjects, in what is by now the understood double sense, both as agents of and subjects to power. These problems of subjects and bodies involve, as the sociologist of science Bruno Latour has suggested, "acts of differentiation and identification, not differences and identities. The words 'same' and 'other' are the consequences of trials of strength, defeats and victories. They cannot themselves describe these links."[6] The problem of identity that I want to explore here, a problem that slavery at once poses and exacerbates, is a problem of such trials of recognition.

II.

Although the primary aim of *The Devil in America* is to argue in favor of slavery, its subtitle gives a breathtakingly indiscriminate indication of its proposed scope and of the topics the text correlates:

Spirit-Rapping—Mormonism;
Woman's Rights Conventions and Speeches;
Abolitionism;
Harper's Ferry Raid & Black Republicanism;
Defeat of Satan,
And Final Triumph of the Gospel.

Attributed to a Reverend Gladney, president of the Aberdeen Female College in Mississippi, the work ranges from nasty satires about abolition and women's rights agitation to attacks on any other mode of reform that entangles the question of rights and the problem of the body, including the natural rights proposed by Thomas Paine and the biological origins that had recently been advanced by Charles Darwin. In each case, the reform activity is exposed as part of a plot by Satan, who has sent demons on specific missions to destroy the United States of America. The Demon of Atheism, for instance, has been sent to use "Philosophers" and "sons of science" to "prove that men and monkeys are the same."[7] The faith that maintains the difference between men and monkeys will be assailed by an atheism that asserts a frightening sameness among species, that indeed erodes differences as such. Everywhere heightening anxieties about inheritance and embodiment, property and identity, the work thus relays both a counter-history of abolition as a strategy by the Devil to destroy the union, and a deep anxiety about maintaining a series of differences, differences each imagined to entail the next, between men and monkeys, men and women, white and black, North and South, master and slave. Such differences might almost be considered constitutive of antebellum American culture.[8]

The mission of the Demon of Fanaticism, for example, is to destroy American women: "Teach her to hate the sphere for her design'd, / And prove that she is treated as a slave / While from the rights of man she is debarr'd."[9] Staging the unnaturalness of natural or equal rights, the poem argues that a woman barred from "the rights of man" is saved from the clutches of the demonic atheist Thomas Paine. Not unexpectedly, the narrator cites the proper alternative, the sentimental ideal of domestic life: "'Tis hers to crown with joy the quiet home, / The infant mind with her own image stamp . . . / In short, to act on earth an angel's part" (D, 72). The angelic mission of the white woman is to stamp an image of herself on the tabula rasa of the infant mind, or, to shift the metaphor, to become the coin of the realm she rules by reproducing her own image. This passage presents reproduction not as a biological process, but as a mechanical stamping; the mother's task becomes the reproduction of identity, a reproduction that does not allow for difference or deviation or, as we will see in a moment, for the accident or mixture of biology or blood.

Satan proposes a perversely similar stamping of identity onto the interiors of bodies, as he instructs his demons on how to arouse dissension in the North by producing abolitionists. But Satan's proposal mixes bodies and identities in just the way that "angelic" reproduction avoids. The demons are first to "work upon the mind," and "there an idol-image firmly fix":

> A negro image let that idol be,
> Whose shadow dark cast on the souls of men,
> Shall give a kindred hue to all within . . .
> And all whose surface white [shall] have hearts within
> Tinged with the hue of Ethiopian's skin. (D, 77)

Fixing an "idol-image" on the mind involves not merely the internalizing of that image, but also an internal mixing of images and bodies. The exterior "hue" of the "Ethiopian" thus becomes "kindred" to the interior of the superficially white abolitionist, as if enacting an extraordinary version of miscegenation. That first the mind, then the soul, then the heart will be "tinged" with the color of the skin also intimates a link between the logic of miscegenation and the logic of sentimentality: both involve the impression of, and mixing of, external and physical states in the interior state of the heart. But the incongruity of stamping or fixing identity on the heart as a tinging of the skin suggests an anxious mixing of images and bodies and raises again the question that *The Devil in America* works to disavow in its "stamping" or "fixing" of identities in bodies: where does identity get located, in the heart or on the skin, the interior or the exterior? Responding to this question evokes, in the first instance, a translation of biological reproduction into replication (images replicating themselves), and, in the second, a sort of internal miscegenation (images and skins mixing with hearts and generating monstrous kindred).

Addressing, for a different purpose, the disjunctive relation between interiors and bodies, the abolitionist journal *The Slave's Friend* tells young readers that "the chestnut has a dark skin. . . . But its *kernel* is all white and sweet. The apple, though it looks so pretty, has many little black grains at the heart. . . . Now little boys and girls can't be abolitionists until they get rid of all these black grains in their hearts."[10] In this garden account of bodies, the chestnut's black skin gets overlooked because of a "sweet" white interior; but the apple's white interior is flawed by a black heart. Acquiring abolitionist citizenship apparently is accomplished through expelling the heart's black grains of slavery. But what marks this contrast of pro- and anti-slavery discourses is the *lack* of contrast: at *heart*, they argue the same perspective; at heart, they call for a white interior. Both pro- and anti-slavery writings exhibit, from different sides, the tension between attempts to locate and inscribe the black/white identity of and in the body and attempts to escape such a biologized essentialism, or biological design or destiny.

Such biologized destinies have been used to link the identities of white women and slaves, linked because their bodies mark their identities as subjected rather than as subjects. The problem raised in both instances, it has recently been suggested, is that "the extent to which the body designates identity" in feminist-abolitionist discourse makes for the "difficulties and resistance inherent in acknowledging the corporeality of personhood. The bodies feminists and abolitionists wish reclaimed, and the bodies they exploit, deny, or obliterate in the attempted rescue, are the same."[11] Yet if this account of reclaiming and denying the body points to an essential tension in both pro- and anti-slavery work, the identification of corporeality and personhood, rather than not being acknowledged, is placed squarely at issue in these works. Whether the struggle is over the identity of the body or the identity that the body represents—"body" and "identity," again, appearing as objects of struggle, not fixed terms—such a struggle both unites and opposes pro- and anti-slavery arguments, and beyond that, foregrounds the complex problem of the body and embodiment. Further, the corporealizing and transcendentalizing double impulse of sentimental discourse at once installs identity in bodies and makes bodies the signs of an identity that transcends them.

Similar attention to the transmission of identity through the body appears, of course, in other popular discussions of the problem of embodiment in mid-century America. For example, Orson Squire Fowler, the popularizer of phrenology and family reformation, promoted the belief that what mothers looked at during pregnancy could shape the characters of their unborn children. He preached a mode of identity at once fixed by the contours of the skull yet malleable, after a phrenological diagnosis of the skull's characteristics.[12] This paradox resembles the paradox of anti-slavery battles in which identity is an essentialist matter of natural bodies (for men, women, slaves, or children), even as the identity located in these bodies must be reformed or transcended.

An extraordinary range of cultural issues involving the question of how the body conveys or contains identity is communicated in this paradox. Yoking several of them, *The Devil in America* expands its scope of operation to rail against: "Infidelity, Woman's Rights, Abolitionism, and Spiritualism! . . . Why is it that these monstrous errors are so often united, and that the adoption of one seems necessarily to lead to the embrace of the other?" (D, 183) Rather than offering anything like an explicit answer to this question, the narrator merely suggests that slavery, because it provides the antidote to promiscuous uniting, adopting, or embracing across these different kinds, must be what protects the South: "The prevalence of these isms at the North, and their absence here, cannot be accidents." The North

> must hide its head in shame over the blasphemies of its infidel conventions, the indecencies of its free-love doctrines, the wickedness and inhumanity of its spiritualism and the treason of its abolitionists. The South can boast of "freedom" from all these isms; and the price which it pays for this freedom is the institution of slavery. The South accepts the terms, and thinks it has made, for once, a great "bargain." (D, 185)

What links these "isms"? If each involves a propping of spiritual or erotic or political meanings on the body, each also and more significantly moves to "transcend" the confines of biology/body. In each case, biology does not equal destiny: infidelity, feminism, spiritualism, abolition all involve what might be called a politics of transcendence, a way of attaching significance to identities, meanings, and values beyond the bodily and the physical just where the body and the physical seem most at issue. Combatting the concept that biology equals destiny brings together the wide diversity of "monstrous errors" that include abolition and women's rights along with phrenology, spiritualism, mesmerism, and "free love."[13] And the blasphemy, the indecency, and the treason of these "united errors" is crucially the "embrace" of their uncertain mixture.

The Demon of Discord, sent to foment Civil War, again asserts just this matter of ineradicably separate identities: "'twixt the North and South the question is / Shall black be turned to white and white to black?" Such a topsy-turvy suggestion involves not simply reversing skin color, but inverting the order of the universe, for

> *Since serve some must, which shall the other serve . . .*
> *The question here of right is very plain;*
> *The right of each to slaves is just the same,*
> *With equal right of color and of form.* (D, 77–78)

Equal rights here means that each has the right to "color" and "form," even as one color means slavery and the other ownership. Equal rights, in other words, means separate but equal rights, since an equal "right" to a distinct color or form merely establishes one's place as served or serving. Following this perverse logic, abolishing slavery appears not only as the abolition of an "equal right" to servitude, but also as the abolishing of natural hierarchical differences between male and female spheres and, indeed, the abolition of the difference between male and female.

In calling attention to the "bargain" that the South has made trading monstrous errors for the "equal" rights of slavery, the narrator parodically adapts a "Yankee" term to differentiate the institution of slavery from the nominally "free" labor and "free" trade of Northern capitalism. The narrator further proposes what the North has overlooked in its capitalistic formulations. It has just begun to "learn that *capital* is *kinky heads*,— / Of which the South has all, the North has none!" (D, 141), and this may account for its desire to intervene in the Southern economy. What at first appears an unsurprising exposure of the North's motives—that the concern for liberty and liberation is a cover for economic jealousy—turns out to be somewhat more surprising. If "capital *is* kinky heads," this is because the pro-slavery argument works to return capital to its physical root—"capital," after all, derives from caput or head. That is, the pro-slavery argument here insists on an identity between the body and the economy, just the identification that the disembodying and impersonal working of capitalism seems to complicate.[14] In such a move of embodiment, it may become possible to see how these errors intersect: "Where Atheism and Pantheism . . . Fourierism and Tribunism, Materialism and Mesmerism have leavened the public mind, and free thinking, free love, and free license are almost as much in vogue as 'free soil, free niggers, and Fremont,' we may well expect a monstrum horrendum" (D, 187).[15] Restoring a monstrous body to such disembodied and disembodying practices, the narrator anticipates a monstrous birth out of convulsions at once political and bodily, in what appears as a birth announcement of the Civil War.

III.

The question of how bodies are reproduced in slavery discourse is raised again in *The Devil in America* as the Demon of Discord condemns abolitionists for exploiting images of slavery's bodies. He describes how "overcharged pedagogues" have

frightful pictures to the children showed
Of monsters holding lashes in their hands . . .
Till infant tears were trickling down their cheeks;
And pictures on the mind engraved for life. (D, 135)

Such permanent engraving of monstrous images on the infant mind appears as another version of *The Devil in America*'s earlier account of how incorporating images into bodies produces abolitionists. In this production of infant abolitionists, "trickling" tears correspond to the internal engraving of pictures of the lash. We can begin to uncover what is at stake here in a sentimental pedagogy linked to picturing, the body and the lash, and the stark physicality of seeing as engraving impressions, by considering in more detail the program of showing "frightful pictures" to children.[16]

While a pedagogical concern about molding the minds of children might have appeared as a reason for not telling them about slavery, early abolitionists saw the matter differently: young readers of *The Slave's Friend*, which indeed showed monsters with whips, were told to "read it through very carefully and *think* while you *read*. Fix the stories so in your memory that you will never forget them. And may God so stamp them upon your heart that you will always *feel* them."[17] *The Slave's Friend* presents reading as a physical act of inscribing stories onto the mind and having them stamped onto the heart. The sentimental progress from seeing to thinking to feeling is accomplished through a process of internalization that again recalls the transformed identity of abolitionists who internalized the image of the "Ethiopian." Reading operates here not merely as a means to correct thinking but as the mode of correct thinking: the refusal to reduce meanings to bodies or to merely physical surfaces (skin color, for instance), and the insistence on thinking and feeling as antidotes to identifying identity with nothing more than the body.[18]

Crucially, whipping and reading get perversely connected as external disciplines made internal, or interiorized. *The Slave's Friend* counterposes pictures of the lash to pictures of whites teaching black children to read. The sentimental lesson juxtaposes these two modes of training—the whip as the external model and reading as the internalized one—and in so doing, contrasts the northern model of managing heads and hearts with the southern. An anti-slavery version of the *New England Primer*, for instance, the *Anti-Slavery Alphabet*, begins, of course, with "A is for Abolitionist," and continues, "W is for the Whipping Post / To which the slave is bound, / While on his naked back the lash / Makes many a bleeding wound."[19] Abolitionist education thus appears as a process of learning to read or to recognize letters of the alphabet through looking at the lash. Internalizing the image of the lash, that is, works as a means of memorizing letters, while letters function as a disciplinary process that at once wards off the lash and keeps it perpetually in view.

Hence these documents about reading uneasily stand in for the body of the slave, even as they represent and reproduce that body. Vexed relations between reading, freeing, and selling recur throughout. Children in *The Slave's*

Friend say, for instance, "I long to see all slaves free; to have children attend Sabbath schools; to have them taught to read, write, and cipher. What a joyful time that will be, Ann! Then . . . all can sing, 'Hail Columbia, happy land'" (SF, 36). This juxtaposition of a liberationist strategy of reading and the potentially coercive effects of reform is indicated by the juxtaposition of freedom *from* slavery and the freedom *to* attend Sunday school, learn to read, and sing patriotic songs. In other words, freedom gets bound up here with a lesson about the allegiance owed to religious and national duty and identity. (Translating the lash into text and icon also meant that national symbols could be read less patriotically: in another issue of *The Slave's Friend* a child's comments conflate the blood raised by the whip with the symbol of the nation that allowed such violence: "The *stripes* in the national flag make me think of the stripes the poor slaves suffer.")[20] And of course, reading *is* a liberationist strategy—a connection perhaps most explicit in the autobiographical writings of Frederick Douglass and salient in other slave narratives.[21] Here, however, it at once subsumes and emphasizes the difference between illiterate slave children and the assumed reader of the text, the slave's friend.

The reading lesson thus appears as part of a crucial anti-slavery lesson in capitalism, precisely the link between abolition and capitalism that *The Devil in America* indicts. The children imagined as readers of *The Slave's Friend* ask, "What can we do?" They are told that to fight slavery means to read, and to earn money to buy books: "By putting the money you earn into the Anti-Slavery treasury, books can be printed" (SF, 37). By vol. 2, no. v: "about 250,000 copies of the Slave's Friend have been published"; the response of the publishers is to promote juvenile anti-slavery societies. Lewis Tappan, the financier-abolitionist, asked rhetorically in 1836, "Does any one doubt the propriety of children associating to form anti-slavery societies? There are already Juvenile Temperance, Missionary, and I believe Peace Societies. . . . Is not slavery as bad as intemperance?" (SF, 66, 68).[22] For children to associate in reform societies is not new—just as linking reading to reform is not a new strategy. Both enterprises join the nineteenth-century American project to incorporate nationalism and religion in reading lessons. And I do not, of course, want to expose reform strategies as based on merely economic motives, nor do I want to suggest that economic strategies "explain" the reform impulse.[23] Rather, I want to point out some implications of their interdependence: the lesson in reading (a necessary lesson in abstraction from merely physical pictures or signs on paper, or from merely corporeal identities) and the lesson in capitalism (the abstraction from physical heads to systems of exchange) are in fact related lessons—what might even be called twin lessons in abolitionist bookkeeping.

To aid in forming the juvenile anti-slavery society, a constitution has been prepared for them: "The object of this Society shall be to collect money for the anti-Slavery cause, to read and circulate The Slave's Friend, to do all in our power to have the free colored people respected and well-treated, and the enslaved set at liberty" (SF, 71–72). The ordering of priorities here marks both the limits of what children might be expected to perform and the function of *The Slave's Friend*: to educate children to raise money as a response to moral trouble. Hence an equivalence is established between the *circulation* of texts and the circulation of money, as if reading and capitalism indicated each other. In fact a competition is set up among the societies to raise money and distribute more literature. The Juvenile Anti-Slavery Society of Rhode Island, for example, is reported to have given $100 to the cause, which translates immediately into 15,000 copies of *The Slave's Friend*. This translation of anti-slavery sentiment into reading *The Slave's Friend* leads to fund-raising to buy more copies of *The Slave's Friend* so more can read it and raise more funds to buy more copies of it.

The grown-up version, the New England Anti-Slavery Society, concentrates on similar questions of freedom and identity, reading and economy. The system of ownership that they seek to overturn in slavery will be reinscribed in the ordering of marriages and families. For them, "Immediate Abolition" means that "every husband shall have his own wife and every wife her own husband," that "parents shall have the control and government of their own children, and that children shall belong to their parents."[24] But this proposed system of family government and control is not exactly compatible with their interest in controlling what amounts to the circulation of children. The reformers explain that abolition "will enable us to take 100,000 infants, who are annually born to slave parents, and doomed to a life of ignorance and servitude—place them in infant schools, and transfer them into primary and sabbath schools; from these into high shools and Bible classes; and . . . from Bible classes into the Christian church. Thus they will become ornaments to society . . . instead of mere animals."[25] What happens to the parents of these 100,000 infants while such a "transfer" takes place? Presumably they will give up their babies to be "ornaments" for northern reformers when they wouldn't want to give them up to be "animals" in southern slavery. Which returns us to the dual concerns of the body and capital we have been sketching throughout. The state-controlled nursery of 100,000 infants accords with the worst imaginings of the pro-slavery faction: capitalist reproduction—the baby factory—has replaced the ideal of the family reiterated in the pro-slavery critique of the monstrous errors of abolition and capital both.

IV.

Not only the reform of families, but also the reform of marriage was seen by some as the natural extension of abolishing slavery. Of course, the destruction of marriages and families through slavery when the family had become the focus of attention as an instrument of both civilization and character formation provided further ammunition for abolitionists. As *The Family and Slavery* explained, "The Family is the head, the heart, the fountain of society, and it has not a privilege that slavery does not nullify, a right that it does not violate." In attacking the destruction of families in slavery, the American

Tract Society not atypically claimed "The family is appointed for the *discipline* of the race." The abolitionist Henry Wright even declared that no one who wanted to "save the world, will overlook the family institution."[26]

The apocalyptic rhetoric that marshalled the family institution in a battle over the "world" was countered by a grimmer view of the confining effects of that institution. As another reformer asserted, *"There are today in our midst ten times as many fugitives from Matrimony as there are fugitives from Slavery."*[27] This fugitive view of marriage was connected to the abolitionist views on slavery in the pamphlet, "Slavery and Marriage: A Dialogue" (1850), attributed to John Humphrey Noyes, founder of the experimental Oneida colony. The characters in this stylized dramatic dialogue, Major South and Judge North, first rehearse the familiar terms of the national debate over slavery. They are interrupted by the proselytizing Mr. Free Church, who adapts the arguments common to both pro- and anti-slavery forces as he attempts to enlist abolitionists in the cause of free love or "perfectionism," an attempt that also mocks them by applying anti-slavery arguments to the abolition of marriage. Mr. Free Church "holds the same opinion about Marriage that [Judge North does] of Slavery, that it is an arbitrary institution and contrary to natural liberty. . . . The catalogue of women's abuses under the tyranny of matrimony, compare very well with the cruel lot of the slaves." The proposed "natural" alternative of "liberty" for women confined by marriage creates as much anxiety for Judge North as his arguments for freedom from slavery have for Major South. Yet to defend the institution of marriage, he unselfconsciously adapts the terms that Major South has previously used to defend slavery: "The *law* protects women," and, besides, "Woman is devotedly attached to marriage"; it's wrong to be "advocating its abolition." As he points out the faulty assumption that legality and rights indicate each other, Mr. Free Church argues that "Marriage separates and breaks up families [so] union at the *altar*, as it is justly called, (considering the cruelty of the sacrifice) mutilates two family circles."

But "the abolition of Marriage," an anxious Judge North contends, still echoing a southern reaction to the proposed abolition of slavery, "would lead to unbridled licentiousness and social ruin." Such anxiety about freedom and lawlessness links the world views of North and South; more important, it grounds the stability of the national social order in the family. Mr. Free Church replies that families would "fare better under a system of free-labor and free-love in Association, than they do under the Marriage system where each family is at the mercy of one man."[28] Through this call for free love and free labor, a call, in effect, for a free market economy in family relations, the tract suggests that the practices of the Marriage system must be repudiated to develop a new social order that would include the abolition of slavery. A Civil War fought for this new order would be fought for the freedom of families.

In linking marriage to slavery, however, the tract invokes the catalogue of women's abuses under the tyranny of matrimony without explicitly addressing how they might be subsumed by the catalogue of women's abuses, abuses of both labor and love, under the tyranny of slavery. That is, as it presents the arbitrary tyranny of matrimony, this tract proclaims the family comparable to slavery, "at the mercy of one man," but refrains from exploring how the family in *slavery* is at the mercy of one man. As other writers show, for the families held in slavery to be at the mercy of one man creates the southern version of the baby factory.[29] The slave system's production of children, for example—a system that crucially generates miscegenation and, often, incest—is the subject of Richard Hildreth's 1836 antislavery novel *The White Slave*. Here the family at the mercy of one man is the plantation at the mercy of Colonel Moore, the "faultless pattern of a true *Virginian* gentleman . . . of liberty, indeed he was always a warm and energetic admirer." Although Colonel Moore "used to vindicate the cause of the French Revolution" and "*the rights of man*," these are the rights of white men: the "gentleman" leaves the rights of his male slaves to an overseer, and appropriates the rights as well as the bodies of the female ones.[30] The French Revolution supplies the model of rebellion with which his son and slave, the young Archy Moore, identifies. Hearing from his father about the "abstract beauty of liberty and equality [it was] the French republicans with whom I sympathized."[31]

As a slave, Archy has difficulty translating these abstractions into the American scene. He learns to sympathize with himself, and to desire liberty and equality, from learning about his family. Southern slave codes decreed that the child follow the condition of the mother, that is, that the racial identity of the mother determine the identity of the child. Such practices suggest that slave children have invisible fathers, as though mothers were alone responsible for reproduction.[32] Archy undergoes a "revolution of feeling" when his dying mother tells him of his paternity. Shocked that he is the "slave of my own father"—and this conflation of relations makes visible the relations implicit in the slave system—Archy explains that "as his slave, his apparent kindness had gained my affection . . . as his son, I soon began to feel that I might claim . . . an equal birth-right with my brethren." The discovery of his father's identity does not change Archy's legal status, but it relocates the abstract question of rights in family identity and introduces the issues of incest and miscegenation that threaten that identity.

To claim an "equal birthright" with his brethren appears, in the peculiar institution of the plantation, as an assertion of sexual desire toward women on the plantation, regardless of birth or relation. Following this logic, Archy falls in love with his half-sister, like him the child of a slave mother:

> Cassy knew herself to be Colonel Moore's daughter; but . . . I had discovered that she had no idea, that I was his son. [His wife] Mrs. Moore was perfectly well informed [but] she discovered in it no impediment to my marriage with Cassy. Nor did I; for how could that same regard for the *decencies of life* . . . that refused to acknowledge our paternity, or to recognize any relationship between us, pretend at the same time . . . to forbid our union?[33]

A refusal to acknowledge the paternity of Cassy and Archy is thus a refusal to acknowledge any biological relationship between them. They cannot legally be related because they have no legal father; their identity can be derived only through the mother. Such disregard for the *"decencies of life"* disavows the "facts" of life involving biological reproduction and translates into miscegenation and incest.

The family boundaries that both miscegenation and incest foreground were well recognized by nineteenth-century legislation. "State criminal codes," as the legal theorist Eva Saks presents it, "usually listed miscegenation next to incest as two crimes of 'blood.'" This problematic association of interracial and intrafamilial crimes of blood was elaborated on by an antebellum Mississippi statesman who declared that "the same law which forbids consanguinous amalgamation forbids ethnical amalgamation. Both are incestuous. Amalgamation is incest."[34] What at once links and produces these crimes of blood is the invisible father. Such generation without a father is perhaps epitomized by Topsy's famous remark, in *Uncle Tom's Cabin*, that she "never was born," since she was "raised by a speculator." Her remark joins the southern logic of fatherlessness and the northern logic of capitalism—she has been born and raised in a system of speculation and exchange.[35] Similarly, in a later version of *The White Slave*, Archy is told that "As slaves could not be married, there could be . . . no widows among them; and as to the children, not being born in lawful wedlock, they could not become fatherless,—for they had no fathers,—being in the eye of the law, as he had heard the learned Judge Hallett observe from the bench, the children of nobody."[36]

But such denying of natural reproduction creates another dilemma for Archy and Cassy. Their father intervenes to prevent their marriage, not out of moral outrage but because his refusal to recognize familial relations, and the miscegenation-incest linkage, allows him to express a competing sexual desire for his daughter. She resists him, and finally forestalls an attempted rape by calling him "father," a name that still has the power to inhibit his sexual performance, although it does not prevent him from threatening future attempts. The family thus becomes almost indiscriminately sexualized when at the mercy of one man since neither miscegenation nor incest taboos prohibit sexual relations. Familial relations collapse into indiscriminate incestuous/miscegenated relations. Even Archy's mother acquires sexual significance: "I describe her more like a lover than a son." Archy resembles his father perhaps most in this matter of desire for both his mother and his sister.[37] Like his father, Archy keeps both desire and reproduction in the family.

V.

One register of the desire to keep reproduction within families is the replication of names that number rather than rename generations of sons. In Lydia Maria Child's novel, *The Romance of the Republic* (1867), Gerald Fitzgerald's name already identifies him as his own son. His two sons (by different mothers) both receive this name. Their resemblance to their father is surpassed only by their resemblance to each other. In such a family, one "could see no difference" between identical sons. This reproduction with no difference, or the identical appearance they have as sons of the same father, bypasses the racial identity each has inherited from his mother, although, until the Civil War, that racial identity codes one as slave and the other as free. The novel repeatedly interrogates such problems of antebellum national identity as it presents the struggle for family identity in a republic at once incestuous and miscegenous.

Both mothers of Gerald Fitzgerald's sons—the northern Lily Bell and the southern Rosa Royal—grow up believing they are white. Only one will have her juridical status redetermined. Since her father never freed her mother, Rosa Royal follows her mother's condition as a slave. She discovers her status after her father's death, when she's put up for sale as part of the moveable goods of the estate she thought to have inherited. Still ignorant that the Louisiana codes of slavery invalidate a marriage contract with a slave, she believes she has escaped her condition by marrying Gerald Fitzgerald. When she finds out that her marriage is a fraud—he has purchased her rather than married her—and that he has not only married the northern Lily Bell and fathered a legitimate heir, but also sold her to the aptly named Mr. Bruteman, she finds herself "in a terrible tempest of hatred and revenge." The children of the two "wives" of Gerald Fitzgerald are lying together: "I looked at the two babes, and thought how one was born to be indulged and honored, while the other was born a slave, liable to be sold by his unfeeling father. . . . Mine was only a week the oldest, and was no larger than his brother. They were so exactly alike that I could distinguish them only by their dress. I exchanged the dresses" (R, 352). The babies are so alike that even their mothers need their "dress" to determine their identity.[38] Not even skin deep, racial difference becomes as superficial as a different garment.

Even the photographs that had just been perfected as a mark of fixing identities are inadequate: because of their similarity, the photograph of the illegitimate son identifies the legitimate one. Locating or fixing identity, as we have seen, was a mid-nineteenth-century preoccupation; and the mid-nineteenth-century inventions of photography and fingerprinting emerge from attempts to fix identity at the surface of the skin, or, as Oliver Wendell Holmes proclaimed of photography, to skin the surface of the visible world.[39] *The Romance of the Republic*, too early for fingerprints, has photographs and tattoos to mark the skins of its characters. The only visible difference between these brothers is the "G. F." tattooed on one son's arm as a register of his identity that he cannot read: he calls himself George Falkner rather than Gerald Fitzgerald, but although he later learns to read the mark of his name on his skin, he still can't read his skin for the sign of whether he is slave or free. The surface does not indicate—for either son—what status they have as subjects of the republic. These competing imperatives of reading the bodily and the extra-bodily foreground the problem of identity and its relation to the problem of the body.

The major conflicts in the novel involve attempts to locate, identify, and claim the lost members of families, most of them lost because of slavery or attempts to escape slavery. In the middle of the novel, for example, two runaway slaves try to leave a ship from New Orleans, significantly called "The King Cotton," as it arrives in Boston. One of the slaves, "passing" as white, is in fact legally "white"; the other masquerades as his slave, but is instead his wife.[40] Detained when they try to land, the stowaways run, and the captain calls after them, "Stop thief!" The theft they commit, of course, is to steal their own bodies.

"There's no safety for property now-a-days," complains the New England shipowner, Mr. Bell. Sending his grandson out to return the runaways, he's unaware that the escaped slave has been substituted for the grandson before him. That is, although both are his grandsons, the one he sends after the runaways could be claimed as a slave, while the runaway could legally inherit Mr. Bell's property, as well as his own brother. As he sends Gerald Fitzgerald to return his brother to slavery, Mr. Bell lectures him, "It is every way for my interest to make sure of returning those negroes; and your interest is somewhat connected with mine."[41] The connections of interest and property more crucially involve what it means to claim a body and to make claims about what the surface of the skin indicates, or, in short, how property and identity are embodied in the novel.

When he later discovers that "the Gerald he had been educating as his grandson was in fact . . . born a slave" (390), Mr. Bell is confronted with an insupportable dilemma: "My property . . . must either go to Gerald, who you say has negro blood in his veins, or to this other fellow, who is a slave with a negro wife" (R, 394). He dies in an apoplectic fit confronting "the vulgar phantom of a slave son" (R, 396). Leaving his grandson to his grandson (a common means, under slavery, of keeping property and identity in the family—Archy Moore, for instance, "belongs" to his brother) has been turned, by their switched identities, into leaving him to himself. His property cannot *go* to Gerald; his property *is* Gerald. The peculiarity of the "peculiar institution"—one that involves the conversion of people into property ("pecu" is the root both of peculiar and pecuniary)—could not be more disturbingly enacted. The issue of property has become the at once peculiar and pecuniary issue of knowing which of your offspring you should leave to which, which is a proper subject and which an object of subjection. Gerald has discovered himself to be not the heir to property, but the property of the heir.[42]

The Civil War brings these mirroring doubles face to face as brothers of the North and South confront each other. When the first Gerald Fitzgerald goes off to fight in the Civil War, he writes home: "Whether I had seen a vision or a reality . . . I saw such a likeness of myself as I never saw excepting in the mirror" (R, 405). This mirrored likeness frightens him: "I thought I had seen myself; and that, you know, is said to be a warning of approaching death" (R, 404–05). The vision of an oncoming doppelganger does prove to be a warning and he dies after a battle in the arms of his brother. When, after his death, this brother/double is discovered, Rosa's husband comments, "I could see no difference . . . his transformation into a gentleman would be an easy process" (R, 413).[43] The paradox here is both that you can *see* no difference (identity is only skin deep) and that he must be *transformed* (seeing no difference is not enough). In its insistent attempts both to tell and remove such differences, A *Romance of the Republic* asks what romance can be had in a republic in which identity is so easily dislocated. As the novel imaginatively traces the consequences of Southern amalgamation, not knowing the difference becomes both a familial and a national issue. The "fraternal" Civil War most violently engages such differences at the level of the national family.

Child's romance of the republic is a romance that combines miscegenation and incest. Like Archy Moore, the young Gerald Fitzgerald falls in love with his own sister. Rather than having the same father, he and his sister have the same mother, Rosa, who intervenes to protect them from committing incest. Rosa has first to explain to her suspicious husband that she loves Gerald Fitzgerald because he is her son and not because she wants him as a lover. (His father, Gerald Fitzgerald, of course, was her lover.) Rosa's son, Gerald Fitzgerald, dies with her daughter's picture on his breast. And her daughter then falls in love with a cousin—we are told improbably that "the dangers of too close relationship are safely diminished" because "nations and races have been pretty thoroughly mixed up in the ancestry of our children" (432). Lydia Maria Child's family romance, in other words, promotes mixture rather than sameness, though its mixture appears as a dizzying proliferation of deviance in a miscegenous family.

The brothers of the *Romance* are not, as in Mark Twain's narrative, simply traded back—instead of being sold down the river, the son of the slave mother is killed in the Civil War; instead of remaining in the still-prejudiced United States, the other goes off to Europe where color might matter less. Neither stays at "home"—neither has a republic to have a romance in. The scandals of the literature we have been examining—its scenarios of incest and miscegenation—bring home to the reader (who has brought this literature home to read) how much this romance is a matter of what happens at home. Part of the post-Civil War attempt to resolve the trauma of families in a miscegenous republic, the novel tries to recover postbellum national identity in the wake of national disintegration. The major struggle, over who can be a subject in this republic, still centers on the problem of embodiment. And, too often, to be identified as white and as a subject appear the same, even in a novel that proposes to open up the republic for all.

The question remains: What happens to identity when to look at another is to look in the mirror? If seeing yourself leads to death, the violence of this recognition suggests the violence of Civil War. And it also suggests the images with which I began: although the identity of slavery can sometimes be turned upside down or washed away, when the doll is turned upside down, we discover that the slave woman and the white woman are the same.[44] Both identities are within its body, and the identities are not only exchangeable, but related. Although these narratives reject the reversibility the doll proposes— where black can become white and white black—beneath the complications and rationalizations of their tales of miscegenation, concealment, and babies switched at birth, lies this obsessional figure of the ambiguity and instability of bodily identity.

Notes

Introduction

1. On the link between decapitation and castration, see, for example, Neil Hertz's discussion of Freud's account of Medusa (in *Sexuality and Psychology of Love*): "the terror of Medusa is thus a terror of castration that is linked to the sight of something." "Medusa's Head: Male Hysteria Under Political Pressure," *Representations* 4 (Fall 1983) 212–13. On Judith and Holofernes, see also Mary Jacobus, *Reading Woman: Essays in Feminist Criticism* (Columbia University Press, 1986) pp. 116–34. On fetishism, see Sigmund Freud, "Fetishism," in *On Sexuality*, vol. 7, (Penguin, 1981), p. 359.

2. Louis Montrose translates the caption this way in "Gender and the Discourse of Discovery," *Representations* 33 (Winter 1991) 4. The engraving by Theodor Galle of a drawing by Jan van der Straet (ca. 1575) he dates as ca. 1580. The woodcuts of cannibal women that inspired this print and that accompanied Vespucci's first published account of his travels, are reproduced in Hugh Honour, *The New Golden Land: European Images of America from the Discovery to the Present Time* (Pantheon, 1975). See Jonathan Goldberg, *Sodometries: Renaissance Texts, Modern Sexualities* (Stanford University Press, 1992, pp. 193–205) for another account of the intersection of cannibalism and sexuality in early accounts of the new world. See also Charles Whitney, "The Naming of America as the Meaning of America: Vespucci, Publicity, Festivity, Modernity," *Clio* 22 (Spring 1993) 195–220. For eroticism and images of the new land, see Margarita Zamora, "Abreast of Columbus: Gender and Discovery" *Cultural Critique* 17 (Winter 1990–91) 127–149. See also Felicity Nussbaum, "'Savage' Mothers: Narratives of Maternity in the Mid-Eighteenth Century" *Cultural Critique* 20 (Winter 1991–92) 123–151; Peter Mason, *Deconstructing America: Representations of the Other* (Routledge, 1990); and Mary Campbell, *The Witness and the Other World: Exotic European Travel Writing, 400–1600* (Cornell University Press, 1988).

3. Michel de Certeau uses this image as his frontispiece in *The Writing of History*. He locates its eroticism in terms of ethnographic fantasies about travel and

cannibalism: "This conquering orgiastic curiosity, so taken with unveiling hidden things, has its symbol in travel literature: the dressed, armed, knighted discoverer face-to-face with the nude Indian woman." Although the symbolic representation of the cultural encounter under the guise of exploration produces titillation and anthropological pleasure, however, he claims that "what is really initiated here is a colonization of the body by the discourse of power." Michel de Certeau, *The Writing of History*, trans. Tom Conley (Columbia University Press, 1988), pp. 232, 233.

Examining the pending violation in such images, according to Montrose, the critic risks reproducing "the appropriation and effacement of both native Americans and women by the dominant discourse of European patriarchy" (p. 3). Similarly, Carolyn Porter argues against Stephen Greenblatt's work for being "complicit in the cultural operations of power it ostensibly wants to analyze." "Are We Being Historical Yet?" *SAQ* 87 (1988) 781.

4. According to Peter Hulme, in *Colonial Encounters: Europe and Native Caribbean, 1492–1797* (Methuen, 1986), cannibalism answers the "widespread desire for the existence of some touchstone of the absolutely 'other'" (83). The threat of cannibalism is "in fact addressed to the body politic itself" (87). For other accounts of personifying the new world, see Bernadette Bucher, *Icon and Conquest: A Structural Analysis of the Illustrations of de Bry's Great Voyage*, trans. Basia Miller Gulati (University of Chicago Press, 1981) and Clare le Corbeiller, "Miss America and Her Sisters: Personifications of the Four Parts of the World," *Metropolitan Museum Bulletin*, nos. 19–20 (1960) 209–223. Patricia Sneed, "On Caribbean Shores: Problems of Writing the History of the First Contact," *Radical History Review* 53 (Spring 1992) 5–11.

5. "The Able Doctor" (BM 5226) appeared in the *London Magazine* (May 1, 1774), and was copied several times, notably by Paul Revere for the June issue of *Royal American Magazine*. The Boston tea party—the masquerading of citizens as "savages"—took place December 16, 1773, after Boston citizens would not let tea be unloaded from British ships, and Thomas Hutchinson, the royal governor, would not allow the ships to leave. After the tea was destroyed, the port of Boston was closed. (The "Boston Petition" was a protest against this port closing.) On January 24, 1774, John Malcomb, the British customs official, was tarred and feathered; he was then taken to the gallows and forced to drink tea. See Joan Dolmetsch, *Rebellion and Reconciliation: Satirical Prints on Revolution* (University of Virginia Press, 1976), pp. 65–68, 178. See also "Bunkers Hill, or the Blessed Effects of Family Quarrels," "The Parricide, A Sketch of Modern Patriotism" (1776), and "The Female Combatants" in Michael Wynn Jones, *A Cartoon History of the American Revolution* (Putnam, 1975). In the last, a half-naked America punches her elaborately dressed mother in the nose and she replies, "I'll force you to obedience you Rebellious Slut." See also Vincent Carretta, *George III and the Satirists from Hogarth to Byron* (University of Georgia Press, 1990), p. 176; Ron Tyler, *The Image of America in Caricature and Cartoon* (Brodnax, 1976), p. 47.

6. Allan Nevins and Frank Weitenkampf, *A Century of Political Cartoons* (Scribner's, 1944), p. 9.

7. Anne Norton, *Reflections on Political Identity* (Johns Hopkins University Press, 1988). See also Elaine Scarry, *The Body in Pain: The Making and Unmaking of the World* (Oxford University Press, 1985). The violence Americans exerted in possessing their country helped to validate their subjective experience of nationalism, proposes Richard Slotkin, in a mythological reading of regeneration through

violence. Slotkin asserts, "The process by which we came to feel an emotional tie to the land was charged with a passionate and aspiring violence"; I want to question whether a national identity that becomes articulated through representations of violence does not become more attached to violence than to the land. *Regeneration Through Violence* (Wesleyan University Press, 1973).

8. Doris Sommer proposes that the national literature of Latin America is founded on the connection between politics and erotics. Developing her argument in the terrain she describes as bordered by Foucault's *History of Sexuality* (Pantheon, 1978) and Benedict Anderson's *Imagined Communities* (Verso, 1983), she finds that "Foucault charts sexual bodies as sites of national production, while Anderson wonders at the libidinal attachment we have to bodies politic." Doris Sommer, *Foundational Fictions: The National Romances of Latin America* (University of California Press, 1991), p. 38. According to Mikkel Borch-Jacobsen, Freud unveiled the "libidinal nature of the political" (*The Freudian Subject*, trans. Catherine Porter, Stanford University Press, 1988, p. 3). Also see George Mosse, *Nationalism and Sexuality: Middle-class Morality and Sexual Norms in Modern Europe* (University of Wisconsin Press, 1985), and Nancy Armstrong, *Desire and Domestic Fiction: A Political History of the Novel* (Oxford University Press, 1989). Cf. also Nancy Armstrong and Leonard Tennenhouse, *The Violence of Representation: Literature and the History of Violence* (Routledge, 1989). And in *Families in Jeopardy: Regulating the Social Body in France, 1750–1910* (Stanford University Press, 1993), Roddey Reid carries out an astute reading of familial discourse and the political and social mechanisms of that nation.

9. "Britania and Her Daughter. A Song," published March 8, 1780, by I. Mills, No. 1 Ratcliff Road near the French Hospital Old Street. It is reprinted in various collections, including Peter Thomas, *The English Satirical Print, 1600–1832: The American Revolution* (Chadwyck-Healey, 1986), p. 213. Thomas also reprints a cartoon called "The World turned upside down, or The Old Woman taught Wisdom," in which the doggerel reads, in part, "Goody Bull and her Daughter together fell out, / Both squabbled and wrangled, and made a damn'd Rout; / Derry Down, etc." In this version of the story, her mother wants her to earn her own bread and America resists, retorting that "If her Mother persisted, she'd turn common Whore." Daughterly rebellion carries the day and the verse ends impertinently: "'tis all a meer Farce, / As I've carried my point, you may now kiss my —— [sic]" (p. 59). See also Bruce Granger, *Political Satire in the American Revolution, 1763–1873* (Cornell University Press, 1960).

10. See the discussion of the concept of the "republican mother" in Linda Kerber, *Women of the Republic: Intellect and Ideology in Revolutionary America* (University of North Carolina Press, 1980), p. 158.

11. Jay Fliegelman, *Prodigals and Pilgrims: The American Revolution Against Patriarchal Authority, 1750–1800* (Cambridge University Press, 1982).

12. Cathy Davidson, *Revolution and the Word: The Rise of the Novel in America* (Oxford University Press, 1986).

13. Several cartoons reproduced in Dolmetsch show a British lion with a severed paw and British ministers examining the bleeding stump—dismemberment and, by extension, castration can be figured through this emblem, though it does not disturb identifications of Britania.

14. "The Colonies Reduced" was produced sometime around 1765 in response to the Townshend Acts. First shown in England, it was then copied by

Benjamin Franklin and reportedly used on his stationery. The legend, *Date Obolum Belisario*, refers to the downfall of the Roman Bellisarius, forced to beg for alms. The ships have broomsticks tied to their masts as a sign that they are for sale. See Charles Press, *The Political Cartoon* (Fairleigh Dickinson University Press, 1981).

The "colonies reduced" can also be read as a response to the 1592 portrait of Queen Elizabeth with her feet on the globe and her head in the clouds (the so-called "Ditchley portrait," by Marcus Gheeraerts the Younger, in the National Portrait Gallery in London). This portrait is discussed by Montrose (pp. 13–14), who develops his discussion of Sir Walter Ralegh and the Amazons "just beyond the receding geographical boundary of *terra incognita*" in terms of the "conceptual shift from *the land as woman* to *a land of women*" (25).

15. The spectator is called to give alms and to read the body parts, but the form of bodily legibility expressed here may emphasize consumption over sympathy.

16. *Over Her Dead Body: Death, Feminity and the Aesthetic*, Elisabeth Bronfen (Routledge, 1992), p. xi. See also Michael Rogin on "political amnesia" during Reagan's presidency, "'Make My Day!' Spectacle as Amnesia in Imperial Politics" in *Cultures of United States Imperialism*, edited by Amy Kaplan and Donald Pease (Duke University Press, 1993), pp. 499–534. Cf. also Klaus Theweleit, who proposes that the "over-explicitness of the fascist language of symbol" works to "safeguard both writer and reader against the experiences they fear." *Male Fantasies: Volume Two; Male Bodies: Psychoanalyzing the White Terror*, trans. Erica Carter and Chris Turner (University of Minnesota Press, 1989), p. 6.

17. Men are also in a homoerotic relation to each other here: France's dagger stabs England frontally as Spain stabs her from behind. Lord Bute, Spain, and the church each hold phallic objects, ready to penetrate the same female buttocks, while Lord Bute urges the other two to "Strike it Home." The erotic energy here is not so much in their not yet accomplished penetration as in their urging each other on.

18. Franklin's best-known print, "Join or Die," refers to a superstition that a snake cut into pieces would survive if the pieces were reunited by sundown. Produced in 1765 as a warning for the colonies to stand united, it was used to galvanize struggles against both Indians and the Stamp Act, and was often reprinted as a masthead in Revolutionary newspapers. A later cartoon by Thomas Gillray, "The American Rattle Snake" (1782), shows a snake coiled around British armies.

19. Sade's *"La philosophie dans le boudoir* is one of the most revealing texts about the revolutionary political unconscious." Lynn Hunt, *The Family Romance of the French Revolution* (University of California Press, 1992), p. 125. See also Frances Ferguson, "Sade and the Pornographic Legacy," *Representations* 36 (Fall 1991).

20. In Joan Scott, *Gender and the Politics of History* (Columbia University Press, 1988).

21. Cf. Anthony Vidler, *The Architectural Uncanny: Essays on the Modern Unhomely* (MIT, 1992). On Lincoln and the house divided, cf. George Forgie, *Patricide in the House Divided: A Psychological Portrait of Lincoln and His Age* (Norton, 1976).

22. Carol Clover, *Men, Women, and Chainsaws: Gender in the Modern Horror Film* (Princeton University Press, 1991), p. 30.

23. Thomas Paine, "Common Sense," reprinted in *The Life and Major Writings of Thomas Paine*, ed. Philip Foner (Citadel Press, 1974), p. 125. Michael

Grossberg comments that "the intimate relationship between political and family change is evident in the readiness of revolutionaries like Tom Paine to describe the crisis with Britain as a domestic quarrel" (7). Michael Grossberg, *Governing the Hearth: Law and the Family in Nineteenth-Century America* (University of North Carolina Press, 1985). Jay Fliegelman's *Prodigals and Pilgrims* studies the influence of familial concepts on political structures, especially as revealed in the literature of the eighteenth century. In the course of an argument about the effects of new forms of the family on both government and novels, he claims that the "new parenting and the constitutional government were intimately related" (161).

24. Cf. Eric Hobsbawm, *The Age of Revolution: 1789–1848* (New American Library, 1964).

25. Juliet Flower MacCannell, *The Regime of the Brother: After Patriarchy* (Routledge, 1991) and Dean MacCannell, "Democracy's Turn: On Homeless Noir" in Joan Copjec, ed., *Shades of Noir: A Reader* (Verso, 1993), pp. 279–298.

26. An example of the translation of revolutionary unrest into familial violence in the French context occurs in the events related in *I Pierre Riviere, Having Slaughtered My Mother, My Sister, and My Brother . . . A Case of Parricide in the Nineteenth Century*, ed. Michel Foucault, trans. Frank Jellinek (University of Nebraska Press, 1975). See the thoughtful commentary, "The Animal, The Madman, and Death" by Jean-Pierre Peter and Jeanne Farret, pp. 175–198. See also Mikkel Borch-Jacobsen, who, in his commentary on what many consider the original model of the "band of brothers" in Freud's *Totem and Taboo*, asserts that "the organization of the group thus reproduces that of the family . . . the libidinal-political economy is analogous to the libidinal-domestic economy (patriarchal as always)." *The Emotional Tie: Psychoanalysis, Mimesis, and Affect*, trans. Douglas Brick et al. (Stanford University Press, 1992) p. 162.

27. According to Lynn Hunt, "most Europeans in the eighteenth century thought of . . . their nations as families writ large" and that often meant reciprocally that "authority in the state was explicitly modeled on authority in the family." Hunt, 5, xiv, 3. On the family/state analogy, see also Roddey Reid, *Families in Jeopardy*; Constance Jordan, "The Household and the State: Transformations in the Representation of an Analogy from Aristotle to James I," *MLQ* 54 (September 1993) 307–321; and Edwin Burrows and Michael Wallace, "The American Revolution: The Ideology and Psychology of National Liberation," *Perspectives in American History*, vol. 6 (Harvard University Press, 1972).

Lynn Hunt decrees that "by *family romance* I mean the collective, unconscious images of the familial order that underlie revolutionary politics" (xiii). See Freud's "Family Romances," vol. 9 of *The Standard Edition of the Complete Works of Sigmund Freud*, trans. James Strachey (Hogarth, 1959), pp. 238–239. Reid finds that "'family' is no prediscursive given but rather a highly productive rearticulation of discursive and nondiscursive relations, which has been realigning bodies, spaces, and subjectivities since the late eighteenth century" (7). Also see Fredric Jameson, "The structure of the psyche is historical and has a history" in *The Political Unconscious: Narrative as a Socially Symbolic Act* (Cornell University Press, 1981) p. 62. The French Revolution affects democracy and the family—the end of patriarchy and the rise of fraternity is also the rise of "contract" (180). On the relation of sexual and social contract, cf. Carol Pateman, *The Sexual Contract* (Stanford University Press, 1988), pp. 12, 36, 114, which derives from Claude Levi-Strauss, *Elementary Structures of Kinship*, trans. Bell and von Sturmer (Beacon, 1969), p. 490: "The rules of kinship and marriage are not made necessary by the social state. They are the social state itself."

28. Hunt claims that "whenever a political message required an allegorical presentation, the allegory almost always centered on female figures" (82). Cf. Marina Warner, *Monuments and Maidens: The Allegory of the Female Form* (Atheneum, 1985), pp. xx, 277; cf. Lynn Hunt, *Politics, Culture, and Class in the French Revolution* (University of California Press, 1984). See also Joan Landes, *Women and the Public Sphere in the Age of the French Revolution* (Cornell University Press, 1988).

29. Hunt, pp. 158, 151, 161 (from a pamphlet published in 1797). The War of 1812, it has been suggested, produced a generational break for the American republic: the sons of the founding fathers, by this view, wanted to have their own war so they could now be fathers as well. Richard Rush (son of Benjamin Rush) gave an oration in favor of the War of 1812 in which he proleptically lamented that if there were no war, "where would be the spirit, where the courage of the slain fathers? Snatched and gone from ignoble sons?" (162). "An Oration, Delivered in the House of Representatives, July 4, 1812" (Washington D.C., 1812), in Stephen Watts, *The Republic Reborn: War and the Making of Liberal America* (Johns Hopkins University Press, 1989). Watts comments that the "son discerned an occasion for equalizing and possibly even surpassing the achievements of the Fathers" (207) and traces the argument about the family allegory of the colonies to references to a "band of 13 brothers" in the *Philadephia Aurora* of 1812. This is not to forget that women *were* political participants in the rhetoric of revolutionary politics. "Remember the Ladies," insisted Abigail Adams in 1776, and her extraordinary contemporaries, such as Mercy Otis Warren and Judith Sargent Murray, made sure almost everyone did. It may be more of a comment on the successful production of an ideological apparatus that repeatedly tries to write women out of politics to notice that despite their emancipatory writings it is easier to locate repression in popular representations of women as political symbols than to find them as participants.

30. In using *Romances of the Republic* as my title I intend to refer to the family romance, in the way that Lynn Hunt uses the term: to talk about the relation between political and familial desires. I also refer to work on history as romance (cf. David Levin, *History as Romantic Art* [Stanford University Press, 1959] or Harry Henderson's *Versions of the Past* [Oxford University Press, 1974]), to the romance vs. novel distinction (still traced best by Richard Chase in *The American Novel and Its Tradition* [Doubleday, 1957]), and to the narratives of romance as seduction.

31. Susan Ridley Sedgwick, *Allen Prescott: or the Fortunes of a New England Boy* (Harper Bros., 1834) II, pp. 26–27. To use a "female figure of speech," as Sedgwick does here, is perhaps to insert the female body into the garment of government. Nonetheless, the passage exhibits some confusion about whether "women are not made to feel its existence" because government invades their "tenderest affections" or because it refrains from invading them. The apparent passivity of the women being fitted by their garment government is undercut when Sedgwick adds: "But let this same garment give token of fracture, decay or uneasy alteration, we should find their tongues move as quickly as their needles" (II, 27).

32. Discussion of the cult of domesticity began with Barbara Welter's "The Cult of True Womanhood, 1820–1860," *American Quarterly* 18 (1966) 151–174.

Feminist critics have continued to question whether focusing on the "separation" of women in nineteenth-century America reinforces the separation, implicitly reasserting a sexual segregation, or produces a necessary corrective, ensuring that, as Gerda Lerner puts it, the majority finds its past. Gerda Lerner, "The Lady and the Mill Girl: Changes in the Status of Women in the Age of Jackson," in *The Majority Finds its Past: Placing Women in History* (Oxford University Press, 1979).

Nancy Cott, for example, whose influential argument about the "bonds of womanhood" presents the "paradox" that the 1830s were simultaneously the decade of the "ideology of domesticity" that kept women in the home, and feminism, which sought roles for women outside the home, usefully summarizes the major feminist treatments of the period, which see women variously as victims of the ideology of domesticity, or as capable of using that ideology for their own ends and discovering in domesticity a source of power and community. Nancy Cott, *The Bonds of Womanhood: "Woman's Sphere" in New England, 1780–1835* (Yale University Press, 1977), pp. 5, 197–206. She notes that the more primary and private the documents that historians examine, the more they argue for the last position. Carroll Smith-Rosenberg revised doctrines of mid-nineteenth-century domesticity by reviewing diaries and letters written by women whose "female world of love and ritual," she argues, provided a powerful alternative to the more constricting worlds of love and ritual men provided. Carroll Smith-Rosenberg, *Disorderly Conduct: Visions of Gender in Victorian America* (Knopf, 1985). See also the essays by Linda Kerber and Alfred Young in Harriet Applewhite and Darline Levy, eds., *Women and Politics in the Age of the Democratic Revolutions* (University of Michigan Press, 1990); and Elaine Crane, "Dependence in the Era of Independence: The Role of Women in a Republican Society" in Jack Green, ed., *The American Revolution: Its Character and Limits* (New York University Press, 1987), pp. 253–275.

33. Kerber, p. 238. She continues, "The notion that a mother can perform a political function represents the recognition that . . . the family is a basic part of the system of political communication and that patterns of family authority influence the general political culture" (283). For a somewhat different account of republican ideology, see Jan Lewis, "The Republican Wife: Virtue and Seduction in the Early Republic," *William and Mary Quarterly* 44 (October 1987) 689–721. Noting that since "eighteenth-century thought [did not] erect a barrier between the private state of the family and the public one of the world, it could dramatize issues of authority in terms of relationships between members of a family," she claims that marriage was the "republican model for social and political relationships" (693, 689). There was a further consequence, however: "In shifting interest from the parent-child nexus to the husband-wife bond, eighteenth-century authors necessarily raised women to a new moral and political stature" (699).

34. *Diary and Autobiography of John Adams*, ed. L. H. Butterfield et al. (Harvard University Press, 1961), 4:123. In *At Odds: Women and the Family in America from the Revolution to the Present* (Oxford University Press, 1980), the social historian Carl Degler has argued that what he calls the "modern American family" emerged between the revolution and 1830 (8). Tracing the decline of parental influence in arranging nineteenth-century marriages, Degler reiterates that the "order of the state" was seen to rest on childrearing (14). See his discussion of the nineteenth-century New England minister Frances Wayland's theories of childrearing (97). For further analyses of Wayland and, more generally, of childrearing in the period, see Richard Brodhead, *Cultures of Letters: Scenes of Reading*

and Writing in Nineteenth-Century America (University of Chicago Press, 1993) esp. chap. 1, "Sparing the Rod: Discipline and Fiction in Antebellum America"; Michael Rogin, *Subversive Genealogy: The Politics and Art of Herman Melville* (Knopf, 1984), pp. 187–192; and Bernard Wishy, *The Child and the Republic* (University of Pennsylvania Press, 1968). See also Mary Ryan, *Cradle of the Middle Class: The Family in Oneida County, New York, 1800–1860* (Cambridge University Press, 1981), pp. 24–26.

35. Michael Grossberg uses the term "republican family" as "the label that identifies most precisely the context and content of the changes that began to alter American households in the 1780s and 1790s and into the next century" (6). Whereas in the colonial period, "the family was seen as a public institution tightly integrated into a well-ordered society," or as "a little commonwealth," after the American Revolution there was a "crucial transition of the family from a public to a private institution. The economic moorings of the household shifted from production toward consumption . . . A new domestic egalitarianism emerged to challenge patriarchy. Other alterations included companionate marriage practices and contractual notions of spousal relations, an elevation of childhood and motherhood to favored status within the home, an emphasis on domestic intimacy as a counterweight to marketplace competition, and a more clearly defined use of private property as the major source of domestic autonomy." Along with these changes, the "new concept of the family" meant that "heightened emotional and affective bonds and socialization duties were seen by almost all Americans as crucial to national well-being" (pp. 4–6). See also John Demos, *A Little Commonwealth: Family Life in Plymouth Colony* (Oxford University Press, 1970).

36. For a different emphasis on the relation of the family to a social structure see Jurgen Habermas, *The Structural Transformation of the Public Sphere*, trans. Thomas Burger with Frederick Lawrence (MIT Press, 1989). He remarks on "the ambivalence of the family as an agent of society yet simultaneously as the emancipation from society" (55).

37. David Hoffman, *Miscellaneous Thoughts on Men, Manners, and Things; by Anthony Grumbler, of Grumbleton Hall, Esq.* (1837), quoted in Maxwell Bloomfield, *Lawyers in a Changing Society, 1776–1876* (Harvard University Press, 1976), p. 91.

38. Grossberg, p. 9. He does not find that this empowers women, however: "The distinction between the male authority to govern the household and female responsibility to maintain it and nurture its wards . . . perpetuated patriarchy in republican society" (27). John and Virginia Demos describe the "maternal associations" that arose in the 1820s and 1830s and the thousands of books on childrearing published after 1825 as indicative of a "deep anxiety" about family government in "Adolescence in Historical Perspective," reprinted in *The American Family in Social-Historical Perspective* (St. Martin's Press, 1973), pp. 209–221. See also Carl Kaestle, *Pillars of the Republic: Common Schools and American Society, 1780–1860* (Hill and Wang, 1983), and Monica Kiefer, *American Children Through Their Books 1700–1835* (University of Pennsylvania Press, 1948).

39. George Forgie, *Patricide in the House Divided: A Psychological Interpretation of Lincoln and His Age* (Norton, 1979), p. 18. Anne Norton finds that "Americans of the antebellum period were preoccupied by the revision of traditional familial roles and by the perceived decay of the family" (266). In *From Colonies to Commonwealth: Familial Ideology and the Beginnings of the American Republic*

(Johns Hopkins, 1985), Melvin Yazawa claims instead that "the familial paradigm lost much of its explanatory power as a result of the Revolution" since "republicanism seemed to require a depersonalization of the diverse public patterns of authority and subordination, patterns found ultimately not in affection but in 'mechanics'" (3–4). For another discussion of the invention of "patriarchal authority" in the postrevolutionary period, see Cynthia Jordan, *Second Stories: The Politics of Language, Form, and Gender in Early American Fictions* (University of North Carolina Press, 1989), pp. 18–23.

40. John Quincy Adams, "Address . . . on the Occasion of Reading the Declaration of Independence on the Fourth of July 1821," reprinted in Arthur Shaffer, *The Politics of History: Writing the History of the American Revolution, 1783–1815* (Precedent, 1975). George Bancroft argued similarly that the inclination toward the principles of democracy was not a matter of learned but of instinctive behavior: "it is not education that teaches the mother to love her child . . . the principle applies equally to political truth; there is an instinct of liberty . . . and our fathers listened to it and took counsel of it." Bancroft, "An Oration Delivered before the Democracy of Springfield, July 4, 1836" (Merriam, 1836), p. 18.

41. The states will cooperate because they are "political brethren." Appropriately grateful for the political opportunities that have been opened for him at least partially through reliance on these familial metaphors, Jackson closes by "thank[ing] God . . . that he has given me a heart to love my country with the affection of a son." Jackson in 1837, reprinted in *Memoirs of General Andrew Jackson* (James C. Derby & Co., 1845) by "anon., a citizen of New York," pp. 226, 241.

42. In *Foundational Fictions*, Doris Sommer finds "the romantic novel as perhaps the most significant discursive medium for national development" (84). There is a practical aspect to such a strategy: "Marriage not only projected an ideal state, but also helped to realize the family alliances that supported national governments" (88).

43. Catherine Sedgwick, *The Linwoods, or "Sixty Years Since" in America* (Harper & Bros., 1835) (II, 285). For a further treatment of the novel, see Chapter 3. Several early national sources make similar points about, for example, how "marriage has ever been considered by every wise state the sinew of its strength and the foundation of its true greatness," declaring, indeed, "the absolute necessity of marriage for the service of the state." "The Reflector No. 1," *Ladies Monitor*, November 17, 1801, p. 92 and "Reflections on Marriage," *Pennsylvania Magazine*, September 1775, p. 408, reprinted as "Letters on Marriage" in *The Works of the Rev. John Witherspoon . . .* , 2d ed. (Philadelphia, 1802), IV, 161–183 (quoted in Jan Lewis, 709).

44. Catherine Sedgwick, *The Linwoods* (I, 53).

45. Michel Foucault, "Governmentality," *Ideology and Consensus*, 6 (Autumn 1979), 17. Reprinted in *The Foucault Effect: Studies in Governmentality*, ed. Graham Burchell et al. (University of Chicago Press, 1991), pp. 87–104.

46. Ruth Bloch argues, for instance, that the "movement toward a more personal, domestic, and feminized definition of morality in the 1780s and 1790s was linked to a greater acceptance of institutional public order," an order found through "churches, schools, and families." "The Gendered Meanings of Virtue in Revolutionary America," *Signs* 13 (1987) 37–58.

47. The nineteenth-century American publishing industry focused on women

as authors, readers, and subjects, as the call went out for women to "save your country" by reforming at home. We have seen how the "melange of politics, popular literature, and family affairs illustrates the centrality of domesticity in the national system of values." Mary Ryan argues that the maternal organizations and "Mother's Magazines" in the 1820s and 1830s, which seemed to indicate that the empire of the mother had already been established, instead preceded the transfer of authority in childrearing from male to female in the 1840s and 1850s, and that early nineteenth-century publication of various tenets of the cult of domesticity preceded and perhaps even caused its formation. Indeed, she argues, the publishing industry proclaimed a "new set of domestic norms" and pushed a "premature" image of the modern family, which they might be said to have created by describing.

Seeking to trouble the relation between producers and consumers of this domestic literature in *Empire of the Mother*, Ryan denigrates historians' reliance on "house-keeping manuals, ladies magazines and mother's books" because she finds them prescriptive rather than descriptive, indicating desires rather than practices. While Ryan wants to "solve" the "gnarly conceptual problems that lurk in the relationship between women and the family," her method of proceeding is somewhat ambivalent; she wants to "relax this fixation on the relationship between women and the family," while at the same time she calls for a more critical analysis of the "institution of the family." Mary Ryan, *Empire of the Mother: American Writing About Domesticity, 1830–1860. Women and History*, Nos. 2/3. (Haworth Press, 1982), pp. 2, 3, 8, 40, 97, 137. For good discussions of mothers in nineteenth-century American literature, see Stephanie Smith, *Conceived by Liberty: Maternal Images and American Literature* (Cornell University Press, 1994) and Eva Cherniavsky, *That Pale Mother Rising: Sentimental Discourses and the Imitation of Motherhood in 19th-Century America* (Indiana University Press, 1995).

48. This admission into the family made reviewers all the more anxious that the novel be morally sound and they stressed "the potential of the novel as an agent for female acculturation." Nina Baym, *Novels, Readers, and Reviewers* (Cornell University Press, 1984), pp. 245, 49, 98. The novel's place in this relation has been explored by critics who have produced accounts of the early Republic which present women as producers and consumers of literary texts (e.g., Mary Kelley and Mary Ryan) or explain their responses to popular fiction (Nina Baym). In *Sensational Designs* (Oxford University Press, 1985), Jane Tompkins views literary works as "attempts to redefine the social order." She finds that the improbably contrived plots of this fiction "serve as a means of stating and proposing solutions for social and political predicaments." Nancy Cott, in contrast, argues that rather than having "designs upon their readers," such literature becomes popular because "it does not have to persuade . . . it addresses readers who are ready for it" (2). For another provocative exploration of the period, see Karen Halttunen, *Confidence Men and Painted Women: A Study of Middle-Class Culture in America, 1830–1870* (Yale University Press, 1982). The most complete treatment of the novel in this period is by Cathy Davidson in *Revolution and the Word: The Rise of the Novel in America* (Oxford University Press, 1986). For another reading of this material see Susan K. Harris, *Nineteenth Century American Women's Novels: Interpretive Strategies* (Cambridge University Press, 1990), pp. 2–12. In *American Women Writers and the Work of History, 1790–1860* (Rutgers University Press, 1995), Nina Baym argues for the public nature of women's writing about history in the nineteenth century and suggests that the home is an appropriately "public

sphere" (as opposed to the "official sphere" Habermas proposes as the place of politics).

49. In the new *Cambridge History of American Literature* (Cambridge University Press, 1994), Michael Gilmore takes it for granted that fiction and the new nation arose together. Hunt asserts that "the rise of the novel and the emergence of interest in children and a more affective family went hand in hand. It is in fact impossible to tell which—the novel or the child-centered family—was cause and which was effect" (21). Hunt further finds, in 1792 and later, a "literal effacement of the political father" and "a new family romance of fraternity: brother and sister appeared frequently in this iconographic outpouring, mothers rarely, and fathers almost never" (53). Cf. further Anne Dalke, who argues that "the typical grouping of kin in early American fiction is most often a profligate father, a dead mother, an illegitimate daughter, and a legitimate son and heir. The family unit is not dissolved by incest." "Original Vice: The Political Implications of Incest in the Early American Novel," *EAL* 23 (1988) 188. She credits Rogin (in *Fathers and Children* [Knopf, 1975], pp. 20–21, 28, 49) with explaining "the Lockean ideal of the 'natural family'" (191) with contractual family relations and thinks that class is the real issue that incest "covers" for or exposes.

50. A great deal of attention has been paid to American nationalism and some of my notes in the following pages cite and respond to it. What I want to do here is to mention a few recent treatments, while acknowledging the limits of my scope. In *The Wretched of the Earth* (Grove, 1966), Frantz Fanon argues that national culture should make the "history of the nation part of the personal experience of each of its citizens" (21). A number of recent works—such as Slavoj Zizek's *For They Know Not What They Do* (Verso, 1989), Benedict Anderson's *Imagined Communities*, Anne Norton's *Reflections on Political Identity*, George Mosse's *Nationalism and Sexuality* (H. Fertig, 1985), the collection *Nationalisms and Sexualities* (Routledge, 1992)—have attempted to relate personal experiences to political conceptions. Their particular value is to question how groups achieve an identity in commonality and how nations secure this identity along with its desires and embodiments. As Lauren Berlant succinctly summarizes this burgeoning approach, "Modern citizens are born in nations and are taught to perceive the nation as an intimate quality of identity" *The Anatomy of National Fantasy* (University of Chicago, 1991), p. 20. In locating the "counter-memory" of nationalism, I would like to think about its stresses as well as its successes.

The political theorist Anne Norton finds that in the acquisition of national identity perhaps the most effective persuasive tactic may be the use of "[f]amilial metaphors" such as "mother, father, brother" (11). She cautions that, in the United States, received notions of nationalism often appear as a New England tradition and may not be applicable to the South, or to indigenous peoples, or to captive people. Throwing cold water on the personal attributes given to national identifications, John Breuilly asserts in *Nationalism and the State* (St. Martin's Press, 1982) that "to focus upon culture, ideology, identity, class, or modernisation is to neglect the fundamental point that nationalism is, above and beyond all else, about politics and that politics is about power" (1–2). Yet, he goes on to admit, "nationalism clearly builds upon some sense of cultural identity, even if it is the major creator of that sense" (35). In counterposing these critics, I want to suggest that nationalism as a historical enterprise involves something like the relation of literature to culture, in which one finds a reciprocal formation, paradoxically shaping and being shaped, so that while the details of such identities continue to fascinate, a search for origins can deflect attention from the operations in play. See also the essays by Anne Norton and Bonnie Honig in Frederick Dolan and Thomas Dumm, eds., *Rhetorical Republic: Governing Representations in American Politics* (University of Massachusetts Press, 1993).

51. To read literary texts as cultural symptoms can itself still appear as a fraught enterprise. A recent attack on new historicism may help in thinking about my claims: "The way the New Historicists construe the relation between literary texts and the cultural system . . . reduces the social to the status of a function of the cultural and then further reduces the cultural to the status of a text." Hayden White critiques a series of "fallacies" of New Historicism, including the "genetic fallacy," that texts grow out of contexts, the "referential fallacy," that they refer to an "outside" world, and a "culturalist fallacy," that the function of culture is implicitly to produce political and social systems rather than vice versa. In disclaiming referentiality while suggesting that political and social systems produce culture, these last two fallacies contradict each other. This book attempts to show the *relation* of texts and contexts, and attempts to avoid organicism or an impossible-to-achieve account of origins. It does not argue that the "function of culture" is to produce social and political systems, implicitly or otherwise. Rather, a continual interconnection of political, cultural, and social systems produces significant narratives about families and states and I want to unpack, with as much specificity as possible, just how such systems become visible and available to us now in the traces of their interactions, traces most readily available as texts.

Hayden White's article is largely a response to a formulation (and critique) by Elizabeth Fox-Genovese. He asks, "Is the literary text to be accorded any special status as a 'function or articulation' of its context? Does the literary text 'function' as an especially privileged historical datum, not only yielding insight into the nature of its context but also providing a model for the study of that context as well?" (298). He calls the particular material that new historicists use the "episodic, anecdotal, contingent, exotic, abjected, or simply uncanny aspects of the historical record. . . . they appear to escape, transcend, contravene, undermine, or contest the rules, law, and principles of the modes of social organization, structures of political superordination and subordination, and cultural codes predominating at the time of their appearance" (301).

Chapter 1

1. William Gordon, *The Letters of William Gordon*, Massachusetts Historical Society, *Proceedings*, 62 (October 1929–June, 1930), p. 393. Quoted in Lester Cohen, *The Revolutionary Histories* (Cornell University Press, 1980), p. 166.

2. Mason Weems, "God's Revenge Against Adultery," reprinted in *Three Discourses*, (Random House, 1929), p. 143. Subsequent page numbers will be cited parenthetically.

3. Paine's work cost threepence, while William Godwin's *Political Justice* was prohibitively expensive at three guineas. "The Prime Minister, Pitt, is said to have withheld prosecution of Godwin . . . only because he believed the high price of *Political Justice* too high to do much harm. Pitt did not anticipate, however, that clubs of working men would buy the book with collective funds and read it aloud." (McCracken, *Caleb Williams*, pp. ix–x).

4. Mason Weems even peddled a version of Paine's *Complete Works* that contained a reply in the place of the *Age of Reason*. Reported in E. E. Skeel, ed., *Mason Locke Weems, His Works and Ways* (Privately printed, 1929), p. 296.

5. Timothy Dwight, *A Discourse on Some Events of the Last Century* (New Haven, 1801), reprinted in *American Thought and Writing*, eds. Russel Nye and Norman Grabo (Houghton Mifflin, 1965), pp. 265–67.

6. *Ibid.*, p. 268.

7. Clifford Griffin, "Religious Benevolence as Social Control, 1815–1860," reprinted in David Brion Davis, *Ante-Bellum Reform*, (Harper & Row, 1967), pp. 95, 91, 94. The first phrases quoted are by Emory Washburn, speaking on the Bible Society in 1847; the last is from the publications of the Home Missionary Society in 1837.

8. For an excellent discussion of the relation between the family and the institution in the period, see David Rothman, *The Discovery of the Asylum: Social Order and Disorder in the New Republic* (Little, Brown, 1971).

9. Charles Brockden Brown, *Wieland, or The Transformation; an American Tale*, (Kent State University Press, 1977), p. 30.

10. From Thomas Robbins's *Diaries*; quoted by David Ludlum, *Social Ferment in Vermont, 1791–1800* (Columbia University Press, 1939), p. 30.

11. Thomas Paine, *The Life and Major Writings of Thomas Paine*, ed. Philip Foner (Citadel Press, 1974), p. 125.

12. *Ibid.*, p. 19. John Adams similarly echoed the rhetoric of many Revolutionary pamphlets: "The people of America had been educated in an habitual affection for England, as their mother country. . . . But when they found her . . . willing like Lady Macbeth, to 'dash their brains out,' it is no wonder if their filial affections ceased." Reprinted in *American Thought and Writing*, eds. Russel Nye and Norman Grabo (Houghton Mifflin, 1965), p. 89.

13. *Ibid.*, p. 30. In an argument about how gender and nationalism inflect what she calls the "National Symbolic," Lauren Berlant cites Karl Marx using a similar conflation: "A nation and a woman are not forgiven the unguarded hour in which the first adventurer that came along could violate them." *The Eighteenth Brumaire of Louis Bonaparte*, cited in Lauren Berlant, *The Anatomy of National Fantasy: Hawthorne, Utopia, and Everyday Life* (University of Chicago Press, 1991), p. 19.

14. *Ibid.*, p. 214.

15. *Ibid.*, p. 155.

16. Neil Hertz has discussed the French Revolution in terms of, as he describes it, "the representation of what would seem to be a political threat as if it were a sexual threat" in "Medusa's Head: Male Hysteria in the Face of Political Pressure," *Representations* 4 (University of California Press, 1983), p. 43. In her reply to Hertz's article, Catherine Gallagher explains the importance of the threat of the "loose woman" in political discourse with a reading of the patriarchal system of land ownership in which (since it relied so heavily on primogeniture in the eighteenth century) the possibility of illegitimacy was a disturbingly disruptive negation of the system of power. Catherine Gallagher, "Reply to Hertz," *Representations* 4, p. 51. For further exploration of the relations of family structure, inheritance, and property distributions, see Lawrence Stone, *The Family, Sex, and Marriage in England 1500–1800* (Harper & Row, 1979). For an interesting discussion of the treatment of

illegitimacy during the French Revolution, see Crane Brinton, *French Revolutionary Legislation on Illegitimacy* (Harvard University Press, 1953).

17. Dwight, p. 269.

18. Henry Cabot Lodge, *Life and Letters of George Cabot* (Little, Brown, 1878), pp. 160, 78.

19. John Miller, *Crisis in Freedom: The Alien and Sedition Acts* (Little, Brown, 1952), p. 40.

20. Miller, pp. 41, 43. Timothy Dwight also presented political alliance with France in these terms: "To ally America to France is to chain living health and beauty to a corpse dissolving with the plague . . . the touch of France is pollution, her embrace is death" ("Discourse in Two Parts" [1812], quoted in Leon Howard, *The Connecticut Wits* [University of Chicago Press, 1943], p. 390).

21. *Life and Major Writings of Thomas Paine*, p. 132. George Gibbs, *Memoirs of the Administrations of Washington and John Adams* (Printed for Subscribers, 1846), vol. 2, p. 118.

22. Norman Grabo, for instance, has an interesting account of the plague as it forms the background for *Arthur Mervyn* in the "Historical Essay" of the bicentennial edition. Robert Levine asserts that "in plague-stricken Philadelphia, Mervyn experiences an American version of the Reign of Terror" ("Arthur Mervyn's Revolutions," *Studies in American Fiction* 12 [1984], 152). See also Robert Ferguson, "Yellow Fever and Charles Brockden Brown: The Context of the Emerging Novelist," *Early American Literature* 14 (1980), 293–305. For an intriguing study of the conjunction between political attitudes and the treatment of disease in America, see Martha Banta, "Medical Therapies and the Body Politic," *Prospects* (1983). A similar approach to politicized methods of "treatment" informs the chapter on Benjamin Rush in Ronald Takaki, *Iron Cages: Race and Culture in Nineteenth Century America* (University of Washington Press, 1979). Rush's violent defense of his often murderous method of bleeding and purging is explored in detail by J. H. Powell, *Bring Out Your Dead: The Great Plague of Yellow Fever in Philadelphia in 1793* (University of Pennsylvania Press, 1949). See also William Hedges, "Benjamin Rush, Charles Brockden Brown, and the American Plague Year," *Early American Literature* 7 (1973) 295–311.

23. In making such an argument, I have been influenced by the adaptation of Michel Foucault's analyses to literary criticism, and especially by the treatment of Foucault in Mark Seltzer's *Henry James and the Art of Power* (Cornell University Press, 1984).

24. Charles Brockden Brown, *Arthur Mervyn, or Memoirs of the Year 1793*, (Kent State University Press, 1980), p. 21. Subsequent references will be cited parenthetically, preceded by AM.

25. Norman Grabo, *The Coincidental Art of Charles Brockden Brown* (University of North Carolina Press, 1982) p. 105. For another account of Philadelphia in the 1790s, see Henry May, "Philadelphia and the World," in *The Enlightenment in America* (Oxford University Press, 1976). He reports that the "plague was blamed by different sufferers on God's anger with irreligion, contagions brought by the French, neglect of urban conditions . . . or the mistakes of Enlightenment doctors" (p. 222). For two methodologically different but complementary analyses of Philadelphia during this period see E. Digby Baltzell, *Puritan Boston and Quaker Philadelphia* (Beacon Press, 1979), and Carl and Jessica Bridenbaugh, *Rebels and Gentlemen, Philadelphia in the Age of Franklin* (Oxford University Press, 1968).

See also Robert Levine, *Conspiracy and Romance: Studies in Brockden Brown, Cooper, Hawthorne, and Melville* (Cambridge University Press, 1989).

26. Alternately, the action of the novel has been viewed as proceeding from the malignant agency of Arthur. See, for instance, Emory Elliott, "Narrative Unity and Moral Resolution in *Arthur Mervyn*," *Critical Essays on Charles Brockden Brown*, ed. Bernard Rosenthal (G. K. Hall, 1981).

27. And it also seems reminiscent of the career of Benjamin Rush, who acted as both moral and physical physician to Philadelphians in the 1790s. For Rush's relationship with his apprentice/son see Takaki, *Iron Cages.*

28. Alan Axelrod, *Charles Brockden Brown: An American Tale* (University of Texas Press, 1983), p. 154.

29. *Ibid.*, p. 141. Axelrod concludes that "the complexities of inherited familial and political ties are absent from this novel. They are replaced by the . . . nexus of cash" (pp. 146–47).

30. Grabo, p. 103.

31. This notion was enforced in law as early as 1636 when Connecticut enacted legislation requiring single persons to reside with families. The intent if not the form of such legislation was repeated through the time of the young republic. See Robert Bremner, ed., *Children and Youth in America, 1600–1835*, vol. 1 (Harvard University Press, 1970).

32. According to Michel Foucault, there is a direct connection between measures taken to control plagues and the rise of disciplinary institutions generally in the eighteenth century. "The plague-stricken town," Foucault argues, "provided an exceptional disciplinary model"; the "plague is met by order . . . the penetration of regulation into even the smallest details of everyday life" (*Discipline and Punish: The Birth of the Prison*, trans. Alan Sheridan [New York: Pantheon, 1977], pp. 207, 197–198). Such penetration of regulation, focused, however, on the disciplinary model of the family, marks, I will be arguing, the administration of the Philadelphia plague.

33. Mathew Carey, *A Short Account of the Malignant Fever, lately prevalent in Philadelphia* (Philadelphia, November 14, 1793), p. 34. Subsequent references will be cited parenthetically in the text, preceded by SA.

34. Reprinted in David Lee Clark, *Charles Brockden Brown: Pioneer Voice of America* (Duke University Press, 1952), p. 61. Further biographical parallels exist with Brown's nursing of his good friend Dr. Elihu Hubbard Smith, who caught the disease from "an Italian gentleman, a stranger in the city, whom he received, when infected with the disease, into his own house" (p. 149, essay on Brown in Jared Sparks, *Dictionary of American Biography*, 1836). Brown seems to be rewriting this tragedy and giving it a happy ending in his description of Dr. Stevens's act of taking in the sick Arthur Mervyn. See also Grabo, "Historical Essay," pp. 453–55.

35. See Jay Fliegelman, *Prodigals and Pilgrims: The American Revolution Against Patriarchal Authority, 1750–1800* (Cambridge University Press, 1982) for a discussion of the symbolic importance of the figure of the prodigal son in the period. John Miller reports a contemporary newspaper account of the plague as "corrective": "Our cities have been punished in proportion to the extent of Jacobinism" (p. 40).

36. Miller, p. 163. In the language of the act approved June 25, 1798, "It shall become lawful for the President of the United States at any time during the contrivance of this act, to *order* all such *aliens* as he shall judge dangerous to

the peace and safety of the United States . . . to depart out of the territory of the United States." The breathlessness of the continuation of these sentiments, approved July 14, 1798, is striking: "That if any person shall unlawfully combine or conspire together, with intent to oppose any measure or measures of the government of the United States, which are or shall be directed by proper authority, or to impede the operation of any law of the United States, or to intimidate or prevent any person holding a place or office in or under the government of the United States, from undertaking, performing or executing his trust or duty; and if any person or persons, with intent as aforesaid, shall counsel, advise, or attempt to procure any insurrection, riot, unlawful assembly, or combination, whether such conspiracy, threatening, counsel, advice, or attempt shall have the proposed effect or not, he or they shall be deemed guilty of a high misdemeanor. . . . That if any person shall write, print, utter or publish, or shall cause or procure to be written, printed, uttered or published, or shall knowingly or willingly assist or aid in writing, printing, uttering or publishing any false, scandalous and malicious writing or writings against the government of the United States, or either house of the Congress of the United States, or the President of the United States, with intent to defame the said government, or either house of the said Congress, or the said President, or to bring them or either or any of them, into contempt or disrepute; or to excite against them, or either or any of them, the hatred of the good people of the United States, or to stir up sedition within the United States, or to excite any unlawful combinations therein, for opposing or resisting any law of the United States, or any act of the President of the United States, done in pursuance of any such law, or of the powers in him, vested by the constitution of the United States, or to resist, oppose or defeat any such law or act, or to aid, encourage or abet any hostile designs of any foreign nation against the United States, their people or government, then such persons . . . shall be punished." "Alien and Sedition Acts," in *The Public Statutes at Large of the United States of America from the Organization of the Government in 1789 to March 3, 1845, arranged in chronological order* . . . [etc.] vol. 1 (Little, Brown, 1850), pp. 570–571, 577–578, 596–597.

37. The Bushhill hospital was, after all, someone's home, which the committee appropriated for the duration of the plague. For another account of the workings of the committee, see "Minutes of the Proceedings of the Committee Appointed 14th September 1793 by the Citizens of Philadelphia . . . to attend to . . . the Malignant Fever" (1794). The Frenchman who took over the hospital was the extraordinary philanthropist Stephen Girard; his biographer speculates that he had been exposed to the disease in St. Domingo, an early source of his wealth. Stephen Simpson, *Biography of Stephen Girard* (Thomas Bonsal, 1832), pp. 55–62.

38. Jacques Donzelot, *The Policing of Families*, trans. Robert Hurley (Pantheon, 1979), pp. 82–95.

39. David Rothman, *The Discovery of the Asylum*, pp. 234–35, 236, 153, 218.

40. Takaki, pp. 275–76.

41. Charles Keshian discusses Brown's politics in "The Political Character of the Novels of Charles Brockden Brown" (Ph.D. dissertation, University of California at Berkeley, 1973). See also Warner Berthoff, "The Literary Career of Charles Brockden Brown" (Ph.D. dissertation, Harvard University, 1954) for an informed discussion of the contemporary context of Brown's stance as an author and his political and literary productions.

42. It would take a further investigation to determine the possible connections between Philadelphia's financial instability and the instability of the family depicted in the novel. Such an investigation might begin with the question of the supposedly forged banknotes (AM, 208).

43. See Michael Warner, *The Letters of the Republic* for an excellent discussion of publication and *Arthur Mervyn* (Harvard University Press, 1991).

Chapter 2

1. Humphrey Marshall, "The Aliens: a patriotic poem . . . occasioned by the *Alien* bill, now before the senate" (Philadelphia: May 15, 1798). See also Jared Gardner, "Alien Nation: Edgar Huntly's Savage Awakening," *American Literature* 66 (September 1994) 429–461, for a discussion of the relation of the Alien and Sedition Acts to the novel and to other repressions of the period.

2. Carwin claims to want to be at Mettingen because "in this delightful region the luxuriances of nature had been chastened by judicious art" and then complains that he has been "self-expelled from a scene . . . in which all the muses and humanities had taken refuge." *Wieland, or The Transformation; an American Tale* (Kent State University Press, 1977), pp. 199, 211. Subsequent citations to *Wieland* will be given parenthetically in the text, preceded by W.

3. Michael Gilmore, "Calvinism and Gothicism: The Example of Brown's *Wieland*," *Studies in the Novel* 9 (Summer 1977) 110; Larzer Ziff, "A Reading of *Wieland*" *PMLA* 51 (March 1962); Michael Davitt Bell, "'The Double-Tongued Deceiver': Sincerity and Duplicity in the Novels of Charles Brockden Brown," *Early American Literature* 9 (Fall 1974) 144; William Hedges, "Charles Brockden Brown and the Culture of Contradictions," *Early American Literature* 9 (Fall 1974) 119.

4. For an account of *Wieland* along these lines, see Edwin Fussell, "*Wieland*: A Literary and Historical Reading," *Early American Literature* 18 (Fall 1983).

5. The practice of looking for the "guilty" party is carried out even in "deconstructive" readings such as Walter Hesford's "'Do You Know the Author?': The Question of Authorship in *Wieland*," *Early American Literature* 17 (Winter 82/83).

6. This is a central issue of George Forgie's *Patricide in the House Divided* (New York: Norton, 1979), and is also discussed by Eric Sundquist in *Home As Found: Authority and Genealogy in Nineteenth-Century Fiction* (Johns Hopkins University Press, 1979).

7. See Lester Cohen, *The Revolutionary Histories* (Cornell University Press, 1981), esp. pp. 50, 5, 14, for a good discussion of the problems facing contemporary historians of the Revolution.

8. Edwin Burrows and Michael Wallace, "The American Revolution: The Ideology and Psychology of National Liberation," *Perspectives in American History*, Vol. 6 (Harvard: Charles Warren Center, 1978), pp. 167–68.

9. Further, according to Fliegelman, Rousseau's educational theories as expounded in novels like *Emile* and *La Nouvelle Heloise* were as significant as his *The Social Contract* in influencing the tendencies of education and politics in America. It is important to remember here that the novel was frequently considered as an educational tool; in eighteenth-century England, the novel was only acceptable insofar as it was pedagogical. *Prodigals and Pilgrims: The American Revolution Against Patriarchal Authority* (Cambridge University Press, 1982), pp. 12–16, 29–31.

10. Fliegelman, p. 5. See also pp. 93–106. He claims that "by implying that the obedience due Britain was synonymous with the debt of nature owed by a child to his or her progenitor, the analogy, in effect, bound the colonies more securely to their parent than could either the rule of force or civil law" (94).

11. Whatever changes may have been literally effected in the government, however, children were still encouraged not only to value the nation as they valued their families but to view George Washington as a father. See Bernard Wishy, *The Child and the Republic* (University of Pennsylvania Press, 1968).

12. *The Discovery of the Asylum: Social Order and Disorder in the New Republic* (Little Brown, 1971), pp. 85, 97, 121, 157, 234, 152–53. See also Michael Ignatieff who argues that "the penitentiary was conceived of as a machine for the social production of guilt": "The same psychological assumptions that inspired . . . faith in human perfectibility, served, when applied to questions of punishment, to validate the notion that criminals were defective mechanisms whose consciences could be remodelled. . . . The social anxieties of the middle class in the 1790s ensured that this hard faith in human malleability soon received operational formulation at the hands of the medical profession, in asylums for the insane, Houses of Industry for paupers, hospitals for the sick, and penitentiaries for the criminal." Further, "the reformative ideal had deep appeal for an anxious middle class because it implied that the punisher and the punished could be brought back together in a shared moral universe" which satisfied "a heartfelt middle-class desire for a social order based on deferential reconciliation." A *Just Measure of Pain: The Penitentiary in the Industrial Revolution, 1750–1850* (Pantheon, 1978) p. 213.

13. There is a prison in the novel, but its prisoner, Wieland, escapes repeatedly and is not "reformed" at all.

14. There has been much critical attention to the sexual attraction Clara feels for Carwin and for her brother. David Brion Davis, for example, claims that "Carwin had saved Clara from an incestuous relation with her brother" (*Homicide in American Fiction* [Cornell University Press, 1957], p. 90). What has not been focused on is the parallel between that "sexual" tension and the representations of deism and revolution in sexual terms during this period. Instead, many critics read the novel as psychological or moral commentary. Alexander Cowie, for example, asserts that "at times *Wieland* seems more like an exposure of the author's unconscious than a reasoned attempt to communicate with the reader logically." "Historical Essay," *Wieland*, p. 327. For a suggestive reading of incest in other novels of the period see Anne Dalke, "Original Vice: The Political Implications of Incest in the Early American Novel," *American Literature* 23 (1988) 188–201.

15. Suggesting the unlocatable threat of the Bavarian Illuminati (with which secret organization he is often linked, especially because of his apprenticeship under Ludloe in *Carwin the Biloquist*), it is Carwin's mysterious appropriation of voices, voices that are "inexplicably and unwarrantedly assumed," and even more important, his assumption of the desires that go along with those voices, that makes him most feared by Clara. Pleyel has already accused Clara of being in love with Carwin when he hears the conversation between them that Carwin projects. Wieland has already prepared himself to hear the voices that he hears. For the history of the fear of the Illuminati in America, see Vernon Stauffer, *New England and the Bavarian Illuminati* (Columbia University Press, 1918).

16. Clara similarly turns from affection to violence when she immediately imagines Pleyel's corpse after he has failed to keep an engagement (W, 82–83).

17. Pleyel, like Paine, is a "champion of intellectual liberty and rejected all guidance but that of his reason" (W, 25).

18. The language of Wieland's account of his journey to God also incongruously echoes several passages in Jonathan Edwards' "Personal Narrative." In this conversion narrative, Edwards reports that as he "walked abroad alone . . . for contemplation . . . God's excellency appeared in every thing." Wieland too reports walking outside alone: "My mind was contemplative. . . . The author of my being was likewise the dispenser of every gift with which that being was embellished" (W, 166). Jonathan Edwards, "Personal Narrative," in *Representative Selections*, eds. Clarence Faust and Thomas Johnson (Hill and Wang, 1965), p. 60.

19. David Brion Davis, *Homicide in American Fiction, 1798–1860* (Cornell University Press, 1957), pp. 9, 22.

20. Timothy Dwight, *Theology Explained and Defended, in a Series of Sermons* (New York, 1846) III:356. Cited by Davis, 8.

21. For an interesting discussion of the frailty of cause-and-effect relations in the novel see Mark Seltzer, "Saying Makes it So: Language and Event in Brown's *Wieland*," *Early American Literature* 13 (1978) pp. 71–81. See also William Scheick, "The Problem of Origination in Brown's *Ormond*," in *Critical Essays on Charles Brockden Brown*, ed. Bernard Rosenthal (G. K. Hall, 1981), pp. 126–41. For a history of nineteenth-century American treatments of insanity, see Ruth Caplan, *Psychiatry and the Community in Nineteenth-Century America* (Basic Books, 1969).

22. "An Account of a Murder Committed by Mr. J—— Y——, upon His Family, in December, A.D., 1781," *New York Weekly Magazine*, vol. 2, no. 55 (July 1796) 20. Repr. *Philadelphia Minerva* 2.81, 82 (August 20 and 27, 1796). Blaming the Indians has a long history in the United States. William Bradford, for instance, blamed internal problems in the Plymouth colony on the external threat of the Indians, who usefully alleviated the psychological threats of faith by posing a physical one. As long as he could blame the Indians for tensions within the colony, he could ignore the divisive internal battles over commerce, settlement, and religion. See also Richard Slotkin: "The crowning irony of the witchcraft delusion is that the Puritans' hysterical fear of the Indian devils led them to behave precisely like the Indians." *Regeneration Through Violence: The Mythology of the American Frontier, 1600–1860* (Wesleyan University Press, 1973), p. 142.

23. Axelrod, p. 59. This source was recognized as early as 1801 by an anonymous reviewer in the *American Review and Literary Journal*. Axelrod comments further that "the blackest irony of James Yates's actions is that in performing what he sees as God's will he commits an atrocity worthy of the stereotyped godless American Indian" (p. 58).

24. Stephen Mix Mitchell, *Narrative of the Life of William Beadle* (Windsor, VT: Spooner, 1795), pp. 20, 21, 31, 15. Another parallel to *Wieland* occurs with a servant girl who survives the massacre of the family: Beadle sends her on an errand during his murderous activities at home; in *Wieland*, she hides in the closet.

25. *Ibid.*, pp. 10, 6, 21, 24, 18, 15.

26. *Ibid.*, pp. 20, 12.

27. *Ibid.*, p. 16.

28. Pleyel mentions Carwin's "*transformation* into a Spaniard" (W, 68).

29. Walter Hesford, "'Do You Know the Author?': The Question of Authorship in *Wieland*," *Early American Literature* 17 (1982/83) 239. For another account of Clara as author see Cynthia Jordan, *Second Stories: The Politics of Lan-*

guage, Form, and Gender in Early American Fictions (University of North Carolina Press, 1989), pp. 78–97.

30. These reactions again seem directly connected to the contemporary American fears of Revolution. For a useful treatment of the novel in this historical context, see Edwin Fussell, *"Wieland*: A Literary and Historical Reading," *Early American Literature* 18 (1983) 171–86.

Chapter 3

1. John Adams, letter to Hezekiah Niles, February 13, 1818; repr. in *American Thought and Writing*, vol. 2, eds. Russel Nye and Norman Grabo (Houghton Mifflin, 1965), p. 89. A typical attempt to soften this chastising image of England as Lady Macbeth may be found in the writings of Samuel Seabury, a Loyalist who wrote to Alexander Hamilton in 1774 that Great Britain was not "an old, wrinkled, withered, worn-out hag, whom every jackanapes . . . may insult with impunity," but a "vigorous matron . . . with strength and spirit sufficient to chastise her undutiful and rebellious children." From *Letters of a Westchester Farmer*, quoted in Bernard Bailyn, *The Ideological Origins of the American Revolution* (Harvard University Press, 1967), p. 137.

2. Hector St. John de Crevecoeur, "Distresses of a Frontier Man," from *Letters from an American Farmer* (New York: E. P. Dutton, 1957), p. 200. James Fenimore Cooper portrays a similar scene in *The Last of the Mohicans* when the massacre is about to begin: "The savage spurned the worthless rags, and . . . dashed the head of the infant against a rock" (1826), ed. William Charvat (Houghton Mifflin, 1958), p. 189.

3. See, for example, the discussion of the rise of the "republican family" by Michael Grossberg in *Governing the Hearth: Law and the Family in Nineteenth Century America* (University of North Carolina Press, 1985), pp. 4–11. He claims that the "'republican family' is the label that identifies most precisely the context and content of the changes that began to alter American households in the 1780s and 1790s and into the next century" (6). The period from the Revolution to 1830 saw the rise of a bourgeois family concerned with both commercial and political manifestations of its desires. Changes in the manifestations of those desires may be traced, I will argue, in the differing depictions of the family in the succeeding novel forms of gothic, historical, and sentimental or domestic fiction.

4. In his study of representations of the American Revolution, *A Season of Youth: The American Revolution and the Historical Imagination*, Michael Kammen suggests that the absence of mothers in many historical novels occurs because "breaking the bonds of Mother England is part of the authors' intended symbolism—weaning colonial children from matronly Brittania. But also, when the mother dies quite young in these novels she invariably leaves behind some strange problem about her origins, and more particularly, a serious question about her relationship to the hero's father" (Cornell University Press, 1976), p. 180.

5. For a discussion of familial metaphors for the Civil War, see Anne Norton, *Alternative Americas: A Reading of Antebellum Political Culture* (University of Chicago Press, 1986), esp. pp. 240–73. She asserts that "Americans of the antebellum period were preoccupied by the revision of traditional familial roles and by the perceived decay of the family. The familial conflicts metaphorically employed

to describe the national conflict are fraternal, oedipal, sexual, and intergenerational" (266).

6. See Neil Hertz, "Medusa's Head: Male Hysteria Under Political Pressure," in *The End of the Line: Essays on Psychoanalysis and the Sublime* (Columbia University Press, 1985), pp. 179–91, for an account of this perception. Writing a preface to his lugubriously titled pamphlet, "A Bone to Gnaw for the Democrats" (1795), William Cobbett sought to dissuade readers from proceeding: "If you are of that sex, vulgarly called the fair, but which ought always to be called the divine, let me beseech you, if you value your charms, to proceed no further. *Politics* is a mixture of anger and deceit, and these are the mortal enemies of beauty." Cobbett's attempt to divorce women from politics was seconded metaphorically when Cooper spoke of America as a domestic figure in *Notions of the Americans*: "Retired within the sacred precincts of her own abode, she is preserved from the destroying taint of excessive intercourse with the world. . . . She must be sought in the haunts of her domestic privacy" (1828), ed. Robert Spiller (New York: 104–5).

7. In *Patricide in the House Divided: A Psychological Interpretation of Lincoln and His Age* (Norton, 1979), George Forgie quotes Gouverneur Morris's characteristic statement: "AMERICANS—he had no child—BUT YOU!" (38). A typical eulogist, John van Buren, asserted that "Providence denied him children, that he might be the father of his country." B. M. Dusenberry, ed., *Monument to the Memory of General Andrew Jackson, Containing Twenty-Five Eulogies and Sermons Delivered on the Occasion of His Death* (Philadelphia, 1846), p. 104. Quoted by Michael Rogin in *Fathers and Children: Andrew Jackson and the Subjugation of the American Indian* (Knopf, 1975), p. 272. See also William Bryan, *George Washington in American Literature* (Columbia University Press, 1951).

8. In addition to Rogin and Forgie, see David Rothman, *The Discovery of the Asylum: Social Order and Disorder in the Early Republic* (Little, Brown, 1971) and Michael Ignatieff, *A Just Measure of Pain: The Penitentiary in the Industrial Revolution, 1750–1850* (Pantheon, 1978). See also John Kasson, *Civilizing the Machine: Technology and Republican Values in America, 1776–1900* (Penguin, 1977).

9. Rufus Choate, "Oration Before the Young Men's Democratic Club," in the Boston *Daily Advertiser*, July 7, 1858, quoted by Forgie, p. 20. See also Monica Kiefer, *American Children Through Their Books 1700–1835* (University of Pennsylvania Press, 1948). She traces changes in the New England Primer's alphabet: In 1749, W = "Whales in the Sea, / God's voice obey." In 1800, W = "By Washington / Great deeds were done." In John Ely's *The Child's Instructor* (1791), Little Billy visits Washington and then announces, "Americans . . . Begin with the infant in the cradle; let the first word he lisps be Washington." The title page of Mason Weems's *Life of Washington* (1809) announced "Lisp! Lisp! his name, ye children yet unborn! / And with like deeds your own great names adorn." With all the lisping they were called upon to do, the question of how to reach adulthood remained rather problematic for Americans of the early republic. Forgie claims that the "central fact" of what he calls the "post-heroic generation" was that they were "born second," automatically barred from participation in what Edward Everett claimed was "the great political consummation of the ages" (62, 20). See also Sacvan Bercovitch on the nineteenth-century historian George Bancroft, who produced such accounts, in "How the Puritans Won the American Revolution," *Massachusetts Review* 17 (1976) 597–630. As these "post-heroic" sons had the founders for their fathers, so they had the Union for their inheritance—"the beautiful house

of our fathers," said Rufus Choate—and were left with the task of maintaining what they had to interpret as the wishes of their fathers with regard to it. Historians have discovered a strong sentiment in the early republic that the American Revolution was incomplete and that it was necessary to complete it by carrying out the mission of the founding fathers, a sentiment that fueled "manifest destiny" (westward expansion) as well as industrialization. At the same time that mission could be carried out through education. See, for instance, John and Virginia Demos, "Adolescence in Historical Perspective," in *The American Family in Social-Historical Perspective* (St. Martin's Press, 1973), pp. 209–21. After 1825, they explain, there were thousands of books on childrearing where few had been published before, and they locate the source in nationalism: "Most of the concern which was evident in these books related to problems of authority . . . because—so many people thought— parental authority was steadily on the wane. In describing the average home, the writers of the childrearing books repeatedly used words like 'disorder,' 'disobedience,' 'licentiousness,' and, above all, 'indulgence'" (211).

10. Forgie, pp. 4, 5. See also Gilmore, "Eulogy as Symbolic Biography" and the chapter on Washington, "George Washington and the reconstituted family," in Jay Fliegelman, *Prodigals and Pilgrims: The American Revolution Against Patriarchal Authority, 1750–1800* (Cambridge University Press, 1982).

11. The issue of slavery made this especially problematic, as Eric Sundquist has discussed in "Slavery, Revolution and the American Renaissance," *The American Renaissance Reconsidered*, eds. Walter Michaels and Donald Pease (Johns Hopkins University Press, 1985), pp. 1–33.

12. These metaphorical formulations continued to be potent in later writings of the early republic. In *A Season of Youth*, Michael Kammen asserts that "imaginative writers have consistently perceived the American Revolution as a national *rite de passage*" (189).

13. In his eulogy for Jackson, George Bancroft announced that "his reverence for Washington surpassed his reverence for any human being" (repr. in *Memoirs*, p. 252). Jackson managed to associate himself with Washington to the point that one eulogist suggested that Washington should be called the first Jackson. Another declared that Jackson could not be compared "with the other heroes of the past. But there *is* one name—one immortal name—one hallowed name, that furnishes a parallel. I would blend the renown of Jackson with the mild glory of Washington. Of each it may be said, he lives but once in an age. . . . Washington was the father—Jackson the saviour of his country . . . Jackson *filled the measure of his country's glory*. And hereafter the true American will find it difficult to determine whether his patriotic emotions are more strongly awakened at the tomb of Mount Vernon, or the grave of the Hermitage." George Barstow, "Eulogy on the Life and Character of Andrew Jackson on the 12th of July, 1845" (Manchester, New Hampshire), p. 7. Anne Norton discusses invocations of Washington during the Civil War, pp. 112, 240.

14. Notably by Jay Fliegelman and George Forgie. See also Ronald Paulson, *Representations of Revolution 1789–1820* (Yale University Press, 1983).

15. The development of free choice in marriage combined with an increasing emphasis on the responsibility of parents in childrearing has been linked to the novel by Lawrence Stone. Tracing the appearances of affective individualism and companionate marriage in the eighteenth century, Stone remarks that "romantic love and the romantic novel grew together after 1780" (*The Family, Sex and Marriage in England, 1600–1800*, [Harper & Row, 1979], pp. 318, 284). Stone notes

further that the growth of "affective individualism" and the rise of "companionate marriage" seemed to be caused by the "incompatibility of domestic patriarchy with contractual obligation" (165), and he asserts that the legal, political and educational changes of the eighteenth century were "consequences of changes in ideas about the nature of family relations" (217). The apparent coincidence of the concept of romantic love with the appearance of the novel form so concerned with exploring it may further be connected with what has been called the age of revolution. Cf. Eric Hobsbawn, *The Age of Revolution: 1789–1848* (NAZ, 1964).

16. In the 1820s, as George Forgie and others have demonstrated, the deaths of the last of these "fathers" accentuated the moral and symbolic dilemma of how to proceed with a sense of legitimation while perpetuating an image of paternal benevolence. See also Richard Buel, *Securing the Revolution: Ideology in American Politics, 1789–1815* (Cornell University Press, 1972) and Edwin Burrows and Michael Wallace, "The American Revolution: The Ideology and Psychology of National Liberation" *Perspectives in American History*, vol. 6 (Harvard University Press, 1972) pp. 167–306.

17. And seems to lie behind R.W.B. Lewis's thesis in *The American Adam* (University of Chicago Press, 1955); Michael Kammen's discussion of the figure of the prodigal son in *A Season of Youth*, as well as Fliegelman's; Forgie's discussion of the attempt of politicians and writers of the early republic to define themselves in terms of their "fathers"; and Michael Rogin's study of Andrew Jackson's use of "paternal" rhetoric in *Fathers and Children*.

18. Isaac Mitchell's use of the family in his novel, *The Asylum*, (1804) may be a transition between the differing uses of the family in gothic and sentimental/domestic narratives (later republished as *Alonzo and Melissa or the Unfeeling Father: An American Tale* [Andrus and Son, 1851]). Far from the center of familial conflicts in historical novels, the mothers of these families are usually absent—often for suspicious reasons that may paradoxically make their absences central to the plot. (See note 4.) And rather than representing strong patriarchal figures to be rebelled against, the fathers of these families are ineffectual. Instead of threatening their children, they are helpless before the attempts of their children to kill one another. The family structure in these novels is still dynastic—the whole thrust of the novels remains the desire to have marriages take place (at whatever cost). The cost represents the Revolutionary impulse: the "old" family must die for the new one to take its place. Siblings must fight one another for inheritance and the choice of a marriage partner in part because the firstborn has no special rights and the parents have no particular say. This is the legacy of the American Revolution—and of the contemporary political order. Finally, it may be that an Oedipal model of revolution only works within the structure of an "aristocratic" family, a family still invested with patriarchal hierarchy and with the residues of primogeniture and family estates. The "democratic" family, the family in which the struggle for power supercedes any struggle to depose fathers or experience rites of passage, appears frequently in these novels to be the family for which the Revolution is fought.

19. Cyrus Barton, "An Address . . . before Republicans . . . July 4, 1828" (Newport, 1828), p. 16.

20. Forgie, p. 17.

21. Catherine Maria Sedgwick, *The Linwoods; or, "Sixty Years Since" in America* (Harper & Brothers, 1835) I, 163. Subsequent references will be cited parenthetically.

22. Sedgwick acknowledges that political or military subjects are "outside" a

woman's sphere, but she acts differently. For example, although she claims not to be able to describe battles, since she cannot "conceal the weak and unskilled woman" (xii), she proceeds to describe several bloody battles.

23. According to Jan Lewis, "Marriage was the very pattern from which the cloth of republican society was to be cut." "The Republican Wife: Virtue and Seduction in the Early Republic," *William and Mary Quarterly* 44 (October 1987) 689.

24. *Early Critical Essays (1820–1822) by James Fenimore Cooper* (Scholar's Facsimiles and Reprints, 1977), p. 97.

25. Michael Grossberg describes marriage in this period as a "reciprocal union of interests" (19) and argues that "early nineteenth-century legal theories" consecrated "the separation of the republican family and the state" (26).

26. As John McWilliams has pointed out, it does seem odd that George Washington should be so concerned with the affairs of a family that is nominally opposed to his own cause. In *Political Justice in a Republic: James Fenimore Cooper's America* (University of California Press, 1972), McWilliams notes that "George Washington travels miles into the mountains in order to liberate [a] British captain from Washington's own troops" (51). Harvey Birch, Washington's agent, more often watches over the family, controlling from the margins a scene in which he cannot act in his true character. Just out of sight, just beyond the grasp of the Virginia horse, as ephemeral as loyalties in the neutral ground, there seems no logic to his risking his life to interfere in Captain Wharton's execution.

27. The sexual overtones to Frances's position between the opposed figures of her brother and her lover indicate again the barely concealed theme of incest that accompanies attempts to consolidate family loyalties.

28. Peyton is determined to "show the world a bridegroom . . . who is equal to the duty of arresting the brother of his bride," but Frances asks, "Will the world comprehend this refinement?" (418)

29. Isabella has a similar sense of the combination: "America and her liberties was my earliest passion. . . . Dunwoodie was my next and last" (280). The Wharton sisters have imbibed their political loyalties slightly differently. While they live in British-occupied New York, "whether or not it was owing to the fact that Frances received none of the compliments which fell to the lot of her elder sister, in the oft repeated discussions on the merits of the war, between the military beaux who frequented the house, it is certain their effects on the sisters were exactly opposite" (25).

30. The ironic rejoinder: "Surely you forget that it is honor enough for a colonist to receive ruin from the hand of a child of Britain" (267).

31. As Barbara Welter has suggested, "The frequency with which derangement follows loss of virtue [in these novels] suggests the exquisite sensibility of woman, and the possibility that . . . her intellect was geared to her hymen, not her brain." Sarah Wharton's sensibility is so exquisite that she doesn't even need to lose her hymen. Barbara Welter, "The Cult of True Womanhood, 1820–1860," pp. 156, 157. The threat of social change was found especially in writers and reformers like Mary Wollstonecraft, Frances Wright, and Harriet Martineau who "were condemned in the strongest possible language—they were read out of the sex" (173). Novels were also exceedingly suspect, especially gothic and sentimental fiction: "The nineteenth century knew that girls *could* be ruined by a book" (166). Cooper's women all refer to the cult of true womanhood, remembering, no matter

their wilderness surroundings, that the "science of housekeeping affords exercise for the judgment and energy" characteristic "of a superior mind" (Lydia Sigourney, *Letters*, p. 27).

32. We learn, for example, that "the law of the neutral ground is the law of the strongest" (177), or that "there is but one tribunal to appeal to for a nation's rights; it is power, and we now make that appeal" (132).

33. John McWilliams, p. 54. For Cooper's sources, see also Bruce Rosenberg, *The Neutral Ground: The Andre Affair and the Background of Cooper's* The Spy (Greenwood, 1994).

34. "The county of West-Chester, after the British had obtained possession of the island of New York, became common ground, in which both parties continued to act for the remainder of the war of the revolution. A large proportion of its inhabitants, either restrained by their attachments, or influenced by their fears, affected a neutrality they did not feel" (12). These attachments include property: the scene of the Wharton household is "sufficiently near to both armies to make the restitution of stolen goods no uncommon occurrence in that vicinity. It is true, the same articles were not always regained; but a summary substitute was generally resorted to, in the absence of legal justice, which restored to the loser the amount of his loss, and frequently with no inconsiderable addition for the temporary use of his property. In short, the law was momentarily extinct in that particular district, and justice was administered subject to the bias of personal interests, and the passions of the strongest" (13). The unfixed nature of property is presented as the most disquieting side effect of war since both familial and property relations are disrupted.

35. Harvey Birch of course foreshadows Melville's Israel Potter—both unsung heroes and unknown soldiers. Ambivalence about whether the revolution counts permeates Melville's account: the hearthstone at the end of the novel provides an odd balance to the Bunker Hill monument at the beginning. Both monuments are in "Potter's field"—one celebrated and one forgotten (and an impediment for the man who wants to plow the field). Ending July 4, 1826, after forty years, the narrative at once questions whether the intervening years count and endorses the revolution as part of the "Young America" movement. Israel's chameleon identity means that as he changes his clothes he is repeatedly confused with how he dresses: a ghost, a British sailor, an American sailor, and finally, his "true" self, the beggar in rags. Are these, like Emerson's representative men, the true representatives of revolution? *Israel Potter: His Fifty Years of Exile* ([1855] Northwestern University Press, 1982). See the discussions by Forgie and by Harry Henderson in *Versions of the Past* (Oxford University Press, 1974).

36. Birch says, typically: "none know me but my God and *Him*" (248), leaving unclear which he worships more.

37. The "pledge" of Birch's "fidelity" is finally that he "would not take the gold" (453). The Whartons think that "love of money is a stronger passion than love of his king" and fear they will be betrayed by Birch since, after all, "no love will withstand the temptation of money" (65). Although Henry Wharton teases Frances with the comment that "there must be one love that can resist any thing" (65), the novel enforces a bleak vision of a neutral ground where the desire for money and property motivates, at one time or another, almost all the characters.

38. "Does your excellency think I have exposed my life, and blasted my character, for money? . . . No, no, no—not a dollar of your gold will I touch;

poor America has need of it all!" (391). Birch cannot have children and cannot marry, but he arranges marriages and children, providing fatal information on Colonel Wellmere and helping Henry Wharton escape. An "agent" and even a surrogate for Washington, he may be seen, like Washington, to adopt where he cannot have children (those of the Wharton family, those of the country as a whole).

39. Cathy Davidson, *Revolution and the Word: The Rise of the Novel in America* (Oxford University Press, 1986), p. 23.

40. What Cooper would also have to mention, had he given Birch his allotment of novels, is that what made books cheap and profitable for these hawkers was the absence of an international copyright law, which meant that most of the books would have been pirated British texts. Publishers found the need to pay American authors royalties discouraging, which made it difficult for an American author to make a living, and is why Cooper doubted that he could make money. His publisher at first printed very few copies of *The Spy*, and was surprised that the novel did so well. Cooper announces in the preface that the first volume was in print for months before the second volume was written.

41. Davidson, p. 24.

42. However, he does introduce commerce into the home and functions as a transitional figure in the movement from aristocratic to bourgeois forms.

43. Cooper complains that the lack of a "good, wholesome, profitable and continued pecuniary support" is what holds back American literature in *Notions of the Americans* (Carey & Lea, 1828) II, pp. 444–45. He comments accurately that "the fact that an American publisher can get an English work without money, must, for a few years longer, (unless legislative protection shall be extended to their own authors,) have a tendency to repress a national literature." While American law required citizenship for copyright protection, English law just stipulated prior publication in England.

44. According to Cathy Davidson, "Cooper received no financial renumeration from the English edition of *Precaution* and learned from this experience . . . to become a shrewd entrepreneur of literature" (269, n. 11). See also Richardson Wright, *Hawkers and Walkers in Early America* (Boni and Liveright, 1927).

Chapter 4

1. "An inversion by means of which what is effectively an *immanent*, purely textual operation—the 'quilting' of the heterogeneous material into a unified ideological field—is perceived and experienced as an unfathomable, *transcendent*, stable point of reference concealed behind the flow of appearances and acting as its hidden cause" (18). Zizek derives his sense of "quilting points" from Lacan's *"point de capiton"* in *The Four Fundamental Concepts of Psychoanalysis* (Hogarth, 1977), p. 112. Slavoj Zizek, *For They Know Not What They Do: Enjoyment as a Political Factor* (Verso, 1991). Cf. also *Sublime Object of Ideology* (Verso, 1989), Chap. 3: "'Nation' is a pre-modern leftover which functions as an inner condition of modernity itself, as an inherent impetus of its progress," he says; "there is always a kind of 'surplus of the Real' that sticks to it" (20).

2. Such a view has been challenged by recent works such as Lauren Berlant's

The Anatomy of National Fantasy: Hawthorne, Utopia, and Everyday Life (University of Chicago Press, 1991). Placing Hawthorne in the midst of the political activism of his day, Berlant draws on Foucault's formulation of "counter-memory" to describe the "material of popular memory in which public or national figures, bodies, monuments and texts accrue a profusion of meanings" (6).

3. Hawthorne's investment in the attributes of domesticity in a haunted house clearly organizes *The House of the Seven Gables* and appears as a fascination with domestic symbols in the embroidery of *The Scarlet Letter*. It also serves as a significant feature of unfinished romances like *The Ancestral Footprint*—in which the bloody foot of the past leaves its mark on the threshold of the house you would inhabit—or even the panegyric to England, *Our Old Home*.

4. The temptation may be to distinguish a "good" Hawthorne whose allegories and symbols remain ambiguous and do not easily resolve into political debates from a "bad" Hawthorne who can only be read as symptomatic of fraught political positioning, but I'd like to posit a Hawthorne whose attention to political detail, if not the canny commentary it has sometimes been found to be, nonetheless organizes an anxiety about political positioning. While the stories may frustrate interpretation with their allegorical insistences, the extent to which they remain allegory seems an appropriate point of departure rather than a goal of analysis. That is, rather than making it the goal of my analysis to expose flattening allegories, I want to ask what stresses fracture these stories. The stories have been read as political allegory by Evan Carton in "Hawthorne and the Province of Romance," *ELH* 47 (1980), 331–54 and in *The Rhetoric of American Romance: Dialectic and Identity in Emerson, Dickinson, Poe, and Hawthorne* (Johns Hopkins University Press, 1985); see also Seymour Gross, "'Lady Eleanore's Mantle' as History," *JEGP* 54 (1955); Neal Frank Doubleday, *Hawthorne's Early Tales* (Duke University Press, 1972); and John McWilliams, "'Thorough-Going Democrat' and 'Modern Tory,'" *Studies in Romanticism* 15 (1976). The most elaborate treatment of the stories is that of Michael Colacurcio in *The Province of Piety: Moral History in Hawthorne's Early Tales* (Harvard University Press, 1984). Colacurcio's study of the "Legends" begins with reminders of Hawthorne's patriotic commercial endeavors. While editing the *American Magazine of Useful and Entertaining Knowledge*, he presented the lives of "eleven Revolutionary Worthies as well as a very carefully wrought account of the Boston Tea Party" (389). In addition to the more well-known "My Kinsman, Major Molineux," "Endicott," and "The Grey Champion," there is the children's version of American history in *Grandfather's Chair*. But, continues Colacurcio, "within the limits of the ironic vision, the whole story is in the 'Legends'" (389).

5. Nathaniel Hawthorne, "Old Esther Dudley," in *Twice-told Tales* (Centenary edition), eds. William Charvat, Roy Harvey Pearce, and Claude Simpson (Ohio State University Press, 1974), p. 302. Further references to "The Legends of the Province House" will be to this edition and will be cited parenthetically in the text.

6. Jay Fliegelman, *Prodigals and Pilgrims: The American Revolution Against Patriarchal Authority, 1750–1800* (Cambridge University Press, 1982).

7. The new offspring had new difficulties with achieving their "filial autonomy." As I have discussed in prior chapters, along with a change in political rhetoric there was a change in educational language and trends. Given that the mind of a child was now seen as a tabula rasa where national ideologies could be freshly inscribed, fictional practices repeatedly sought to establish a pattern for

national childrearing. Since the success of the Revolution, which apparently enforced the transformed family compact in which children should be trained to succeed if not supplant their parents, the metaphorical family had become problematic. If the "fathers" of America were heroes, what was there left for the children to become? Cf. Forgie, Watts, and Fliegelman. The confusing combination of breaks and continuities with the "parent" country was in part representative of the political situation after the War; very generally speaking, Federalists and then Whigs tried to retain ties to England, while their opponents, Republicans and then Democrats, wanted to make everything new and "American."

8. For a history of the "Young America" movement, see John Stafford, *The Literary Criticism of 'Young America': A Study of the Relationship of Politics and Literature, 1837–1850* (University of California Press, 1952). See also Priscilla Wald, *Constituting Americans: Cultural Anxiety and Narrative Form* (Duke University Press, 1995), especially chap. 2, on *The United States Magazine and Democratic Review* and the Young America movement (pp. 106–22).

9. At least one story appeared under an alias. The first story, "Howe's Masquerade," appeared in vol. 2, no. 6 (May 1838) between "True Principles of Commercial Banking" and "The Discovery of America by the Norsemen." (Of course this was a time of passionate interest in banking—the Panic of 1837 and subsequent depression had obsessed national political debates, and had arguably helped depress sales of Hawthorne's first edition of *Twice-told Tales* [March 1837]). Located between commerce and geographical origin, Hawthorne's story launches national ambivalence. The next issue, vol. 2, no. 7 (June 1838) contained a piece called "The Political Crisis" that told the story of the "Revolution of 1837 . . . when the Republican party succeeded, after a fearful strugle, in overthrowing the old Federal ascendancy which had . . . threaten[ed] the speedy termination of the 'American Experiment' in failure and disgrace" (312).

10. From O'Sullivan's introduction to the first number of the *United States Magazine and Democratic Review* (Langtree and O'Sullivan, 1837), p. 8. Hawthorne had been receiving $1 per page for stories in *The Token* or *The New England Magazine*; in promising him as much as $5 per page, O'Sullivan also promised him that "as this magazine will have a vast circulation throughout the Union, and it will occupy so elevated a literary rank, it will afford to [you] the acquisition of distinction." Hawthorne was to publish eight pieces in fifteen months there, starting with the first issue (from "Historical Introduction" to *Twice-told Tales*, pp. 497, 499, 515).

11. For a stimulating account of how questions of origin and discrimination serve to invest objects and architecture, see Anthony Vidler's dissection of haunted houses in *The Architectural Uncanny: Essays in the Modern Unhomely* (MIT, 1992).

12. The present-tense setting and frame place these stories uncomfortably closer to the surface of a present-tense anxiety for Hawthorne's audience than stories like "My Kinsman, Major Molineux." Grouping these stories with other fictions of ambivalent history—for instance, Cooper's ambivalence about the project of patriotism and the profit from expressing your patriotism—shows Hawthorne's participation in, rather than transcendence of, such anxieties.

13. "For it was the policy of Sir William Howe to hide the distress and danger of the period, and the desperate character of the siege, under an ostentation of festivity" (243). For an account of the source, see Fumio Anza, "The Mischianza

Ball and Hawthorne's 'Howe's Masquerade,'" *Nathaniel Hawthorne Journal* 4 (Microard Editions, 1974).

14. After the story of the masquerade, the narrator becomes disturbed by the figure of a stage-driver "reading a penny paper of the day." He makes attempts to represent him problematic by "presenting a figure which could nowise be brought into any picture of 'Times in Boston' seventy or a hundred years ago" (255). His daily paper presents an instant history that allows for no historical distance, as his profession as a stage-driver stands for the closing of physical distances. And the newspaper, like the *Democratic Review*, stands for an undifferentiated presentation of current events specifically relevant to the problem of a democracy. An aristocracy or a monarchy creates hierarchy and difference: men must refer to the king for power and identity. In a democracy, these differences are levelled: each man refers to himself. The narrator finds this leveling everywhere: democracy poses a crucial problem of representation.

15. The colonials had stocked the garrison with arms and troops, so that the change meant a loss of their possessions as well as of their control over the town. Tremendous tensions erupted in a series of events, from the sacking of Governor Hutchinson's house to the Boston Massacre. Focusing on the portrait as emblematic of the decision, the narrator manages to make a concrete and charged situation as nebulous as a ghost story: "The following is as correct a version of the fact as the reader would be likely to obtain from any other source; although, assuredly, it has a tinge of romance approaching to the marvellous" (258).

This story first appeared in the *Democratic Review* right after a review of Tocqueville's *Democracy in America*: "The aristocratic principle can, therefore, never acquire any dangerous influence among us, and in the only shape in which it can display itself, that of opposition to the democratic tendencies of our institutions, may occasionally operate as a salutary check upon abuse or accidental error" (347).

16. Other works of the period, as we will see, make quicker connections between political identities and lethal consequences. Their narrative tensions do not depend on a moment of choice, since the choice has almost always been made at some moment prior to the novel's action.

17. For a somewhat different account of such narrative instability see Teresa de Lauretis "The Violence of Rhetoric: Considerations on Representation and Gender" in Nancy Armstrong and Leonard Tennenhouse, eds., *The Violence of Representation: Literature and the History of Violence* (Routledge, 1989), pp. 239–258.

18. This story appeared in an issue of the *Democratic Review* that contained a dramatization of the fate of Major Andre ("West Point—A Tale of Treason") and a memorial sketch Hawthorne wrote about his friend and ex-Bowdoin classmate Jonathan Cilley, who introduced O'Sullivan to Hawthorne's work and encouraged him to solicit it for the magazine (vol. 3, no. 12 [Dec. 1838]).

19. Neal Frank Doubleday, among others, has complained that the moral of the story is too bald and asks why Hawthorne would give "what was a moral conviction a political cast"? Neal Frank Doubleday, *Hawthorne's Early Tales* (Duke University Press, 1972).

20. According to Colacurcio, "Hawthorne somehow connected the moral climate of the smallpox epidemic with that of revolution" (438). He discusses Increase Mather's warnings about the smallpox epidemic of 1721 and points out

that the story omits what stood out for later writers as the salient detail: the smallpox inoculation promoted by Cotton Mather (427, 430). The connection of plague and politics shows up in the sources as well: "What emerges is that the eighteenth-century 'Opposition' is everywhere obsessed with the 'health' of the body politic; that social disorder everywhere figured itself as infectious disease; and that the 'Puritan' contribution was the sense that such political disease could be as much a 'scourge'; as an outbreak of the pox" (p. 637, n. 14). For the conjunction of medical and political language in the period, see also Caroline Robbins, *The Eighteenth-century Commonwealth* (Harvard University Press, 1959); Bernard Bailyn, *Ideological Origins of the American Revolution* (Harvard University Press, 1967), and Gordon Wood, *The Creation of the American Republic* (University of North Carolina Press, 1969).

21. First appeared in *Democratic Review* vol. 5 no. 13 (January 1839), an issue that contained the "Trials of Woman."

22. "Lucian and His Age," *United States Magazine and Democratic Review* II (1842), pp. 225–26; quoted by Forgie, pp. 93–94.

23. *The Reign of Reform, or the Yankee Doodle Court*, Mrs. Margaret Botsford, pp. 6, 8, 12, 39, 42–43. The disorder of his sexual and political activities extends to Jackson's interior decorating schemes. Not only has he turned government "topsy-turvy" ("the rabble have the sovereign sway"), he has even remodeled the White House: "Could not the plain old *'Tennessee farmer'* have been satisfied with what his predecessors (who were all infinitely greater than he) thought sufficient . . . ?" Recalling the better days of the father of the country, Washington, one says, "My soul is sick of the *Contrast*." Jackson called forth the author's "poison pen" by refusing a pension to *her* father, a Revolutionary veteran: "luxury . . . has rendered the *'Hero's'* heart callous to calls of humanity." By reneging on his duty to her father, the author implies, Jackson has abandoned the principle of the Father.

24. *New England Galaxy*, February 18, 1825, p. 2. Reprinted in "Historical Introduction" to James Fenimore Cooper, *Lionel Lincoln, or The Leaguer of Boston*, eds. Donald and Lucy Ringe (State University of New York, 1984), p. xxviii.

25. John McWilliams makes a case for the realistic, even modern, sense of battle in *Lionel Lincoln* in "Lexington, Concord, and the 'Hinge of the Future,'" *American Literary History* 5 (Spring 1993) 1–29.

26. Lydia Maria Child, *The Rebels, or Boston Before the Revolution* (Cummings, Hillard and Co., 1825).

27. Anonymous review in *Literary World*, July 27, 1850. A *Godey's* review of September 1850 contradicts the earlier one: Child "has been very successful in connecting an interesting domestic tale with the thrilling events which preceded the American Revolution." Cited by Nina Baym in *Novels, Readers, and Reviewers*, p. 238. Commenting on this review, Nina Baym claims that "the historical novelist tended to sacrifice the fictional story to the historical narrative rather than accepting his artistic responsibility as a novelist to make up an original fiction, and thereby 'really' wrote history rather than a historical novel" (238).

28. George Dekker, *James Fenimore Cooper: The American Scott* (Barnes and Noble, 1967), p. 35.

29. James Kirk Paulding, *The Old Continental, or, The Price of Liberty* (Cady & Burgess, 1851) I, 149. Further references will be cited parenthetically.

30. As if this were not difficult enough, he continues, "You must figure in broad daylight . . . you must receive the approbation of the great Washington" (I, 34).

31. John Neal, *Seventy-Six*, *"Our Country—Right or Wrong"* (1823; York Mail-Print, 1971), II, 258, 242, 243.

32. Robert Montgomery Bird, *The Hawks of Hawk-Hollow* (Carey, Lea and Blanchard, 1835), I, 6. Further references will be cited parenthetically.

33. Jessie Gilbert's son was changed with the still-born son of her stepmother—to save it from the Gilbert brothers who wanted to kill the child for being Colonel Falconer's son—and then sent to the West Indies. Colonel Falconer married Jessie Gilbert, but denied the marriage in order to marry for money. He concealed this from his subsequent children: "Why should I have filled him with shame, staining him who was innocent of his father's crimes, with the disgrace of his birth?" (II, 209).

34. Mason Weems, *Life of George Washington*, ed. Marcus Cunliffe (Harvard University Press, 1962), pp. 69, 74, 133.

35. J. V. Ridgely, "George Lippard's *The Quaker City*: The World of the American Porno-Gothic," *Studies in the Literary Imagination* 7 (Spring 1974) 77–94.

36. George Lippard, *Blanche of Brandywine, or September 11, 1777; A Romance of the Revolution* (T. B. Peterson, 1846), p. 114. Further references will be cited parenthetically.

37. Scarry, *Body in Pain*, 127.

38. Mark Carnes, *Secret Ritual and Manhood in Victorian America* (Yale University Press, 1989), p. 120. I am indebted to Heather Roberts and other seminar participants for several insights about fraternal identification in Lippard, for productively engaging the topics of violence, sexuality, and nationalism, and for not laughing at me for making them read *Blanche of Brandywine*.

39. George Mosse, *Nationalism and Sexuality: Respectability and Abnormal Sexuality in Modern Europe* (Howard Ferlig, 1985), p. 80. (I'd like to note also Klaus Theweleit's work on German nationalism in these terms. See *Male Fantasies: Volume Two; Male Bodies: Psychoanalyzing the White Terror* (University of Minnesota, 1989). And, of course, Richard Slotkin, *Regeneration Through Violence: The Mythology of the American Frontier* (Wesleyan University Press, 1973).

40. *Reflections on Political Identity* (Johns Hopkins University Press, 1988), pp. 7, 17.

41. Jean Laplanche and J. B. Pontalis, "Fusion/Defusion (of Instincts)" *The Language of Psychoanalysis* trans. Donald Nicholson-Smith (Norton, 1973), pp. 180, 181.

42. The significance of the dark versus the light woman has been investigated elsewhere and I do not propose to solve it here. The standard political/sexual symbolism holds that the dark woman, frequently "tainted" (if only by rumor) and almost invariably the locus of sexual attraction, gives way to the pure white chaste one, who functions as the locus for marriage and chivalric deeds. See, for instance, Leslie Fiedler, *Love and Death in the American Novel* (Criterion, 1960). If, as was frequently the case in Cooper and elsewhere, the former was practical and the latter ineffectual, this separation still furthered a perverse American vision of expansionism, industrialization, and the frontier in which the darker brother or sister must be sacrificed so the lighter can represent civilization. (In *Blanche*, however, the darker brother wins.) In the crossing of dark and light bodies, as I argue in the next chapter, a form of miscegenation through violence occurs.

43. The horrors of the family do not deter the Frazier brother and sister. One marries a sister, the other chooses one of the brothers. But the rival Walford brother

destroys the marriage by setting a trap that makes Blanche's mother appear unfaithful. The husband does not ask for an explanation: *"he thought her false"* and "fled
from her sight, as from a polluted thing" (32). She dies soon after. The duelling
between the brothers is "one of the many, dark and terrible pictures which marked
the era of revolutionary terror, and bloodshed time of civil war" (72). Dave Walford
acknowledges the war, but thinks of more substantial goals; as he tells his brother,
"These are times of battle, Walter—the strongest hand bears the purse away!" (71).

44. Blanche Walford and Rose Frazier are cousins, born of a brother and sister
who escaped political murder in Scotland. David and Walter Walford, twin sons of
Rose's uncle Philip, and bitter rivals in love and war, fight over Rose. The Tory
Dave kidnaps her; his brother, the rebel Walter, is killed by their father on the
battlefield at Brandywine. Blanche represents both victory and death for Percy—
"For that lovely form, death would be willingly faced" (123)—but he finally decides
to kidnap her (mirroring Dave Walford's kidnapping of Rose) and tells her that since
she has refused his more generous offers, "now you shall accept the love of a
sensualist" (190).

Chapter 5

1. James Fenimore Cooper, *The Last of the Mohicans* (State University of
New York [1826]) p. 22. All subsequent references to the novel are to this edition
and will be cited parenthetically.

2. I am suggesting that the notion of regeneration through violence points to
the work of this ritualized violence but does not quite register the ways in which
problems of generation and gender are bound up with these rituals. Richard
Slotkin, *Regeneration through Violence: The Mythology of the American Frontier*
(Wesleyan University Press, 1973).

3. For example: "The foremost Indian bounded like a stricken deer, and fell
headlong" (70) or "a Delaware leaping high into the air, like a wounded deer,
fell . . . dead" (329). The word "kind," from middle English "kinde," primarily
means "nature, race, origin" (synonyms are order, genus, race). An archaic meaning of gender, however, is also "kind." See Donna Harraway, "Gender for a Marxist
Dictionary: The Sexual Politics of a Word," for a discussion of the "gender identity
paradigm": "Words close to gender are implicated in concepts of kinship, race,
biological taxonomy, language, and nationality." *Simians, Cyborgs, and Women:
The Reinvention of Nature* (Routledge, 1991) pp 127–148.

4. By Leslie Fiedler, who concentrates on the "scandal" of Cora's mixed blood
and of Uncas's posthumous marriage with her. Leslie Fiedler, *Love and Death in
the American Novel* (Criterion Books, 1960), pp. 204–5.

5. I am indebted to Mark Seltzer for this phrase. See Mark Seltzer, "The
Love-Master" in *Engendering Men*, eds. Michael Cadden and Joseph Boone (Routledge, 1990), pp. 214–34.

6. Drawing on the accounts of this myth by John Heckewelder, who was
Cooper's source for much of his information about the Indians, Richard Slotkin
applies this myth to the deer slaying in *The Pioneers* and to Natty Bumppo's acquisition of the name "Deer Slayer." Richard Slotkin, *Regeneration Through Violence*,
pp. 46, 306. John Heckewelder, *An Account of the History, Manners, and Customs
of the Indian Nations* (Abraham Small, 1819), p. 251. While Slotkin finds this an
allegory about the regeneration of a cultural order through the violent absorption of

a natural one, I want to trace the natural as already imbricated with the mark of the cultural. Daniel Peck also discusses Heckewelder in *A World By Itself: The Pastoral Moment in Cooper's Fiction* (Yale University Press, 1977), p. 126.

7. Indeed, it is the cultural work of rendering inevitable—of lending ideology the invulnerable banality of the hard fact—that his account may be seen at once to examine and reinforce or conserve. Philip Fisher, *Hard Facts: Setting and Form in the American Novel* (Oxford University Press, 1985).

8. Slotkin, *The Fatal Environment: The Myth of the Frontier in the Age of Industrialization, 1800–1890* (Wesleyan University Press, 1989), p. 89. Cooper is fond of the sort of neutral territory he depicts in *The Spy*, a neutral territory that has been called the land of the American romance, where these distinctions are often violently refigured. The whole action of *Last of the Mohicans* takes place in territory disputed between French and English: the Indian claims to the land are made to seem incidental to this dispute.

9. Gamut's extravagantly constructed body and the treatment he receives seem designed to bring the comic relief of Washington Irving's Ichabod Crane. Like Gamut, Ichabod Crane is

> a native of Connecticutt, a state which supplies the Union with pioneers for the mind as well as the forest, and sends forth yearly its legions of frontier woodsmen and country schoolmasters. . . . He was tall, but exceedingly lank, with narrow shoulders, long arms and legs, hands that dangled a mile out of his sleeves, feet that might have served for shovels, and his whole frame most loosely hung together.

Crane's talent is also like Gamut's: the "singing-master of the neighborhood," his voice, with its "peculiar quavers," "resounded far above all the rest." Washington Irving, "Legend of Sleepy Hollow," in *The Sketch Book* (1820) (New American Library, 1961), pp. 332, 334. Sending forth such notably inept schoolmasters, Connecticut gets vilified as the source of an inept model of education and religion. While Gamut's profession is singing—"I teach singing to the youths of the Connecticutt levy" (57)—his singing often creates or accompanies danger: he almost always begins in and even precipitates perilous moments. In the cave, his singing is succeeded by and almost blends with the screams of the horses, "that horrid cry" first thought to be supernatural (60).

10. Their entry into the woods is also sexualized as they approach a path "which might, with some little inconvenience, receive one person at a time" (21), a "dark and tangled pathway" which they enter by "penetrating the thicket" (22).

11. Natty tells Duncan to wash off his Indian disguise before he sees Alice: "young women of white blood give the preference to their own colour." After he "availed himself of the water," "every frightful or offensive mark was obliterated, and the youth appeared again in the lineaments with which he had been gifted by nature" (258). By this point, to appear in the "lineaments" of his own color seems another choice of disguise. On improvisatory identification as a tactic of power, see Stephen Greenblatt, "Improvisation and Power," *Literature and Society: Selected Papers from the English Institute, 1978* (Johns Hopkins University Press, 1980), pp. 57–58.

12. Cooper may derive his attention to the beaver, "those sagacious and industrious animals," from George Henry Loskiel, a missionary-anthropologist who describes "The *Beaver* of North America" in similarly anthropomorphic terms, com-

menting on the "amazing sagacity of these animals, displayed in building their dwellings, in their whole oeconomy." George Henry Loskiel, *History of the Mission of the United Brethren Among the Indians in North America*, trans. from the German by Christian La Trobe (Brethren's Society for the Furtherance of the Gospel, 1794), p. 81.

13. John Heckewelder, *An Account*, p. 234.

14. A later version of the threat of these transposed positions shows up in "Circumstance" (1860), a story by Harriet Prescott Spofford about a woman caught in the grasp of a panther known as the "Indian devil." The woman is terrified of being eaten because her body would continue to exist inside a creature who threatens her both as a beast and as a stand-in for the Indian. Edgar Huntly acts out a reversal of the ingestion of both flesh and qualities when he eats the panther he finds in the cave in Charles Brockden Brown's *Edgar Huntly*. To eat the body of the panther that threatened his life seems a more direct version of Richard Slotkin's concept of internalizing the wilderness in order to rejuvenate the culture that presents itself as oposed to it. The instances I am treating here of disguise and transposition seem related but act in thematically and politically different ways. Harriet Prescott Spofford, "Circumstance," reprinted in *Provisions*, ed. Judith Fetterley (Indiana University Press, 1986); Charles Brockden Brown, *Edgar Huntly, or Memoirs of a Sleep-Walker* (Penguin, 1988), p. 160.

15. Jane Tompkins, *Sensational Designs: The Cultural Work of American Fiction* (Oxford University Press, 1985), pp. 116, 118, 117. While I agree with her point that "an obsessive preoccupation with systems of classification—the insignia by which race is distinguished from race, nation from nation, human from animal, male from female—dominates every aspect of the novel," I argue with her conclusion that the novel works to reassert "'natural' divisions" (105).

16. The most absurd mixture of disguises and substitutions may be the rescue of Uncas from the Huron camp which involves Natty Bumppo, who has been disguised as the bear, disguising himself as David Gamut, Uncas disguising himself as the bear, and David Gamut remaining behind in the Indian camp poorly disguised as Uncas.

17. And "all clergymen." See Ann Douglas for this identification of the audience of women novel-readers and a clergy who "might be better employed" (4). *The Feminization of American Culture* (Knopf, 1977). For a account of Cooper's use of history in the novel, see Ian Steele, "Cooper and Clio: The Sources for 'A Narrative of 1757,'" *Canadian Journal of American Studies* (Winter 1989) pp. 121–35.

18. William Cobbett, *A Bone to Gnaw for the Democrats* (Philadelphia, 1795), pp. 3–4. I do not want to ignore the possibility that both prefaces could be read as provocation, as an invitation to read a forbidden text that sets out to create a Pandora-like desire in the female reader. But I also think that reading them as invitation does not change the way that these prefaces ward off women. They also work as a curious reversal of the warnings for women, especially young ones, to be wary of novel reading.

19. Associations between families and a national genealogy line up imperfectly, since citizens are not children and the nation not a family, yet the analogy repeatedly appears in the early republic to present the family as a model or a metaphor for the nation, or as a form of explanation, an agent, or an instrument to make political and historical change seem natural. Jay Fliegelman scrutinizes the status of this analogy and how it works to structure political language in *Prodigals*

and Pilgrims: The American Revolution Against Patriarchal Authority (Cambridge University Press, 1982). Heckewelder tells how the American Revolution was explained to the Native American: "Disputes having arisen between Great Britain and her North American colonies, and a congress being chosen by the latter, it appointed commissioners . . . for the purpose of explaining the nature of the dispute to them" (136). After telling them not to get involved, "they next proceeded to state the cause from whence the dispute had originated, calling the same a family dispute, a quarrel between a parent and his child." The Indians pledged that "they would remain neutral during the 'contest between the parent and the son'" (140). But a new war chief of the Delawares reinterpreted the scenario: "'You see a great and powerful nation divided! You see the father fighting against the son, and the son against the father!' . . . At first I looked upon it as a family quarrel . . . at length it appeared to me, that the father was in the right; and his children deserved to be punished a little! . . . from the many cruel acts his offspring had committed from time to time, on his Indian Children" (216–17).

20. Magua even sees Cora as a dismembered piece of her father's body: he follows up his proposal by saying that while Munro would "sleep among his cannon, his heart would be within reach of the knife of le Subtil" (105). In a more conventional version of declaring a new family allegiance through marriage, when Duncan proposes to marry Alice he asks Munro for the "honour of being your son" (157).

21. Much of the violence of Cooper's novel gets directed against a potentially redemptive future generation. The Indian woman who dies in the cave, for example, gets introduced as "the wife of one of my bravest young men" (256). Philip Fisher notes that violence against women in Cooper tends to prevent marriages and that the "many unaccomplished marriages tend to thin out the future in advance." *Hard Facts*, pp. 56–58.

22. The statue was removed from the Capitol in 1958. See Richard Drinnon, *Facing West: The Metaphysics of Indian-Hating and Empire-Building* (University of Minnesota Press, 1980), pp. 131–33.

23. Cooper's several sources included Jonathan Carver, who wrote as a witness to the massacre, and Humphreys' *Life of Putnam*, which is even more graphic about the bodies of slaughtered women left behind. Jonathan Carver, *Travels Through the Interior Parts of North-America, in the Years 1766, 1767, and 1768* (London, 1778). These and other sources are discussed on pp. 361–65 of the "Explanatory Notes" to the SUNY edition of *Last of the Mohicans*.

24. The passage echoes the danger posed in "The Distresses of a Frontier Man," Crèvecoeur's classic descriptions of frontier violence in which he imagines that "it is necessary for the good of Britain that my children's brains should be dashed against the walls of the house." Hector St. John de Crèvecoeur, *Letters from an American Farmer* ([1782] Dutton, 1957), p. 201.

25. Heckewelder, pp. 249, 254. The whites make a different connection, as we have seen, between human and animal identities, in which they categorize the Indians as beasts. In his other work, Heckewelder cites an Indian chief who looks forward to a time "when your own descendants will testify against you!—will say: we were taught by our parents to believe this!—we were told when we had killed an Indian, that we had done a *good* act!—had killed a wild beast, &c." (xi). He inveighs against "a rabble, (a class of people generally met with on the frontiers) who maintained, that to kill an Indian was the same as killing a bear" (130). John

Heckewelder, *Narrative of the Mission of the United Brethren Among the Delaware and Mohegan Indians from its Commencement in the Year 1740 to the Close of the Year 1808 . . . by John Heckewelder who was many Years in Service of that Mission* (McCarty and Davis, 1820).

26. According to one of Cooper's sources, the Iroquois proposed to the Delaware, "One nation shall be the *woman*. We shall place her in the midst and the other nations who make war shall be the man and live around the woman." George Henry Loskiel, *History of the Mission of the United Brethren Among the Indians in North America*, trans. from the German by Christian La Trobe (Brethren's Society for the Furtherance of the Gospel, 1794), p. 25. Heckewelder explains that it "must be understood that among these nations wars are never brought to an end but by the interference of the weaker sex. The men, however tired of fighting, are afraid of being considered as cowards if they should intimate a desire for peace." He continues, "They say also that the whites speak too much, and that much talk disgraces man, and is fit only for women," *Account*, pp. 56–57, 58, 189. For Slotkin, in contrast, Cooper "uses sexual analogy to establish the immutability of racial character—nonwhite can become white only to the degree that women can become men" (*Fatal*, 90).

27. In his history of the Iroquois, Francis Jennings explains that the "woman" "seems to have meant originally a nation that was assigned a political role of neutrality so as to be able to assume the peacemaker's role when warring tribes wanted to end their strife without losing face. . . . In the mid-eighteenth century the woman metaphor became corrupted by European notions of female subordination, which were wholly at odds with such Iroquois customs as the power of clan matrons to make and unmake chiefs." Francis Jennings, *The Ambiguous Iroquois Empire: The Covenant Chain Confederation of English Colonies* (Norton, 1984), pp. 45–46.

28. Nationalism, according to Benedict Anderson, can be understood by examining "the larger cultural systems that produced it" rather than "self-consciously held political ideologies." Through these cultural systems, but predominantly through language, the means of transmitting cultural systems, "nation-ness" can be "assimilated to . . . all those things one cannot help," such as race and gender. Benedict Anderson, *Imagined Communities*, pp. 19, 131, 133. In "The Nazi Myth," Jean-Luc Nancy and Philippe Lacoue-Labarthe describe how the notion that national identity can be transmitted through language runs violently into the problem of race: "The race, the people, is linked to *blood*, not to language" (308). Jean-Luc Nancy and Philippe Lacoue-Labarthe, "The Nazi Myth," *Critical Inquiry* 16 (1990) 291–312.

Chapter 6

1. I first learned about this doll from Harryette Mullen. I would like to thank Harryette as well as Lauren Berlant, Rick Bogel, Laura Brown, Jonathan Culler, and, especially, Mark Seltzer for assistance with this chapter.

2. This story has been discussed by Carolyn Karcher, in a talk on Child at the 1989 American Studies Association convention in Miami, and by Karen Sanchez-Eppler, in "Bodily Bonds: The Intersecting Rhetorics of Feminism and Abolition," who comments that if the "liberating tears" of Mary French "offer . . . a perfect emblem for sentimental fiction's power to emancipate, that emblem includes the

recognition that the freedom it offers depends upon the black being washed white." *Representations* 21 (1987) pp. 20–21. The fear of stolen and disguised children shows up in various narratives. In its first issue, *The Liberator* announced, "There were kidnapped during the past year . . . MORE THAN FIFTY THOUSAND INFANTS, the offspring of slave parents!!!!" (vol. 1, no. 1, Boston, Massachusetts, January 1, 1831). In the sensational novel *Ida May*, the slave trader "stained [the white child's] skin with a sponge . . . until it was the color of a dark mulatto" (58). She is discovered when a fellow slave "took some water to wash ye . . . 'cause yer was *dat* dirty . . . how I did jump when I find *de black wash off!*" (129) Mary Pike, pub. as Mary Langdon, *Ida May, A Story of Things Actual and Possible* (Derby, 1855).

3. The very recourse to "white" interiors indicates the reembodiment of identity—as if the body were turned inside out and relations of body and identity not so much transcended as relocated. It's neither new to point out that abolition was predominantly a white enterprise, nor, I think, particularly helpful to express retrospective outrage about what now appear as racist assumptions of abolitionists. In looking at both pro- and anti-slavery writings, I want instead to explore how certain bodies and families get constituted in a fantasy of national identity. See, for instance, the analysis by Ronald Walters: especially in their use of "family as a metaphor for social harmony," "the antislavery and Southern proslavery arguments often bore deep similarities"; the desire of pro-slavery forces for "social, racial and sexual hierarchy" could not, however, fit with the "egalitarian" desire of abolitionists to "reconcile industry with order and morality." *The Anti-Slavery Appeal: American Abolitionism after 1830* (Johns Hopkins University Press, 1976), p. 148.

The sentimental appeals made by abolitionist works like Stowe's *Uncle Tom's Cabin* were often countered by refutations that opposed industrial slavery in the north to southern chattel slavery. For example, Caroline Rush's *North and South, or Slavery and Its Contrasts, a Tale of Real Life: "Truth is" Stronger "Than Fiction"* (Crissy and Markley, 1852), asks readers rhetorically "whether the 'broad-chested, powerful negro,' or the fragile, delicate girl, with her pure white face, is most entitled to your sympathy and tears" (128). In a perverse reversal, the novel presents the sale of a white infant to a Southern planter for $10,000—insisting, perhaps paradoxically, both on the mother's sorrow at her loss and on the tremendous advantage for the child who will be raised on a southern slaveholding plantation rather than in a northern city (where most of its siblings are battered to the point of madness or death): "the bondage of poverty forces a lady to give up her child . . . here is another proof of the slavery that exists in the North" (238).

4. The attention to exterior marks of identity coincided with a fascination with photography, phrenology, pseudo-scientific racism, and, later, eugenics. See, for example, "Science, Polygenesis, and the ProSlavery Argument" in George Frederickson, *The Black Image in the White Mind: The Debate on Afro-American Character and Destiny, 1817–1914* (Harper & Row, 1971).

5. The word "miscegenation" was coined in 1864 by David Croly, in *Miscegenation: The Theory of the Blending of the Races, Applied to the White Man and the Negro*. The earlier term, "amalgamation," implies that the "mixture" produces a new whole, whereas miscegenation emphasizes the mixing of distinct races. The criminalization of interracial relations began in the colonial period. Maryland passed a miscegenation statue in 1661 that made marriage between white women and black men illegal because it would produce legally free children. And it contin-

ued well after the end of slavery. In *Green v. State* (Alabama, 1877), a black man and a white woman were sent to jail for being married, in the name of preserving marriage and the home. Denying legitimacy to this union, the presiding judge announced, "It is through the marriage relation that the *homes* of a people are created. . . . These homes, in which the virtues are most cultivated and happiness most abounds, are the true *officinae gentium*—the nurseries of the States." Cited in Eva Saks, "Representing Miscegenation Law," *Raritan* 8 (Fall 1988) 42, 54. See also the discussion of the republican family and slavery in Michael Grossberg, *Governing the Hearth: Law and the Family in Nineteenth-Century America* (University of North Carolina Press, 1985), pp. 134–38.

6. Bruno Latour, *The Pasteurization of France* (Harvard University Press, 1988), p. 169.

7. *The Devil in America*, p. 23. Further references will be included parenthetically in the text preceded by D.

8. American political culture, according to Anne Norton, is determined by oppositions such as "white and black, East and West, North and South, man and woman," that reflect "the twinned American inheritance of Enlightenment and Reformation" and "have created a network of meaning through the articulation of difference." Anne Norton, *Alternative Americas: A Reading of Antebellum Political Culture* (University of Chicago Press, 1986), p. 3.

9. The satanic destruction of women seems easy:

> *To make a fool of her, my plan is this:*
> *Her first persuade her wrongs are very great . . .*
> *Without a right to rule, or even vote,*
> *And thus placed on a level with the slave.* (D, 72–3)

In these passages the identification abolitionist women found with slaves as they tried to claim "rights" gets at once mocked and reestablished. There is a varied and still growing literature on the attraction of women to the abolitionist cause. See, for example, Blanche Hersch, *The Slavery of Sex: Feminist-Abolitionists in America* (University of Illinois Press, 1978), and Jean Fagan Yellin, *Women and Sisters: The Antislavery Feminists in American Culture* (Yale University Press, 1969). Other treatments of the subject proceed from the standpoint of either abolition or feminism, therefore of course privileging the perspective they adopt in claiming that a movement for women's rights made the rights of others matter, or that abolition was the moral imperative through which women realized that they might have rights. The crisis of this identification, in the nineteenth century as well as today, is the implication that one matters more than another. Most famously, the alliances among women's rights advocates and abolitionists shattered after the Civil War over the issue of women's right to vote, which was (typically) opposed to that of the freed (male) slave. Advocacy of the former was presented as a betrayal of the latter. A less public instance was the division of the American Anti-Slavery Society in the 1830s over the inclusion of women as officers, notably the participation of the feisty Abby Kelly.

Shortly after her expulsion from the "old" organization, Abby Kelly wrote to the *National Anti-Slavery Standard* about her outrage that "such imputations to abolitionists, as 'no church,' 'no Bible,' 'no ministry,' 'no marriage,' 'woman out of her sphere,' and 'infidelity' [are made] by those who are sustaining an institution which denies the Bible, the church, the Sabbath, the ministry and marriage, to millions of their fellow countrymen, and throws more than a million American women out of the sphere of humanity, making them beasts of burden." She goes on to celebrate the fact that Anti-Slavery societies are not confined to slavery; they modestly promote not only "temperance, moral reform, and the sanctity of the Sabbath," but, in seeking to abolish "Drunkenness, licentiousness, profaneness, [and] infidelity," seek finally the "Abolition of all vice and sin in the land and the world" (May 20, 1841).

In Lydia Maria Child's first signed editorial for the *National Anti-Slavery Standard*, she asks, "Why has woman nothing to do with politics? Is she not bought and sold and brutalized . . . ?" (New York City, June 11, 1840). Angelina Grimke, the first woman to address any senate in the United States, explained to the Massachusetts legislature in May 1838, "All women have to do with this subject, not only because it is moral and religious, but because it is *political.*" For an extended account of woman's political rights and responsibilities and woman's "sphere," see her debate with Catherine Beecher, beginning with Grimke, *An Appeal to the Christian Women of the South* (New York, American Anti-slavery Society, 1836), followed by Beecher, *An Essay on Slavery and Abolition with Reference to the Duty of American Females* (2d ed., Henry Perkins, 1837), and ending with Grimke, *Letters to Catherine Beecher* (Knapp, 1838), in which she makes the typical claim that "the investigation of the rights of the slave has led me to a better understanding of my own" (114).

10. *The Slave's Friend* vol. 1 (Williams, 1836), p. 11.

11. Karen Sanchez-Eppler, "Bodily Bonds." Responding to the criticism that sentimental fiction "provides an inappropriate vehicle for the project of educating the public to slavery's real terrors" (14), Sanchez-Eppler argues that its effectiveness derives from its power as "an intensely bodily genre" in which the "tears of the reader are pledged . . . as a means of rescuing the bodies of slaves" (15). Still, she finds problematic sentimental fiction's "reliance on the body as the privileged structure for communicating meaning"; although it usefully "reinscribes the troubling relation between personhood and corporeality that underlies the project of both abolition and feminism" (22), the certainty of its inscription can be dismantled by miscegenation, which stands "as a bodily challenge to the conventions of reading the body, thus simultaneously insisting that the body is a sign of identity and undermining the assurance with which that sign can be read" (24).

12. His bestselling book, *Phrenology*, presented graduated lists of dominant and recessive traits with pictured examples and advice about how to respond to or compensate for inadequacy or overabundance in each instance. Orson Squire Fowler and Lorenzo Niles Fowler, *Phrenology* (rep. Chelsea House, 1980). See also John D'Emilio and Estelle Freedman, *Intimate Matters: A History of Sexuality in America* (Harper & Row, 1988).

13. After the First National Woman's Rights Convention at Worcester, Massachusetts (October 23, 1850), which included Lucy Stone, Frederick Douglass, Lucretia Mott, William Lloyd Garrison, and Wendell Phillips, the *New York Herald* reported an "awful combination of Socialism, Abolitionism, and Infidelity" (cited in *National Anti-Slavery Standard*, November 1850). Northern reformers were eager to discuss how tactics from revivals, temperance agitation, and even mesmerism and phrenology, could assist them.

14. It may be worth noting here how closely the pro-slavery critique of the impersonal and insubstantial workings of capitalism gets repeated in, for instance, Marxian critiques of capitalist impersonality. On the pro-slavery critique of capital-

ist impersonality, see George Fitzhugh, *Cannibals All! or Slaves Without Masters* (1857), ed. C. Vann Woodward (Harvard University Press, 1960).

15. A parody of the presidential campaign slogan of John Fremont, nominated for the Republican ticket in 1856: "Free Soil, Free Labor, Free Speech, Free Men, Fremont." (In this same presidential campaign William Seward coined the fateful phrase "irrepressible conflict.")

16. "But the pictures! the pictures!! these seem to have been specially offensive. And why, unless it is because they give specially distinct impressions of the horrors of slavery?" *Fourth Annual Report of . . . Massachusetts Anti-slavery Society* Jan. 20, 1836 (Knapp, 1836), p. 20. The dissemination of information about abolition especially occupies the Demon of Abolition. He describes how

> *The anti-slavery papers multiplied*
> *Each striving to depict the blackest scenes*
> *And satiate the public appetite . . .*
> *And works of fiction too were much employ'd,*
> *Selecting incidents and coloring well*
> *Such scenes as might the feelings most affect, . . .*
> *Thus work'd our lying legions everywhere*
> *Through papers, pamphlets, sermons, and reviews,*
> *Through novels, poems, and books made for schools,*
> *Through teachers, preachers, and professors learn'd,*
> *Through orators, editors, and statesmen,*
> *Through societies and in conventions,*
> *In college walls and legislative halls,*
> *Till agitation everywhere was felt.* (D, 134, 139–40)

This incantation is of course the dark side to the celebration that marks the upswelling of popular sympathy against slavery in the north. The major source for Theodore Weld's *American Slavery As It Is: The Testimony of a Thousand Voices* (Boston, 1842), which helped spur that sympathy, was, however, advertisements in southern newspapers.

17. *The Slave's Friend*, p. 96. Future references will be cited parenthetically preceded by SF.

18. In *The Child and the Republic*, Bernard Wishy discusses changes in childrearing practices along the lines of a move from physical discipline to internalized models (University of Pennsylvania Press, 1968). On discipline and character formation in the early republic, see also Richard Brodhead, "Sparing the Rod: Discipline and Fiction in Antebellum America," *Representations* 21 (Winter 1988) 67–96.

19. *Anti-Slavery Alphabet* (Printed for Anti-slavery Fair, 1846).

20. *The Slave's Friend*, vol. 2 (Williams, 1837), p. 20. The magazine's lessons in reading and diction include what amounts to a dictionary of anti-slavery. Young readers are taught "Never to call a colored person a NEGRO"; "Never to call a colored *man* a BOY"; and told that "Immediatism," or "immediate emancipation"—the unconditional freeing of the slaves which was at the time still a scandalous suggestion even for the north—"means, *doing a thing right off* . . . ": "If you are a good child, and do your duty, as soon as you know it, you are an immediatist"; while "gradualism" "means, doing a thing very slowly. . . . When you don't want to do a thing, you know you ought to do, and must do" (SF, 96, 97, 105, 106).

21. See, for example, Eric Sundquist's introduction to *Frederick Douglass: New Literary and Historical Essays* (Cambridge University Press, 1990), pp. 8–11, for discussions of reading and reform in Douglass.

22. Asked while guiding children in a Chatham St. Chapel meeting. See Walters, *The Anti-Slavery Appeal* (91–100) for an analysis of the involvement of abolition with antebellum concepts of the importance of women and children in reform.

23. In a series of significant articles, the historian Thomas Haskell argues that abolition depended upon a certain style of responsibility derived from capitalism. In "Convention and Hegemonic Interest in the Debate over Anti-slavery," he claims that "abolition was part of a broader effort to tame the market by setting limits to the pursuit of self-interest." *American Historical Review* 92 (October 1987), p. 550. In "Capitalism and the Origins of Humanitarian Sensibility," he asserts that the market functions as an "agency of social discipline" for "education and character modification." *American Historical Review* 90 (June 1985), p. 864.

24. They comment that under slavery, "Every year, 100,000 infants—a large proportion the offspring of pollution and shame—are born, and doomed to horrors of bondage." *Annual Report of Board of Managers of New England Anti-Slavery Society*, January 9, 1833 (Garrison and Knapp, 1833), pp. 17, 14. More typical is this protest: "We saw [slaves] held incapable of contracting even marriages, and liable to have that relation, at any moment, set at nought . . . we saw men putting those asunder whom God had joined together—tearing the husband from the wife—the wife from the husband—the parent from the child—yea, even the sucking babe from the bosom of his mother." A *Full Statement . . . to the Committee of the Legislature of Massachusetts . . . respecting Abolitionists and the Anti-Slavery Society* (Massachusetts Anti-Slavery Society, 1836), p. 4.

25. *Annual Report of New England Anti-Slavery Society*, p. 19.

26. *The Family and Slavery* (Cincinnati, n.d.), p. 23; Henry Wright, in the *Liberator*, March 7, 1838; cited in Walters, *Anti-Slavery Appeal*, pp. 92, 95.

27. Stephen Pearl Andrews, *Love, Marriage, Divorce, and the Sovereignty of the Individual . . .* (1853), p. 85, cited in Walters, p. 93.

28. "Slavery and Marriage: A Dialogue," [attrib. John Humphrey Noyes,] 1850) pp. 8, 13, 9. This discussion, of course, parodies the women/slaves debate (referred to in note 3). For a good contextual explanation of Noyes and the Oneida colony (1848–1879) see D'Emilio and Freedman, *Intimate Matters*, pp. 118–20. See also the discussion by Ann Braude in *Radical Spirits: Spiritualism and Women's Rights in Nineteenth-Century America* (Beacon, 1989). She cites the medium Mrs. Julia Branch declaring at the Rutland Free Convention of 1858 that "the slavery and degradation of woman proceed from the institution of marriage" (71).

The call for women's rights was also connected to slavery by Southerners: The pro-slavery novelist Caroline Rush attacks "that most horrible of all slaveholders, the tyrannical husband": "If you want to see slavery, in its worst form—the slavery that . . . holds in lifelong chains its wretched victims, you have only to visit the homes of many married people. . . . How many women are irrevocably tied to men. . . . Oh! freedom, thou art a jewel." Her narrator explains, "(. . . I will say, in this parenthesis, where our masters can't see it, Oh! fellow women, stand up for your rights and don't obey: don't yield up every thought to your owners.) The laws of slavery are all formed for the man and against the woman." [Caroline E. Rush], *North and South, or Slavery and Its Contrasts*, pp. 163–65.

29. For a discussion of the family in slavery, see Eugene Genovese, "'Our Family, White and Black': Family and Household in the Southern Slaveholders' World View," and Catherine Clinton, "'Southern Dishonor': Flesh, Blood, Race, and Bondage," in Carol Bleser, ed., *In Joy and in Sorrow: Women, Family, Marriage in the Victorian South, 1830–1900* (Oxford University Press, 1991). Catherine Clinton comments that "both the sexual dynamics of slavery and the racial dynamic of sexuality" must be considered in treating slavery as a "distinctive system of *reproduction* in the plantation South" (53). Genovese cites the pro-slavery argument: "Slavery *in the family* will be their happiest condition" (79). The pro-slavery John Fletcher asserted that "we are the property of the great family of man, and are under obligations . . . to the national community of which we form a part, and so on down to the distinct family of which we are a member." In answering the question of how a family could hold its members as property, he explained "if a man has absolute property in himself, he must surely have the right to alienate that property" (85). John Fletcher, *Studies on Slavery, in Easy Lessons* ([1852] Mnemosyne Publishing, 1969), pp. 182–83.

30. Richard Hildreth, *The Slave; or Memoirs of Archy Moore* (Eastburn, 1836), vol. 1, pp. 4, 5. Orlando Patterson proposes that Southerners' attraction to chivalry (and, perhaps, their interest in the French Revolution) was because of, and not in spite of, their system of slavery. *Slavery and Social Death: A Comparative Study* (Harvard University Press, 1982), pp. 94–97.

31. Hildreth, vol. 1, p. 14.

32. Hence, see, for instance, Frederick Douglass for a typical assertion that "I never knew my father." However, see also Herbert Gutman, *The Black Family in Slavery and Freedom* (Pantheon, 1976) for an analysis of how tenacious were both marital and family bonds.

33. Hildreth, vol. 1, pp. 20, 21, 22.

34. Eva Saks comments, "The taboo of too different (amalgamation/miscegenation) is interchangeable with the taboo of too similar (incest), since both crimes rely on a pair of bodies which are mutually constitutive of each other's deviance, a pair of bodies in which each body is the signifier of the deviance of the other" (53–54). For a discussion of the "sensuality" of the "captive body," see Hortense Spillers, "Mama's Baby, Papa's Maybe: An American Grammar Book," *Diacritics* (Summer 1987), p. 67. For the suggestion that "abolition's sexual propaganda" appeared as the pornography of slavery, see Peter Walker, *Moral Choices: Memory, Desire, and Imagination in Nineteenth-Century American Abolition* (Louisiana State University Press, 1978), pp. 288–90.

35. Harriet Beecher Stowe, *Uncle Tom's Cabin, or Life Among the Lowly* in *Harriet Beecher Stowe, Three Novels* (Library of America, 1982), p. 282. In the opening act of Dion Boucicault's *The Octoroon*, the grumbling Pete says of the children under his feet, "Guess they neber was born . . . dem black tings never was born at all; dey swarmed one morning on a sassafras tree in the swamp; I cotched 'em" (3). Dion Boucicault, *The Octoroon, or Life in Louisiana* (1861; Mnemosyne reprint, 1969).

36. Hildreth, p. 340.

37. Hildreth, vol. 2, pp. 48–49, vol. 1, p. 6. His sentiments about paternity undergo a further shock when he becomes a father. Like his own father, he is

"father of a slave!" The only power he shares with his father is that of murdering his son; while his father has nearly beaten him to death for having run away, Archy wants to kill his own son to keep him from being a slave.

38. For a thorough treatment of the novel see Carolyn Karcher, "Lydia Maria Child's *A Romance of the Republic*: An Abolitionist Vision of America's Racial Destiny," in *Slavery and the Literary Imagination: Selected Papers from the English Institute, 1987*, eds. Deborah McDowell and Arnold Rampersad (John Hopkins University Press, 1989), pp. 81–103. In *Pudd'nhead Wilson*, of course, the identity of the exchanged brothers is revealed by their "natal autographs," or their finger-prints.

39. Stuart Ewen discusses Holmes in a section called "Skinners of the Visible World," *All-Consuming Images: The Politics of Style in Contemporary Culture* (Basic Books, 1988). Oliver Wendell Holmes called the photograph a *"mirror with a memory"* in "The Stereoscope and the Stereograph," *Atlantic Monthly* (June 1859); reprinted in Beaumont Newhall, ed., *Photography: Essays and Images* (1980) 53–54; cited in Ewen.

40. The issue of recognizing a legislated racial identity is confronted by the only working-class abolitionist in the novel, Joe Bright, who becomes one when he discovers that he's been "passing" for himself. He sees an ad for a "stout mulatto slave, named Joe; has light sandy hair, blue eyes, and ruddy complexion . . . and will pass himself for a white man": "'By George!' said I, 'That's a description of *me*. I didn't even know before that I was a mulatto.' Well, it's just as bad for those poor black fellows as it would have been for me; but that blue-eyed Joe seemed to bring the matter home" (R, 322). Eva Saks comments that the phenomenon of passing, "blacks who passed as white," implies an "ontological corollary: whites who passed as white" (41). The Gerald Fitzgerald who gets sold as a slave discovers himself to be, as he is finally informed, "unmixed white." The other Gerald, Rosa's son, has to "take the case home to myself" (382) when he learns of what might be called his "mixed white" identity. In this novel's disturbing proliferation of applied identities, identities and identifications (with others, with oneself) are almost obsessively reen-acted.

41. Lydia Maria Child, *A Romance of the Republic* (Ticknor and Fields, 1867), p. 311. Further references will be cited parenthetically preceded by R.

42. In a brief essay on "The Declaration of Independence," Jacques Derrida notes that the act of declaring "we are and ought to be free and independent" constitutes the self that can make the declaration. What's left out of the Declaration of Independence, and, it has been argued, what makes it incomplete, are the passages on slavery excised by the Continental Congress. "Declarations of Independence," *New Political Science* 15 (1986) 7–15.

43. The narrator comments that nothing "made this favored band of colored people forgetful of the brethren they had left in bondage" (R, 401). Yet they serve Rosa's children, who don't know that *they* could be legally claimed as slaves. It's important to note here that I'm not accusing Lydia Maria Child of racist practices: she sacrificed as much as, if not more than, any other white abolitionist. See Carolyn Karcher, *The First Woman in the Republic: A Cultural Biography of Lydia Maria Child* (Duke University Press, 1994). Still, the question of the "transforma-tion into a gentleman" leads to a difficult issue of the novel—the question of how its anti-slavery impulse retains traces of the subtle racism we have seen informing earlier reform efforts. When Tulipa, the black slave of Rosa's father, is discovered,

"her own little episode of love and separation, of sorrow and shame, was whispered only to Missy Rosy" (R, 379). We don't hear her story after the moment of being stolen by Mr. Bruteman. The romance of the republic is not her romance—she's not only not a subject in this narrative, but she's quickly returned to a state of servitude as she is re-employed as a domestic by Rosa (R, 398).

Rosa's other former servants have "places provided for them, either in the household, or in [her husband's] commercial establishment. Their tropical exuberance made him smile . . . he said to his wife . . . 'It really seemed as if we were landing on the coast of Guinea with a cargo of beads'" (R, 398). As northern reformers, they still find themselves using the labor of others—and Rosa's identity as a slave descended from quite different acts of landing on the coast of Guinea seems forgotten as they imagine themselves to be missionaries colonizing a dark continent.

44. Elizabeth Fox-Genovese, *Within the Plantation Household: Black and White Women in the Old South* (University of North Carolina Press, 1989).

Bibliography

"An Account of a Murder Committed by Mr. J_____ Y_____, upon His Family, in December, A. D., 1781." *New York Weekly Magazine*, July 1796, vol. 2, no. 55.

Adair, Douglas. *Fame and the Founding Fathers* (New York: Norton, 1974).

Adams, John Quincy. "Address . . . on the Occasion of Reading the Declaration of Independence on the Fourth of July 1821" (City of Washington: Davis & Force, 1821).

Albanese, Catherine. *Sons of the Fathers: The Civil Religion of the American Revolution* (Philadelphia: Temple University Press, 1976).

Alexander, John. *Render Them Submissive: Responses to Poverty in Philadelphia, 1760–1800* (Amherst: University of Massachusetts Press, 1980).

Alien and Sedition Acts (1798), in *The Public Statutes at Large of the United States of America from the Organization of the Government in 1789 to March 3, 1845, arranged in chronological order . . . [etc.]* vol. 1. (Boston: Little, Brown, 1850).

Anderson, Benedict. *Imagined Communities: Reflections on the Origins and Spread of Nationalism* (London: Verso, 1983).

Andrews, Stephen Pearl. *Love, Marriage, Divorce, and the Sovereignty of the Individual . . .* (New York, 1853).

Anon., *Memoirs of General Andrew Jackson* (Auburn, New York: James C. Derby & Co., 1845) by "anon., citizen of New York."

Anti-Slavery Alphabet (Philadelphia: Printed for Anti-slavery Fair, 1846).

Applewhite, Harriet and Darline Levy, eds. *Women and Politics in the Age of the Democratic Revolutions* (University of Michigan Press, 1990).

Armstrong, Nancy. *Desire and Domestic Fiction: A Political History of the Novel* (Oxford University Press, 1989).

Armstrong, Nancy and Leonard Tennenhouse. *The Violence of Representation: Literature and the History of Violence* (New York: Routledge, 1989).

Axelrod, Alan. *Charles Brockden Brown: An American Tale* (Austin: University of Texas Press, 1983).

Axtell, James. *The School Upon a Hill: Education and Society in Colonial New England* (New Haven: Yale University Press, 1974).

Bailyn, Bernard. *The Ideological Origins of the American Revolution* (Cambridge: Harvard University Press, 1967).

Balibar, Etienne. "The Nation Form: History and Ideology" in Etienne Balibar and Immanuel Wallerstein, *Race, Nation, Class: Ambiguous Identities*, trans. Chris Turner (London: Verso, 1991).

Baltzell, E. Digby. *Puritan Boston and Quaker Philadelphia: Two Protestant Ethics and the Spirit of Class, Authority, and Leadership* (New York: Free Press, 1979).

Bancroft, George. "An Oration Delivered before the Democracy of Springfield, July 4, 1836" (Springfield: Merriam, 1836).

Banta, Martha. *Imaging American Women: Idea and Ideals in Cultural History* (New York: Columbia University Press, 1987).

———. "Medical Therapies and the Body Politic," *Prospects* (1983).

Barker-Benfield, G. J. *The Horrors of the Half-Known Life: Male Attitudes Toward Women and Sexuality in Nineteenth-Century America* (New York: Harper and Row, 1976).

Barnes, Gilbert. *The Anti-slavery Impulse: 1830–1844* ([1933] New York: Harcourt, Brace, & World, 1964).

Barstow, George. "Eulogy on the Life and Character of Andrew Jackson on the 12th of July, 1845" (Manchester, New Hampshire).

Barton, Cyrus "An Address . . . before Republicans . . . July 4, 1828" (Newport, 1828).

Baym, Nina. *American Women Writers and the Work of History, 1790–1860* (New Brunswick, New Jersey: Rutgers University Press, 1995).

———. *Novels, Readers, and Reviewers: Responses to Fiction in Antebellum America* (Ithaca: Cornell University Press, 1984).

———. *Woman's Fiction: A Guide to Novels by and about Women in America, 1820–1870* (Ithaca: Cornell University Press, 1978).

Beaumont, Gustave de. *Marie, or Slavery in the United States*, trans. Barbara Chapman ([1835] Stanford, 1958).

Beecher, Catherine. *An Essay on Slavery and Abolition with Reference to the Duty of American Females*, 2d ed. (Philadelphia: Henry Perkins, 1837).

Bell, Michael Davitt. *The Development of American Romance: The Sacrifice of Relation* (Chicago: University of Chicago Press, 1980).

———. *Hawthorne and the Historical Romance of New England* (Princeton: Princeton University Press, 1967).

Bell, Susan. *Women, The Family and Freedom: The Debate in Documents* (Stanford: Stanford University Press, 1983).

Bender, John. *Imagining the Penitentiary: Fiction and the Architecture of Mind in Eighteenth-Century England* (Chicago: University of Chicago Press, 1987).

Benson, Lee. *The Concept of Jacksonian Democracy: New York as a Test Case* (Princeton: Princeton University Press, 1961).

Berens, John. *Providence and Patriotism in Early America, 1640–1815* (Charlottesville: University Press of Virginia, 1978).

Berg, Barbara. *The Remembered Gate: Origins of American Feminism; The Woman and the City, 1800–1860* (New York: Oxford University Press, 1978).

Berlant, Lauren. *The Anatomy of National Fantasy: Hawthorne, Utopia, and Everyday Life* (Chicago: University of Chicago Press, 1991).

Bloch, Ruth. "The Gendered Meanings of Virtue in Revolutionary America," *Signs* 13 (1987), 37–58.

Bloomfield, Maxwell. *American Lawyers in a Changing Society, 1776–1876* (Cambridge: Harvard University Press, 1976).

Blumin, Stuart. *The Emergence of the Middle Class: Social Experience in the American City, 1760–1900* (New York: Cambridge University Press, 1989).

Bode, Carl. *The Anatomy of American Popular Culture, 1840–61* (Berkeley: University of California Press, 1959).

Borch-Jacobson, Mikkel. *The Emotional Tie: Psychoanalysis, Mimesis, and Affect,* trans. Douglas Brick et al. (Stanford: Stanford University Press, 1992).

———. *The Freudian Subject*, trans. Catherine Porter (Stanford: Stanford University Press, 1988).

Braude, Ann. *Radical Spirits: Spiritualism and Women's Rights in Nineteenth-Century America* (Boston: Beacon, 1989).

Bremner, Robert, ed. *Children and Youth in America*, vol. 1, 1600–1865 (Cambridge: Harvard University Press, 1970).

Breuilly, John. *Nationalism and the State* (New York: St. Martin's, 1982).

Bridenbaugh, Carl. *Cities in Revolt: Urban Life in America, 1743–1776* (New York: Knopf, 1955).

Bridenbaugh, Carol and Jessica Bridenbaugh. *Rebels and Gentlemen: Philadelphia in the Age of Franklin* (New York: Reynal and Hitchcock, 1942).

Bridges, William. "Family Patterns," *American Quarterly* 17 (Spring, 1965).

Bronfen, Elisabeth. *Over Her Dead Body: Death, Feminity and the Aesthetic* (New York: Routledge, 1992).

Brooks, Van Wyck. *The Flowering of New England, 1815–65* (New York: E. P. Dutton, 1937).

Brown, Charles Brockden. *Arthur Mervyn, or Memoirs of the Year 1793*, bicentennial edition, ed. Sydney Krause, (Kent State University Press, 1980).

———. *Edgar Huntly, or Memoirs of a Sleep-Walker* (New York: Penguin, 1988).

———. *Wieland, or The Transformation; An American Tale*, bicentennial edition (Kent State University Press, 1977).

Brown, Gillian. *Domestic Individualism: Imagining Self in Nineteenth-Century America* (Berkeley: University of California, 1990).

Brown, Herbert Ross. *The Sentimental Novel in America, 1789–1860* (Durham: Duke University Press, 1940).

Bryan, William. *George Washington in American Literature, 1775–1865* (New York: Columbia University Press, 1952).

Bucher, Bernadette. *Icon and Conquest: A Structural Analysis of the Illustrations of de Bry's Great Voyage*, trans. Basia Miller Gulati (University of Chicago, 1981).

Buel, Richard. *Securing the Revolution: Ideology in American Politics, 1789–1815* (Ithaca: Cornell University Press, 1972).

Burrows, Edwin, and Michael Wallace. "The American Revolution: The Ideology and Psychology of National Liberation," *Perspectives in American History* Vol. 6 (Harvard: Charles Warren Center, 1972).

Butterfield, L. H. et al., eds. *Diary and Autobiography of John Adams*, (Cambridge: Harvard University Press, 1961).

Byrdsall, F. *The History of Loco-foco Democrats* (New York: Burt Franklin, 1842).

Calhoun, Arthur. *The Social History of the American Family From Colonial Times to the Present* (Cleveland: Arthur Clark Co., 1917–19).

Campbell, Mary. *The Witness and the Other World: Exotic European Travel Writing, 400–1600* (Ithaca: Cornell University Press, 1988).

Caplan, Ruth. *Psychiatry and Community in Nineteenth-Century America: The Recurring Concern with the Environment in the Prevention and Treatment of Mental Illness* (New York: Basic Books, 1969).

Carey, Mathew. *A Short Account of the Malignant Fever, lately prevalent in Philadelphia* (Philadelphia, Nov. 14, 1793).

Carnes, Mark. *Secret Ritual and Manhood in Victorian America* (New Haven, Connecticut: Yale University Press, 1989).

Carretta, Vincent. *George III and the Satirists from Hogarth to Byron* (Athens: University of Georgia Press, 1990).

Carton, Evan. *The Rhetoric of American Romance: Dialectic and Identity in Emerson, Dickinson, Poe, and Hawthorne* (Baltimore: Johns Hopkins University Press, 1985).

Carver, Jonathan. *Travels Through the Interior Parts of North-America, in the Years 1766, 1767, and 1768* (London, 1778).

Chambers-Schiller, Lee Virginia. *Liberty: A Better Husband; Single Women in Nineteenth-Century America* (New Haven: Yale University Press, 1984).

Charvat, William. *Literary Publishing in America, 1790–1850* (Philadelphia: University of Pennsylvania Press, 1959).

Cherniavsky, Eva. *That Pale Mother Rising: Sentimental Discourses and the Imitation of Motherhood in 19th-Century America* (Bloomington: Indiana University Press, 1995).

Child, Lydia. *Hobomok and Other Writings*, ed. Carolyn Karcher (New Brunswick: Rutgers University Press, 1989).

———. *The Rebels, or Boston Before the Revolution* (Boston: Cummings, Hillard and Co., 1825).

———. *A Romance of the Republic*. (Boston: Ticknor and Fields, 1867).

Choate, Rufus. *Addresses and Orations* (Boston: Little, Brown, 1878).

Clark, David Lee. *Charles Brockden Brown: Pioneer Voice of America* (New York: AMS Press, 1966).

Clinton, Catherine. *The Other Civil War: American Women in the Nineteenth Century* (New York: Hill and Wang, 1984).

———. "'Southern Dishonor': Flesh, Blood, Race, and Bondage," in *In Joy and in Sorrow: Women, Family, and Marriage in the Victorian South, 1830–1900*, ed. Carol Bleser (New York: Oxford University Press, 1991).

Clover, Carol. *Men, Women, and Chainsaws: Gender in the Modern Horror Film* (Princeton: Princeton University Press, 1991).

Cobbett, William. "A Bone to Gnaw for the Democrats," *Peter Porcupine in America: Pamphlets on Republicanism and Revolution*, ed. David Wilson (Ithaca, New York: Cornell University Press, 1994).

Cohen, Lester. *The Revolutionary Histories: Contemporary Narratives of the American Revolution* (Ithaca: Cornell University Press, 1980).

Colacurcio, Michael. *The Province of Piety: Moral History in Hawthorne's Early Tales* (Cambridge: Harvard University Press, 1984).

Commager, Henry Steele. *The Empire of Reason: How Europe Imagined and*

America Realized the Enlightenment (Garden City, New York: Anchor Press, 1977).

Conrad, Susan, *Perish the Thought: Intellectual Women in Romantic America, 1830–1860* (New York: Oxford University Press, 1976).

Cooper, James Fenimore. *The Last of the Mohicans*, ed. William Charvat (Boston: Houghton Mifflin, 1958).

———. *Lionel Lincoln, or The Leaguer of Boston*, ed. Donald and Lucy Ringe (Albany: State University of New York Press, 1984).

———. *Notions of the Americans* (Philadelphia: Carey & Lea, 1828).

———. *The Spy: A Tale of the Neutral Ground* (New Haven: College and University Press, 1971).

Cott, Nancy. *The Bonds of Womanhood: "Woman's Sphere" in New England, 1780–1835* (New Haven: Yale University Press, 1977).

Crane, Elaine. "Dependence in the Era of Independence: The Role of Women in a Republican Society," in Jack Green, ed., *The American Revolution: Its Character and Limits* (New York: New York University Press, 1987), pp. 253–75.

Craven, Wesley. *The Legend of the Founding Fathers* (New York: New York University Press, 1956).

Crèvecoeur, Hector St. John de. *Letters from an American Farmer* ([1782] New York: Dutton, 1957).

Cross, Whitney. *The Burned-Over District: The Social and Intellectual History of Enthusiastic Religion in Western New York, 1800–1850* (Ithaca: Cornell University Press, 1950).

Curti, Merle. *Probing Our Past* (New York: Harper and Bros., 1955).

———. *The Roots of American Loyalty* (New York: Columbia University Press, 1946).

Dalke, Anne. "Original Vice: The Political Implications of Incest in the Early American Novel," *EAL* 23 (1988) 188–201.

Dalzell, Robert. *Daniel Webster and the Trial of American Nationalism, 1843–1852* (Boston: Houghton Mifflin, 1973).

Dangerfield, George. *The Awakening of American Nationalism, 1815–1828* (New York: Harper and Row, 1965).

Davidson, Cathy. *Revolution and the World: The Rise of the Novel in America* (New York: Oxford University Press, 1987).

Davidson, James. *The Logic of Millenial Thought: Eighteenth-Century New England* (New Haven: Yale University Press, 1977).

Davidson, Philip. *Propaganda and the American Revolution, 1763–1783* (Chapel Hill: University of North Carolina Press, 1941).

Davis, David Brion. *Homicide in American Fiction, 1798–1860* (Ithaca: Cornell University Press, 1957).

———. *The Problem of Slavery in the Age of Revolution, 1770–1823* (Ithaca: Cornell University Press, 1975).

Davis, Leonard. *Factual Fictions: The Origins of the English Novel* (New York: Columbia University Press, 1983).

de Certeau, Michel. *The Writing of History*, trans. Tom Conley (New York: Columbia University Press, 1988).

Degler, Carl. *At Odds: Women and the Family in America from the Revolution to the Present* (New York: Oxford University Press, 1980).

Dekker, George. *The American Historical Romance* (New York: Cambridge University Press, 1987).

————. *James Fenimore Cooper: The American Scott* (New York: Barnes and Noble, 1967).

Dekker, George and John McWilliams, eds. *James Fenimore Cooper: The Critical Heritage* (London: Routledge and Kegan Paul, 1973).

D'Emilio, John and Estelle Freedman. *Intimate Matters: A History of Sexuality in America* (New York: Harper and Row, 1988).

Demos, John. *A Little Commonwealth: Family Life in Plymouth Colony* (New York: Oxford University Press, 1970).

————. "How the Puritans Won the American Revolution," *Massachusetts Review* 17 (Winter 1976) 597–630.

Demos, John and Sarane Bovcock, eds. *Turning Points: Historical and Sociological Essays on the Family* (Chicago: University of Chicago Press, 1978).

Demos, John and Virginia Demos. "Adolescence in Historical Perspective," in *The American Family in Social-Historical Perspective* (New York: St. Martin's Press, 1973), pp. 209–221.

Derrida, Jacques. "Declarations of Independence," *New Political Science* 15 (1986) 7–15.

Dimock, Wai-chee. *Empire for Liberty: Melville's Poetics of Individualism* (Princeton: Princeton University Press, 1990).

Dolmetsch, Joan. *Rebellion and Reconciliation: Satirical Prints on Revolution* (Charlottesville: University Press of Virginia, 1976).

Donovan, Josephine. *New England Local Color Literature* (New York: F. Ungar, 1983).

Donzelot, Jacques. *The Policing of Families*, trans. Robert Hurley (New York: Pantheon, 1979).

Doubleday, Neal Frank. *Hawthorne's Early Tales* (Durham, North Carolina: Duke University Press, 1972).

Douglas, Ann. *The Feminization of American Culture* (New York: Knopf, 1977).

Drinnon, Richard. *Facing West: The Metaphysics of Indian-Hating and Empire-Building* (St. Paul: University of Minnesota, 1980).

Duban, James. *Melville's Major Fiction: Politics, Theology, and Imagination* (Dekalb: Northern Illinois University Press, 1983).

DuBois, Ellen. *Feminism and Suffrage: The Emergence of an Independent Women's Movement in America, 1848–1869* (Ithaca: Cornell University Press, 1978).

Dudden, Faye. *Serving Women: Household Service in Nineteenth-Century America* (Middletown, Connecticut: Wesleyan University Press, 1983).

Duffy, John. *Epidemics in Colonial America* (Baton Rouge: Louisiana State University Press, 1953).

Dwight, Timothy. *A Discourse on Some Events of the Last Century* (New Haven: Yale University Press, 1801).

————. "Discourse in Two Parts" (1812).

————. *Theology Explained and Defended, in a Series of Sermons* (New York: 1846).

Edwards, Jonathan. "Personal Narrative," in *Representative Selections*, ed. Clarence Faust and Thomas Johnson (New York: Hill and Wang, 1965).

Ekirch, Arthur. *The Idea of Progress in America, 1815–1860* (New York: P. Smith, 1951).

Elliott, Emory. *Revolutionary Writers: Literature and Authority in the New Republic, 1725–1810* (New York: Oxford University Press, 1982).

Ellis, Joseph. *After the Revolution: Profiles of Early American Culture* (New York: Norton, 1979).

Elson, Ruth. *Guardians of Tradition: American Schoolbooks of the Nineteenth-Century* (Lincoln: University of Nebraska Press, 1964).

Emerson, Everett, ed. *American Literature, 1764–1789* (Madison: University of Wisconsin Press, 1977).

Epstein, Barbara. *The Politics of Domesticity: Women, Evangelism, and Temperance in Nineteenth-Century America* (Middletown, Connecticut: Wesleyan University Press, 1981).

Faderman, Lillian. *Surpassing the Love of Men: Romantic Friendships and Love between Women from the Renaissance to the Present* (New York: Morrow, 1981).

The Family and Slavery (Cincinnati, n.d.).

Fanon, Frantz. *The Wretched of the Earth* (New York: Grove, 1968).

Ferguson, Frances. "Sade and the Pornographic Legacy," *Representations* 36 (Fall 1991) 1–21.

Ferguson, Robert. "Yellow Fever and Charles Brockden Brown: The Context of the Emerging Novelist," *Early American Literature* 14 (1980) 293–305.

———. *Law and Letters in American Culture* (Cambridge: Harvard University Press, 1984).

Fessenden, Thomas Green. *Democracy Unveiled* (New York: I. Riley, 1806).

Fiedler, Leslie. *Love and Death in the American Novel* (New York: Stein and Day, 1966).

Fisher, Philip. *Hard Facts: Setting and Form in the American Novel* (New York: Oxford University Press, 1985).

Fisher, Sidney. "Legendary and Myth-Making Process in Histories of the American Revolution" *Proceedings of the American Philosophical Association* 51 (1912) 53–75.

Fletcher, John. *Studies on Slavery, in Easy Lessons* ([1852] Miami: Mnemosyne Publishing, 1969).

Fliegelman, Jay. *Prodigals and Pilgrims: The American Revolution Against Patriarchal Authority, 1750–1800* (New York: Cambridge University Press, 1982).

Forgie, George. *Patricide in the House Divided: A Psychological Interpretation of Lincoln and His Age* (New York: Norton, 1979).

Foucault, Michel. "Governmentality," *Ideology and Consensus*, 6 (Autumn 1979), 17. Reprinted in *The Foucault Effect: Studies in Governmentality*, ed. Graham Burchell et al. (Chicago: University of Chicago Press, 1991), pp. 87–104.

———. *Discipline and Punish: The Birth of the Prison*, trans. Alan Sheridan (New York: Pantheon, 1977).

———. *History of Sexuality* vol 1. (Pantheon, 1978).

———, ed. *I Pierre Riviere . . . A Case of Parricide in the Nineteenth Century* (University of Nebraska Press, 1975).

Fourth Annual Report of . . . Massachusetts Anti-slavery Society Jan. 20, 1836 (Boston: Knapp, 1836).

Fox-Genovese, Elizabeth. *Within the Plantation Household: Black and White Women in the Old South* (Chapel Hill: University of North Carolina Press, 1989).

Franzen, Monica and Nancy Ethiel. *Make Way! 200 Years of American Women in Cartoons* (Chicago: University of Chicago Press, 1988).

Fredrickson, George. *The Black Image in the White Mind: The Debate on Afro-American Character and Destiny, 1817–1914* (New York: Harper and Row, 1971).

———. *The Arrogance of Race: Historical Perspectives on Slavery, Racism, and Social Inequality* (Middletown, Connecticut: Wesleyan University Press, 1988).

Freud, Sigmund. "Family Romances," vol. 9 of *The Standard Edition of the Complete Works of Sigmund Freud*, trans. James Strachey (London: Hogarth Press, 1959) pp. 238–39.

———. "Fetishism," vol. 7 of *The Standard Edition of the Complete Works of Sigmund Freud* (London: Hogarth Press, 1955) 21:152–157.

———. *Totem and Taboo* (New York: Routledge, 1950).

Friedman, Lawrence. *Inventors of the Promised Land* (New York: Knopf, 1975).

A Full Statement . . . to the Committee of the Legislature of Massachusetts . . . respecting Abolitionists and the Anti-Slavery Society (Boston: Massachusetts Anti-Slavery Society, 1836).

Gardner, Jared. "Alien Nation: Edgar Huntly's Savage Awakening" *American Literature* 66 (September 1994), 429–461.

Gay, Peter. *The Enlightenment: An Interpretation* (New York: Knopf, 1966).

Gellner, Ernest. *Nations and Nationalism* (Cambridge, Massachusetts: Basil Blackwell, 1983).

Gibbs, George. *Memoirs of the Administrations of Washington and John Adams* (New York: Printed for subscribers, 1846).

Gilmore, Michael. *American Romanticism and the Marketplace* (Chicago: University of Chicago Press, 1985).

Goldberg, Jonathan. *Sodometries: Renaissance Texts, Modern Sexualities* (Stanford: Stanford University Press, 1992).

Grabo, Norman. *The Coincidental Art of Charles Brockden Brown* (Chapel Hill: University of North Carolina Press, 1981).

Granger, Bruce. *Political Satire in the American Revolution, 1763–83* (Ithaca: Cornell University Press, 1946).

Green, Harvey. *The Light of the Home: An Intimate View of the Lives of Women in Victorian America* (New York: Pantheon, 1983).

Greene, Jack P., ed. *The Ambiguity of the American Revolution* (New York: Harper and Row, 1968).

Greven, Philip. *Four Generations: Population, Land, and Family in Colonial Andover, Massachusetts* (Ithaca: Cornell University Press, 1970).

———. *The Protestant Temperament: Patterns of Child-Rearing, Religious Experience and the Self in Early America* (New York: Knopf, 1977).

Griffin, Clifford. *Their Brother's Keepers: Moral Stewardship in the United States, 1800–1865* (New Brunswick, New Jersey: Rutgers University Press, 1960).

———. "Religious Benevolence as Social Control, 1815–1860," in David Brion Davis, ed. *Ante-Bellum Reform* (New York: Harper & Row, 1967).

Grimke, Angelica. *An Appeal to the Christian Women of the South* (New York: American Anti-Slavery Society, 1836).

Gross, Seymour. "'Lady Eleanore's Mantle' as History," *JEGP* 54 (1955) 549–554.

Grossberg, Michael. *Governing the Hearth: Law and the Family in Nineteenth-Century America* (Chapel Hill: University of North Carolina Press, 1985).

Habegger, Alfred. *Gender, Fantasy, and Realism in American Literature* (New York: Columbia University Press, 1982).

Habermas, Jurgen. *The Structural Transformation of the Public Sphere*, trans. Thomas Burger with Fredrick Lawrence (Cambridge, Massachusetts: MIT Press, 1989).

Haller, John, Jr. and Robin Haller. *The Physician and Sexuality in Victorian America* (Urbana: University of Illinois Press, 1974).

Halttunen, Karen. *Confidence Men and Painted Women: A Study of Middle-class Culture in America, 1830–1870* (New Haven: Yale University Press, 1982).

Haraway, Donna. "Gender for a Marxist Dictionary: The Sexual Politics of a Word," in *Simians, Cyborgs, and Women: the Reinvention of Nature* (New York: Routledge, 1991) pp. 127–148.

Hareven, Tamara, ed. *Family and Kin in Urban Communities, 1700–1930* (New York: Viewpoints, 1977).

Harris, Susan K. *19th century American Women's Novels: Interpretive Strategies* (New York: Cambridge University Press, 1990).

Hart, James. *The Popular Book: A History of America's Literary Taste* (New York: Oxford University Press, 1950).

Haskell, Thomas. "Capitalism and the Origins of Humanitarian Sensibility," *American Historical Review* 90 (June 1985) 547–566.

———. "Convention and Hegemonic Interest in the Debate over Anti-slavery," *American Historical Review* 92 (October 1987) 829–878.

Hatch, Nathan. *The Sacred Cause of Liberty: Republican Thought and the Millenium in Revolutionary New England* (New Haven: Yale University Press, 1977).

Hawthorne, Nathaniel. "The Legends of the Province House" in *Twice-Told Tales*, ed. William Charvat, Roy Harvey Pearce, and Claude Simpson (Columbus: Ohio State University Press, 1974).

Hayden, Dolores. *The Grand Domestic Revolution: A History of Feminist Designs for American Homes, Neighborhoods, and Cities* (Cambridge, Massachusetts: MIT Press, 1981).

Heckewelder, John. *An Account of the History, Manners, and Customs of the Indian Nations* (Philadelphia: Abraham Small, 1819).

———. *Narrative of the Mission of the United Brethren Among the Delaware and Mohegan Indians from its Commencement in the Year 1740 to the Close of the Year 1808 . . . by John Heckewelder who was many Years in Service of that Mission* (Philadelphia: McCarty and Davis, 1820).

Hedges, William. "Benjamin Rush, Charles Brockden Brown, and the American Plague Year," *Early American Literature* 7 (1973) 295–311.

Heimert, Alan. *Religion and The American Mind: From the Great Awakening to the American Revolution* (Cambridge: Harvard University Press, 1966).

———. "Moby-Dick and American Political Symbolism" *American Quarterly* 16 (1963) 498–534.

Henderson, Harry. *Versions of the Past: The Historical Imagination in American Fiction* (New York: Oxford University Press, 1974).

Hersh, Blanche. *The Slavery of Sex: Feminist-Abolitionists in America* (Urbana: University of Illinois Press, 1978).

Hertz, Neil. "Medusa's Head: Male Hysteria Under Political Pressure" in *The End of The Line: Essays on Psychoanalysis and the Sublime* (New York: Columbia University Press, 1985), pp. 179–191.

Hewitt, Nancy. *Women's Activism and Social Change: Rochester, New York, 1822–1872* (Ithaca: Cornell University Press, 1984).

Hildreth, Richard. *The Slave or Memoirs of Archy Moore* (Boston: Eastburn, 1836).

Hobsbawn, Eric. *The Age of Revolution: 1789–1848* (New York: New American Library, 1964).

———. *Nations and Nationalism Since 1780: Programme, Myth, Reality* (New York: Cambridge University Press, 1990).

Hoffer, Peter Charles. *Revolution and Regeneration: Life Cycle and the Historical Vision of the Generation of 1776* (Athens: University of Georgia Press, 1983).

Hofstadter, Richard. *The American Political Tradition and the Men Who Made It* (New York: Knopf, 1948).

Honig, Bonnie. "Declarations of Independence: Arendt and Derrida on the Problem of Founding a Republic" in Frederick Dolan and Thomas Dumm, eds. *Rhetorical Republic: Governing Representations in American Politics* (Amherst: University of Massachusetts Press, 1993).

Honour, Hugh. *The New Golden Land: European Images of America from the Discovery to the Present Time* (New York: Pantheon, 1975).

Horsman, Reginald. *Race and Manifest Destiny: The Origins of American Racial Anglo-Saxonism* (Cambridge: Harvard University Press, 1981).

Horwitz, Morton. *The Transformation of American Law, 1780–1860* (Cambridge: Harvard University Press, 1977).

Howard, Leon. *The Connecticut Wits* (Chicago: University of Chicago Press, 1943).

Hulme, Peter. *Colonial Encounters: Europe and the Native Caribbean, 1492–1797* (London: Methuen, 1986).

Hunt, Lynn. *The Family Romance of the French Revolution* (Berkeley: University of California Press, 1992).

Hyneman, Charles, ed. *American Political Writing During the Founding Era, 1760–1805* (Indianapolis: Liberty Press, 1983).

Ignatieff, Michael. *A Just Meaure of Pain: The Penitentiary in the Industrial Revolution, 1750–1850* (New York: Pantheon, 1978).

Irving, Washington. "Legend of Sleepy Hollow," *The Sketch Book* (New York: New American Library, 1961).

Jacobus, Mary. *Reading Woman: Essays in Feminist Criticism* (New York: Columbia University Press, 1986).

Jameson, Fredric. *The Political Unconscious: Narrative as a Socially Symbolic Act* (Ithaca: Cornell University Press, 1981).

Jennings, Francis. *The Ambiguous Iroquois Empire: The Covenant Chain Confederation of English Colonies* (New York: Norton, 1984).

Johnson, Paul. *A Shopkeeper's Millenium: Society and Revivals in Rochester, New York, 1815–1837* (New York: Hill and Wang, 1978).

Jones, Howard. *Revolution and Romanticism* (Cambridge: Belknap Press of Harvard University Press, 1974).

Jones, Jacqueline. *Labor of Love, Labor of Sorrow: Black Women, Work, and the Family from Slavery to the Present* (New York: Basic Books, 1985).

Jones, Michael Wynn. *A Cartoon History of the American Revolution* (New York: Putnam, 1975).

Jordan, Constance. "The Household and the State: Transformations in the Representation of an Analogy from Aristotle to James I" *MLQ* 54 (September 1993) 307–321.

Jordan, Cynthia. *Second Stories: The Politics of Language, Form, and Gender in Early American Fiction* (Chapel Hill: University of North Carolina Press, 1989).

Jordan, Winthrop. "Familial Politics: Thomas Paine and the Killing of the King, 1776," *Journal of American History* 60 (1973) 294–308.

Kaestle, Carl. *Pillars of the Republic: Common Schools and American Society, 1780–1860* (New York: Hill and Wang, 1983).

Kammen, Michael. *A Season of Youth: The American Revolution and the Historical Imagination* (Ithaca: Cornell University Press, 1978).

Kaplan, Amy and Donald Pease, eds. *Cultures of United States Imperialism* (Durham: Duke University Press, 1994).

Karcher, Carolyn. *The First Woman in the Republic: A Cultural Biography of Lydia Maria Child* (Durham: Duke University Press, 1994).

Kasson, John. *Civilizing the Machine: Technology and Republican Values in America, 1776–1900* (New York: Penguin, 1977).

Kasson, Joy. *Marble Queens and Captives: Women in Nineteenth-Century American Sculpture* (New Haven: Yale University Press, 1990).

Katz, Michael B. *Irony of Early School Reform: Educational Innovation in Nineteenth-century Massachusetts* (Cambridge: Harvard University Press, 1968).

Kelly, Mary. *Private Woman, Public Stage: Literary Domesticity in Nineteenth-Century America* (New York: Oxford University Press, 1984).

Kennedy, John Pendleton. *Quodlibet* (Philadelphia: Lea and Blanchard, 1840).

———. *Horse-Shoe Robinson: A Tale of the Tory Ascendancy*, revised ed. (New York: Putnams, 1881).

Kenyon, Cecelia. "Republicanism and Radicalism in the American Revolution" *William and Mary Quarterly* 19 (1962) 153–82.

Kerber, Linda. *Federalists in Dissent: Imagery and Ideology in Jeffersonian America* (Ithaca: Cornell University Press, 1970).

———. *Women of the Republic: Intellect and Ideology in Revolutionary America* (New York: Norton, 1986).

Kerber, Linda and Jane Hart-Mathews. *Women's America* (New York: Oxford University Press, 1982).

Kesler-Harris, Alice. *Out to Work: A History of Wage-Earning Women in the United States* (New York: Oxford University Press, 1982).

Kiefer, Monica. *American Children Through Their Books, 1700–1835* (Philadelphia: University of Pennsylvania Press, 1948).

Kimball, Arthur G. *Rational Fictions: A Study of Charles Brockden Brown* (McMinnville, Oregon: Linfield Research Institute, 1968).

Koch, Adrienne, ed. *The American Enlightenment: The Shaping of the American Experiment and a Free Society* (New York: George Braziller, 1965).

Kolodny, Annette. *The Lay of the Land: Metaphor as Experience and History in American Life and Letters* (Chapel Hill: University of North Carolina Press, 1975).

Kraditor, Aileen. *Means and Ends in American Abolitionism: Garrison and His Critics on Strategy and Tactics, 1834–1850* (New York: Pantheon, 1969).

Landes, Joan. *Women and the Public Sphere in the Age of the French Revolution* (Ithaca: Cornell University Press, 1988).

Laplanche, Jean and J. B. Pontalis. "Fusion/Defusion (of Instincts)" *The Language of Psychoanalysis*, trans. Donald Nicholson-Smith (New York: Norton, 1973).

Laqueur, Thomas. "Memory and Naming in the Great War," in John Gillis, ed. *Commemorations: The Politics of National Identity* (Princeton University Press, 1994), 150–167.

le Corbeiller, Clare. "Miss America and Her Sisters: Personifications of the Four Parts of the World," *Metropolitan Museum Bulletin* ns. 19–20 (1960).

Lerner, Gerda. "The Lady and the Mill Girl: Changes in the Status of Women in the Age of Jackson," in *The Majority Finds its Past: Placing Women in History* (New York: Oxford University Press, 1979).

Levin, David. *History as Romantic Art: Bancroft, Prescott, Motley and Parkman,* (Stanford: Stanford University Press, 1959).

Levine, Robert. *Conspiracy and Romance: Studies in Brockden Brown, Cooper, Hawthorne, and Melville* (New York: Cambridge University Press, 1989).

Levi-Strauss, Claude. *Elementary Structures of Kinship,* trans. Bell and von Sturmer (Boston: Beacon, 1969).

Levy, Leonard and Carl Siracusa, eds. *Legacy of Suppression* (Cambridge: Harvard University Press, 1960).

————. *Essays on the Early Republic, 1789–1815* (Illinois: Dryden Press, 1974).

Lewis, Jan. "The Republican Wife: Virtue and Seduction in the Early Republic," *William and Mary Quarterly* 44 (October 1987) 689–721.

Lewis, Orlando. *The Development of American Prisons and Prison Customs 1776–1845* (New York: Prison Association of New York, 1922).

Lewis, R. W. B. *The American Adam* (Chicago: University of Chicago Press, 1955).

Lippard, George. *Blanche of Brandywine, or September 11, 1777; A Romance of the Revolution* (Philadelphia: T. B. Peterson, 1846).

————. *The Legends of the American Revolution; "1776," or, Washington and his Generals* (Philadelphia: Leary, Stuart & Co., 1876).

Loskiel, George Henry. *History of the Mission of the United Brethren Among the Indian in North America,* trans. from the German by Christian La Trobe (London: Brethren's Society for the Furtherance of the Gospel, 1794).

Lutz, Alma. *Crusade for Freedom: Women of the Anti-Slavery Movement* (Boston: Beacon, 1968).

MacCannell, Dean. "Democracy's Turn: On Homeless *Noir*" in Joan Copjec, ed., *Shades of Noir: A Reader* (London: Verso, 1993) pp. 279–298.

MacCannell, Juliet Flower. *The Regime of the Brother: After Patriarchy* (New York: Routledge, 1991).

Marshall, Humphrey. "The Aliens: a patriotic poem . . . occasioned by the *Alien* bill, now before the senate," (Philadelphia: May 15, 1798).

Marty, Martin E. *Religion, Awakening, and Revolution* (North Carolina: Consortium, 1977).

Mason, Peter. *Deconstructing America: Representations of the Other* (New York: Routledge, 1990).

May, Henry. *The Enlightenment in America* (New York: Oxford University Press, 1976).

Mazlish, Bruce. "Leadership in the American Revolution: The Psychological Dimension" *Leadership in the American Revolution* (Washington, D. C.: Library of Congress, 1974).

McKay, George. *American Book Auction Catalogues, 1713–1934* (New York: New York Public Library, 1967).

McLoughlin, William. "The Role of Religion in the American Revolution: Liberty of Conscience and Cultural Cohesion in the New Nation" *Essays on the American Revolution*, eds. Steven Kurtz and James Hutson (Chapel Hill: University of North Carolina Press, 1973).

McWilliams, John. *Political Justice in a Republic: James Fenimore Cooper's America* (Berkeley: University of California Press, 1972).

———. "'Thorough-Going Democrat' and 'Modern Tory,'" *Studies in Romanticism* 15 (1976) 549–71.

McWilliams, Wilson. *The Idea of Fraternity in America* (Berkley: University of California Press, 1973).

Melville, Herman. *Israel Potter: His Fifty Years of Exile* ([1855] Evanston: Northwestern University Press, 1982).

Merk, Frederick. *Manifest Destiny and Mission in American History; a Reinterpretation* (New York: Knopf, 1963).

Meyers, Marvin. *The Jacksonian Persuasion: Politics and Belief* (Stanford: Stanford University Press, 1957).

Miller, Perry. *Jonathan Edwards* (New York: W. Sloane Associates, 1949).

Mitchell, Isaac. *Alonzo and Melissa, or the Unfeeling Father: an American Tale* (Hartford: Andrus and Son, 1851).

Mitchell, Stephen Mix. *Narrative of the Life of William Beadle* (Windsor, Vermont: Spooner, 1795).

Montrose, Louis. "Gender and the Discourse of Discovery," *Representations* 33 (Winter 1991) 1–41.

Morgan, Edmund. *The Puritan Family; Religion and Domestic Relations in Seventeenth-Century America* (New York: Harper and Row, 1966).

Morris, Richard. *The American Revolution Reconsidered* (New York: Harper and Row, 1967).

Mosse, George. *Nationalism and Sexuality: Middle-class Morality and Sexual Norms in Modern Europe* (Madison: University of Wisconsin Press, 1985).

Mott, Frank Luther. *American Journalism: A History of Newspapers in the U.S. through 250 Years, 1690–1940* (New York: Macmillan, 1941).

———. *Golden Multitudes: Best Sellers in the United States* (New York: Macmillan, 1974).

Nancy, Jean-luc and Philippe Lacoue-Labarthe. "The Nazi Myth," *Critical Inquiry* 16 (1990) 291–312.

Neal, John. *Seventy-Six, "Our Country—Right or Wrong"* (Bainbridge, New York: York Mail-Print, 1971 [1823]).

Nelson, Dana. *The Word in Black and White: Reading "Race" in American Literature, 1638–1867* (New York: Oxford University Press, 1992).

Nevins, Allan and Frank Weitenkampf. *A Century of Political Cartoons* (New York: Scribner's, 1944).

Norton, Anne. *Alternative Americas: A Reading of Antebellum Political Culture* (Chicago: University of Chicago Press, 1986).

———. *Reflections on Political Identity* (Baltimore: Johns Hopkins University Press, 1988).

Norton, Mary Beth. *Liberty's Daughters* (Boston: Little, Brown, 1980).

[Noyes, John Humphrey], attrib. "Slavery and Marriage: A Dialogue," (1850).

Nussbaum, Felicity. "'Savage' Mothers: Narratives of Maternity in the Mid-Eighteenth Century," *Cultural Critique* 20 (Winter 1991–92) 123–151.

Nye, Russel. *Society and Culture in America, 1830–1860* (New York: Harper and Row, 1974).

Paine, Thomas. "Common Sense," reprinted in *The Life and Major Writings of Thomas Paine*, ed. Philip Foner (Secaucus, New Jersey: Citadel Press, 1974).

Parker, Andrew et al., eds. *Nationalisms and Sexualities* (New York: Routledge, 1992).

Pateman, Carol. *The Disorder of Women: Democracy, Feminism, and Political Theory* (Cambridge: Polity Press, 1989).

———. *The Sexual Contract* (Stanford: Stanford University Press, 1988).

Patterson, Orlando. *Slavery and Social Death* (Cambridge: Harvard University Press, 1982).

Paulding, James Kirk. *John Bull in America* (New York: Charles Wiley, 1825).

———. *The Old Continental, or, The Price of Liberty* (New York: Cady & Burgess, 1851).

Paulson, Ronald. *Representations of Revolution, 1789–1820* (New Haven: Yale University Press, 1983).

Pease, Jane and William Pease. *Bound with them in Chains: A Biographical History of the Anti-Slavery Movement* (Westport, Connecticut: Greenwood Press, 1972).

Pickering, James. *James Fenimore Cooper and the History of New York* (Evanston, Illinois: Pickering, 1964).

Pivar, David. *Purity Crusade* (Westport, Connecticut: Greenwood Press, 1973).

Porte, Joel. *In Respect to Egotism: Studies in American Romantic Writing* (New York: Cambridge University Press, 1991).

Powell, J. H. *Bring Out Your Dead: The Great Plague of Yellow Fever in Philadelphia in 1793* (Philadelphia: University of Pennsylvania Press, 1949).

Press, Charles. *The Political Cartoon* (Rutherford, New Jersey: Fairleigh Dickinson University Press, 1981).

Reid, Roddey. *Families in Jeopardy: Regulating the Social Body in France, 1750–1910* (Stanford: Stanford University Press, 1993).

Richards, Leonard. *"Gentlemen of Property and Standing": Anti-Abolition Mobs in Jacksonian America* (New York: Oxford University Press, 1970).

Ridgely, J. V. "George Lippard's *The Quaker City*: The World of the American Porno-Gothic," *Studies in the Literary Imagination* 7 (Spring 1974) 77–94.

Rogin, Michael. *Fathers and Children: Andrew Jackson and the Subjugation of the American Indian* (New York: Random House, 1976).

———. *Subversive Genealogy: The Politics and Art of Herman Melville* (New York: Knopf, 1984).

———. "'Make My Day!' Spectacle as Amnesia in Imperial Politics," in *Cultures of United States Imperialism*, eds. Amy Kaplan and Donald Pease (Durham: Duke University Press, 1993), pp. 499–534.

Romero, Lora. "Vanishing Americans: Gender, Empire, and New Historicism," in *The Culture of Sentiment: Race, Gender, and Sentimentality in Nineteenth-Century America*, ed. Shirley Samuels (Oxford University Press, 1992).

Rosenberg, Bruce. *The Neutral Ground: The Andre Affair and the Background of Cooper's The Spy* (Westport, Connecticut: Greenwood, 1994).

Rothman, David. *The Discovery of the Asylum: Social Order and Disorder in the New Republic* (Boston: Little, Brown, 1971).

Rudolph, Frederick, ed. *Essays on Education in the Early Republic* (Cambridge: Harvard University Press, 1965).

Rush, Benjamin. *Account of the Influences of the Military and Political Events of the American Revolution Upon the Human Body.*

[Rush, Caroline E.] *North and South, or Slavery and Its Contrasts* (Philadelphia: Crissy & Markley, 1852).

Rush, Richard. *An Operation, Delivered in the House of Representatives, July 4, 1812* (Washington D.C., 1812).

Ryan, Mary P. *Cradle of the Middle Class: The Family in Oneida County, NY, 1790–1865* (New York: Cambridge University Press, 1981).

———. *The Empire of the Mother: American Writing About Domesticity, 1830–1860* (New York: Haworth Press, 1982).

———. *Women in Public: Between Banners and Ballots, 1825–1880* (Baltimore: John Hopkins University Press, 1990).

Saks, Eva. "Representing Miscegenation Law," *Raritan* 8 (Fall 1988) 139–69.

Sanchez-Eppler, Karen. *Touching Liberty: Abolition, Feminism, and the Politics of the Body* (Berkeley: University of California Press, 1993).

Scarry, Elaine. *The Body in Pain: The Making and Unmaking of the World* (New York: Oxford University Press, 1985).

Scott, Donald and Bernard Wishy, eds. *America's Families: A Documentary History* (New York: Harper and Row, 1982).

Scott, Joan. *Gender and the Politics of History* (New York: Columbia University Press, 1988).

Sedgwick, Catherine. *The Linwoods, or "Sixty Years Since" in America* (New York: Harper & Bros., 1835).

Sedgwick, Susan Ridley. *Allen Prescott: or the Fortunes of a New England Boy*, (New York: Harper Bros., 1834).

Seltzer, Mark. *Bodies and Machines* (New York: Routledge, 1992).

———. *Henry James and the Art of Power* (Ithaca: Cornell University Press, 1984).

Seton-Watson, Hugh. *Nations and States: An Enquiry into the Origins of Nations and the Politics of Nationalism* (Boulder, Colorado: Westview, 1977).

Shaffer, Arthur. *The Politics of History: Writing the History of the American Revolution, 1783–1815* (Chicago: Precedent, 1975).

Shields, David. *Oracles of Empire: Poetry, Politics and Commerce in British America, 1690–1750* (Chicago: University of Chicago Press, 1990).

Simms, William Gilmore. *Joscelyn, A Tale of the Revolution* (Greenville: University of South Carolina Press, 1975 [1867]).

Simpson, Stephen. *Biography of Stephen Girard* (Philadelphia: Thomas Bonsal, 1832).

Skeel, E. E., ed. *Mason Locke Weems, His Works and Ways* (New York: privately printed, 1929).

Sklar, Kathryn. *Catharine Beecher: A Study in American Domesticity* (New York: Norton, 1976).

Slotkin, Richard. *The Fatal Environment: The Myth of the Frontier in the Age of Industrialization, 1800–1860* (New York: Atheneum, 1985).

———. *Regeneration Through Violence: The Mythology of the American Frontier* (Middletown, Connecticut: Wesleyan University Press, 1973).

Smith, James Morton. *Freedom's Fetters: The Alien and Sedition Laws and American Civil Liberties* (Ithaca: Cornell University Press, 1956).

Smith, Stephanie. *Conceived by Liberty: Maternal Images and American Literature* (Ithaca: Cornell University Press, 1994).

Smith, Wilson, ed. *Theories of Education in Early America, 1655–1819* (Indianapolis: Bobbs-Merrill, 1973).

Smith-Rosenberg, Carroll. *Disorderly Conduct: Visions of Gender in Victorian America* (New York: Knopf, 1985).

———. *Religion and The Rise of the American City: The New York City Mission Movement, 1812–1870* (Ithaca: Cornell University Press, 1971).

Sneed, Patricia. "On Caribbean Shores: Problems of Writing the History of the First Contact." *Radical History Review* 53 (Spring 1992) 5–11.

Somkin, Fred. *Unquiet Eagle: Memory and Desire in the Search for American Freedom, 1815–1860* (Ithaca: Cornell University Press, 1967).

Sommer, Doris. *Foundational Fictions: The National Romances of Latin America* (Berkeley: University of California Press, 1991).

Spencer, Benjamin. *The Quest for Nationality: An American Literary Campaign* (Syracuse: Syracuse University Press, 1957).

Spiller, Robert. *American Literary Revolution, 1783–1837* (New York: New York University Press, 1967).

Spillers, Hortense. "Mama's Baby, Papa's Maybe: An American Grammar Book," *Diacritics* (Summer 1987) 65–81.

Spofford, Harriet Prescott. "Circumstance," reprinted in *Provisions*, ed. Judith Fetterley (Bloomington: Indiana University Press, 1986).

Stafford, John. *The Literary Criticism of "Young America": A Study of the Relationship of Politics and Literature, 1837–1850* (New York: Russell and Russell, 1967).

Stansell, Christine. *City of Women: Sex and Class in New York, 1790–1860* (New York: Knopf, 1986).

Stauffer, Vernon. *New England and the Bavarian Illuminati* (New York: Columbia University Press, 1918).

Stone, Lawrence. *The Family, Sex, and Marriage in England, 1600–1800* (New York: Harper & Row, 1979).

Strasser, Susan. *Never Done: A History of American Housework* (New York: Pantheon, 1982).

Sundquist, Eric. *Home As Found: Authority and Genealogy in Nineteenth-Century American Literature* (Baltimore: Johns Hopkins University Press, 1979).

———. "Slavery, Revolution and the American Renaissance," in *The American Renaissance Reconsidered*, eds. Walter Michaels and Donald Pease (Baltimore: Johns Hopkins University Press, 1985), pp. 1–33.

Sutherland, Daniel. *Americans and Their Servants; Domestic Service in the U.S. from 1890–1920* (Baton Rouge: Louisiana State University Press, 1981).

Takaki, Ronald. *Iron Cages: Race and Culture in Nineteenth-Century America* (New York: Knopf, 1979).

Taylor, William. *Cavalier and Yankee: The Old South and the American National Character* (New York: George Braziller, 1961).

Thernstrom, Stephan and Richard Sennett, eds. *Nineteenth-Century Cities: Essays in the New Urban History* (New Haven: Yale University Press, 1969).

Theweleit, Klaus. *Male Fantasies: Volume Two; Male Bodies: Psychoanalyzing the*

White Terror, trans. Erica Carter and Chris Turner (St. Paul: University of Minnesota Press, 1989).

Thomas, Peter. *The English Satirical Print, 1600–1832: The American Revolution* (Cambridge: Chadwyck-Healey, 1986).

Thompson, Daniel Pierce. *The Rangers, or, The Tory's Daughter* (Boston: B. B. Mussey, 1851).

Tilly, Louise and Joan Scott. *Women, Work and Family* (New York: Holt, Rinehart and Wilson, 1978).

Tise, Larry. *Proslavery: A History of the Defense of Slavery in America, 1701–1840* (Athens: University of Georgia Press, 1987).

Todorov, Tzvetan. *The Conquest of America*, trans. Richard Howard (New York: Harper and Row, 1984).

Tompkins, Jane. *Sensational Designs: The Cultural Work of American Fiction, 1790–1860* (New York: Oxford University Press, 1985).

Twain, Mark. *Pudd'nhead Wilson* (New York: Oxford University Press, 1992).

Tyler, Ron. *The Image of America in Caricature and Cartoon* (Brodnax, 1976).

The United States Magazine and Democratic Review. (Washington, D. C.: Langtree & O'Sullivan, 1837–55).

Vidler, Anthony. *The Architectural Uncanny: Essays on the Modern Unhomely* (Cambridge: MIT Press, 1992).

Wald, Priscilla. *Constituting Americans: Cultural Anxiety and Narrative Form* (Durham, North Carolina: Duke University Press, 1995).

Walker, Peter. *Moral Choices: Memory, Desire, and Imagination in Nineteenth-Century American Abolition* (Baton Rouge: Louisiana State University Press, 1978).

Walters, Ronald. *The Anti-Slavery Appeal; American Abolitionism after 1830* (Baltimore: John Hopkins University Press, 1976).

Warner, Marina. *Monuments and Maidens: The Allegory of the Female Form* (New York: Atheneum, 1985).

Warner, Michael. *Letters of the Republic: Publication and the Public Sphere in Eighteenth-Century America* (Cambridge: Harvard University Press, 1990).

Watts, Stephen. *The Republic Reborn: War and the Making of Liberal America* (Baltimore: Johns Hopkins University Press, 1989).

———. *The Romance of Real Life: Charles Brockden Brown and the Origins of American Culture* (Baltimore: Johns Hopkins University Press, 1994).

Webster, Noah. "On the Education of Youth in America," [1790] reprinted in *Essays on Education in the Early Republic*, ed. Frederick Rudolph (Cambridge: Harvard University Press, 1965).

Weems, Mason. "God's Revenge Against Adultery," reprinted in *Three Discourses*, (New York: Random House, 1929).

———. *Life of George Washington*, ed. Marcus Cunliffe (Cambridge: Harvard University Press, 1962).

Weld, Theodore. *American Slavery As It Is: The Testimony of a Thousand Voices* (Boston: 1842).

Welter, Barbara. "The Cult of True Womanhood, 1820–1860," *American Quarterly* 18 (1966): 151–74.

Welter, Rush. *Popular Education and Democratic Thought in America* (New York: Columbia University Press, 1962).

Whitney, Charles. "The Naming of America as the Meaning of America: Vespucci, Publicity, Festivity, Modernity," *Clio* 22 (Spring 1993) 195–220.

Wiegman, Robyn. *American Anatomies: Theorizing Race and Gender* (Durham, North Carolina: Duke University Press, 1995).

Wilentz, Sean. *Chants Democratic: New York City and the Rise of the American Working Class, 1788–1850* (New York: Oxford University Press, 1984).

Wills, Garry. *Inventing America: Jefferson's Declaration of Independence* (New York: Doubleday, 1978).

Wishy, Bernard. *The Child and the Republic; the Dawn of Modern American Child Nurture* (Philadelphia: University of Pennsylvania Press, 1968).

Wolf, Bryan. *Romantic Re-Vision: Culture and Consciousness in Nineteenth-Century Painting and Literature* (Chicago: University of Chicago Press, 1982).

Wood, Gordon. *The Creation of the American Republic* (Chapel Hill: University of North Carolina Press, 1969).

Wright, Richardson. *Hawkers and Walkers in Early America* (New York: Boni and Liveright, 1927).

Yazawa, Melvin. *From Colonies to Commonwealth: Familial Ideology and the Beginnings of the American Republic* (Baltimore: Johns Hopkins University Press, 1985).

Yeazell, Ruth. "Why Political Novels Have Heroines" *Novel* 18 (Winter 1985) 126–144.

Yellin, Jean Fagan. *Women and Sisters: The Antislavery Feminists in American Culture* (New Haven: Yale University Press, 1989).

Zaller, Robert. "Melville and the Myth of Revolution" *Studies in Romanticism* 15 (Fall 1976) 607–22.

Zamora, Margarita. "Abreast of Columbus: Gender and Discovery" *Cultural Critique* 17 (Winter 1990–91) 127–149.

Ziff, Larzer. *Literary Democracy; the Declaration of Cultural Independence in America, 1837–1861* (New York: Viking Press, 1981).

———. *Writing in the New Nation: Prose, Print, and Politics in the Early United States* (New Haven: Yale University Press, 1991).

Žižek, Slavoj. *For They Know Not What They Do* (London: Verso, 1989).

Index